The Queer Thing About Sin

THE QUEER THING ABOUT SIN

Why the West Came to Hate Queer Love

HARRY TANNER

BLOOMSBURY CONTINUUM
LONDON · OXFORD · NEW YORK · NEW DELHI · SYDNEY

BLOOMSBURY CONTINUUM
Bloomsbury Publishing Plc
50 Bedford Square, London, WC1B 3DP, UK
Bloomsbury Publishing Ireland Limited
29 Earlsfort Terrace, Dublin 2, D02 AY28, Ireland

BLOOMSBURY, BLOOMSBURY CONTINUUM and the Diana logo are trademarks of
Bloomsbury Publishing Plc

First published in Great Britain 2025

Copyright © Harry Tanner, 2025

Harry Tanner has asserted his right under the Copyright, Designs and Patents Act, 1988, to be
identified as Author of this work

All rights reserved. No part of this publication may be: i) reproduced or transmitted in any form, electronic or mechanical, including photocopying, recording or by means of any information storage or retrieval system without prior permission in writing from the publishers; or ii) used or reproduced in any way for the training, development or operation of artificial intelligence (AI) technologies, including generative AI technologies. The rights holders expressly reserve this publication from the text and data mining exception as per Article 4(3) of the Digital Single Market Directive (EU) 2019/790

Bloomsbury Publishing Plc does not have any control over, or responsibility for, any third-party websites referred to or in this book. All internet addresses given in this book were correct at the time of going to press. The author and publisher regret any inconvenience caused if addresses have changed or sites have ceased to exist, but can accept no responsibility for any such changes

A catalogue record for this book is available from the British Library

Library of Congress Cataloguing-in-Publication data has been applied for

ISBN: HB: 978-1-3994-2229-1; eBook: 978-1-3994-2232-1; ePDF: 978-1-3994-2233-8

2 4 6 8 10 9 7 5 3 1

Typeset by Deanta Global Publishing Services, Chennai, India
Printed and bound in Great Britain by Clays Ltd, Elcograf S.p.A.

To find out more about our authors and books visit www.bloomsbury.com and sign up for
our newsletters

For product safety related questions contact productsafety@bloomsbury.com

For Chris and David, and in memory of all the beautiful queer people I'll never meet who believed God hated them for their love.

Contents

	Foreword	viii
1	The Myth of Greek Sex	1
2	How Money Corrupted Love	27
3	Queer as Macedon	47
4	Plato and the Philosophy of the Closet	63
5	Alexander the Straight?	81
6	Love in the Time of the Old Testament	103
7	Toxic Masculinity in Ancient Rome	129
8	The First Christians	157
9	The Birth of Modern Homophobia	183
	Acknowledgements	205
	Notes	206
	Bibliography	236
	Index	251
	Note on the Author	259
	Note on the Type	260

Foreword

When I was a teenager, I believed I was going to hell. For centuries, it was almost universally acknowledged that all gay men would. It wasn't until years later that I asked myself where that idea came from, and why was it that, thousands of years ago when the Bible was written, people decided that queer love was a sin?

It hadn't always been a sin to be queer. In many cities across the ancient world, same-sex love was celebrated. So how did homophobia take root? Why did so many societies start executing men and women for the same love once praised by their philosophers and rulers?

I have personal reasons for wanting to know the answer. My father died when I was two years old and for many years being Christian made me feel whole. Christianity gave me a compass with which to navigate the world and allowed me to commune with the people I'd lost. But that all changed when I fell in love with another boy at school.

The love that upended my world was clandestine and unrequited. Little girls and boys grow up knowing they will get married; they sketch out the geography of their future relationships long before they even feel physical attraction. For queer people, desire arrives unannounced – it comes as a lightning bolt through a clear-blue sky. I knew I couldn't tell anyone. I had to keep it secret from him, from the world, and at times even from myself. It was what Christianity taught me to do.

Around that time, I was given a book published by an evangelical group which showed two Black girls holding hands beneath the title: 'What about same-sex desire?' The answer, printed below the photo, was Lev. 18.22: 'Thou shalt not lie with mankind as with womankind, it is an abomination.' I remember feeling sick with guilt. I became deeply preoccupied with atoning for my sins. Every single night, I begged God to make me straight.

Eventually I went to a lay preacher and confessed everything. Sitting on his cosy, blue sofa, the autumnal light streaming in through the windows, I told him I was gay. He reassured me that he could help, but it had to be a secret — just between us. He handed me a yellow Post-it note with a list of websites that he said could teach me to repress and control my desires. Later, he organized a session for me with another figure in the Church who had written candidly about his own experiences 'suffering' from same-sex desire. Both of them wholeheartedly believed that it was our unique curse as queers to desire other men, but never to act on them. It might sound strange but, to this day, I do not believe they meant any harm — they were trying to be kind.

With their encouragement and advice, I embarked on my very own programme of conversion therapy. With their techniques I set about cultivating the numbness that they promised would save my soul. What happened instead was that, after only a few months, I casually told a friend on a walk down a dirt path that I wanted to take my own life. I wanted to escape, and the only escape from a world without love was death.

Perhaps surprisingly, it was a dead language, ancient Greek, that turned my life around. I remember my teacher opening a battered copy of a Greek tragedy — Sophocles' *Oedipus the King*, I think – and showing me the tiny footnotes beneath the Greek text. 'We call it the *apparatus criticus*,' she said as she traced the foxed pages with her manicured finger, explaining with exemplary patience that those footnotes told us where each and every single word in the play's text had come from. From dozens of different manuscripts, scattered in fragments all over Europe, buried in archives in the Vatican and the Bodleian Library in Oxford, sequestered in great palaces of learning, teams of scholars had pieced together what that tragedian had written for a sun-soaked stage 2,500 years ago.

My teacher looked at me: 'Harry, this stuff did not come in the post. It is our job, as inheritors of the tradition to amend, to fix, to preserve – we pass it on.'

Studying ancient Greek shattered my faith in literal translations of the Bible. I realized that it must have been passed down through the centuries in much the same way as Sophocles' play; it had also been subject to different translations and interpretations which influenced how people understood and read it. Finally, my unshakeable belief that God hated me for who I loved began to waver. And at the same time, I discovered the rich and strange world of ancient Greece – a land where gay men could be heroes and poets, not just sinners.

But it was only when I left for university and threw myself into London's gay scene that, safely separated from the evangelical Christian community, I finally stopped fearing God's retribution. It was around then that I began to ask the question that would lead to this book – I was studying for a PhD in ancient Greek and I no longer thought that homosexuality was a sin, but I still wanted to know why Western culture believed it was for so long.

I wish I could show my teenage self what life is like now. I want to tell him that yesterday I lay in bed with a man I love who held me close in his arms and made all the world seem at peace. I want him to see the Pride flags waving over a million people parading for our rights, I want him to see his own face in that crowd with rainbow paint smeared down his cheek. I want him to know that he won't be alone: help is coming.

As Pride, equal marriage and adoption rights all show, we live in a moment of light — at least for gay men. I was able to move to London and find a queer community; I had the chance to teach myself how to love again. But I've learned from the ancient world that queer communities have existed and flourished throughout history – and that time and time again, they have been destroyed by moralists, puritans and zealots. In the modern world, with increasingly fervent attacks on trans people, we are seeing the same pattern again. Just because we live in a moment of tolerance and acceptance now, it doesn't mean we always will.

Though evangelical Christianity no longer holds the same power over me, I keep returning to that question: how and why did ancient societies turn against their queer citizens? With the world as it is, and with homophobia on the march and back in the pages of the statute books, we need answers.

Writing this book, I've been inspired by my own experiences as a gay man. It is hard enough to rescue any queer life from the ancient world, especially given the purges and revisions of the source material conducted by Romans and Christians alike. But that is even more true for queer women and for trans people. Throughout antiquity, women were subjected to far more stringent controls on their lives than men, and even societies that celebrated love between men remained deeply misogynistic. Where there has been evidence of queer women and trans lives, I have discussed them throughout the book, but inevitably there will be stories and fragments that I've missed. The records are dominated by the voices of the free male citizens of Greece and Rome; the lives of enslaved people and women are still emerging. I do believe, though, that the historical forces that conspire to bring about homophobia for queer men are the same as for all other queer people.

But despite these tragic absences and with the acknowledgement that there's so much more for us to discover, I believe that by looking to the lives of queer poets, prophets, warriors, philosophers and politicians who felt free to love those of their own sex, we might find the origins of the homophobia that has twisted our culture for so long. And if we can understand that, perhaps we can make sure the freedom to love and to live out queer lives never again dies in the West.

ONE

The Myth of Greek Sex

> Happy is the man in love who works out at the gym and comes home and sleeps all day with a beautiful boy.
>
> THEOGNIS OF MEGARA, ELEGIES 1335–6

A MODERN MYTH ABOUT ANCIENT SEX

In 1895, Oscar Wilde was on trial. Standing at the witness box, his long, dark hair neatly arranged about his face, Wilde couldn't completely disguise his skin's wan, waxy quality – the outward sign of the months of mental torture he had endured. A man admired by all, the audacious and eccentric darling of the London stage, had fallen. Charged with gross indecency, his private love life aired for all to see, Wilde's trial had caused a sensation the likes of which had never been seen before. His new audience – a courtroom – listened, glued to their wooden benches, as the prosecuting QC, Charles Gill, put his question: 'What is "the Love that Dare not Speak its Name"?' There was a collective intake of breath. Wilde paused. Then he began to speak:

> The love that dare not speak its name in this century is such great affection of an elder for a younger man as there was between David and Jonathan, such as Plato made the very basis of his philosophy, and such as you find in the sonnets of Michelangelo and Shakespeare.[1]

On hearing this panegyric to same-sex love, the court burst into applause, drowning out the boos and hisses of Wilde's enemies. What is so surprising about this scene from the late 1800s is not just that an audience of Victorians should applaud this speech. It is that Wilde imagined same-sex desire had always been a pairing between an older and a younger man. Wilde was talking about a popular myth about queer love in ancient Greece: that gay love only existed between an older man and a teenager.

Wilde's claims have more to do with his legal predicament than historical fact. So the testimony of one Antonio Migge – the Savoy Hotel's masseur – would suggest. After a brief knock on a hotel room door, in March of 1893, he entered. The sight that met Migge's stunned eyes was none other than Oscar Wilde in bed with a young man who could only have been 'between sixteen and eighteen', as the masseur later testified in court.[2]

Wilde was 38 at the time, over twice the age of his lover. But his interest in younger men did not end at the revolving door of the Savoy Hotel. Wilde's most famous boyfriend, Lord Alfred Douglas, was 20 when they met. The men whom his pimp – Alfred Taylor – was accused of procuring for Wilde rarely exceeded their twenties. Many of the men procured by Taylor were from vulnerable socioeconomic backgrounds, including the valet Charles Parker and his brother William, a groom, both out of work.[3] According to the trial, Wilde had sex with some of them in his family home on Tite Street, which he shared with his wife and children.

When put on trial with his life at stake, Wilde used the example of the ancient Greek philosopher Plato to defend himself. If he could show that the elder philosophers, poets and statesmen of ancient Greece – who were celebrated by the Victorians as the founders of Western civilization – found sex with young men perfectly acceptable, it could provide him with an excuse to do the same. But this involved a certain level of mythologizing, of massaging the facts, about Greek love. Unfortunately, it wasn't enough to save him. Wilde lost. He was imprisoned in Reading and Britain's appetite for convicting homosexual men was renewed. Queer men – among them the art critic More Adey, the journalist Robert Ross and the author Reggie Turner – fled for Paris following Wilde's arrest.

One of Wilde's contemporaries, a man he possibly visited when in Italy, was the pioneering photographer Wilhelm von Gloeden. Von Gloeden lived much of his life in exile from his native Germany on the island of Sicily in the hilltop citadel Taormina. Kaiser Wilhelm II's cabinet had recently been embroiled in a series of high-profile sex scandals between men, and the combination of his ill-health and a less tolerant political climate compelled him to flee.

Taormina is a small city set into the coastline against the backdrop of the deep-blue waters of the Ionian Sea, dotted with palm trees and ancient ruins. It was the perfect getaway from inclement Germany, and gave him the freedom he needed to pursue his passions. At his villa, von Gloeden paid young Sicilian men and, disturbingly, even boys to strip naked and paint their skin with milk and glycerin before taking their photographs. They often posed with imagery from the ancient landscape they had grown up in. The works became a commercial success in von Gloeden's own time. As in the case of Wilde's speech, evoking classical themes shielded von Gloeden from accusations that his work was mere smut.

Between Oscar Wilde, von Gloeden and their contemporaries, the ancient world became a means to legitimize taboo desires, but a myth entered the public consciousness that somehow ancient Greece and Rome were remarkable for sexual relationships between elder mentors and their younger mentees. We assume when looking at ancient Greece and Rome that same-sex desire was culturally different there: rather than some gay men being interested in other men, *all* males were interested in boys. There is very little in the way of reliable, primary evidence to support the existence of ritualized, same-sex sex acts between an older and a younger man.[4] There is certainly visual evidence for equal-age attraction between men in Greece before the year 450 BCE, and there is certainly some visual evidence of sex between older and younger men, but there is not enough to support the claim that such a practice was widespread.

This ritualized account of ancient same-sex desire was only accentuated with the publication of a landmark study by one of British academia's more eccentric figureheads. The Oxford classicist Sir Kenneth Dover, sporting an impressive moustache, liked to tell his students (and readers of his autobiography[5]) the story of the time when he was standing on the edge of a cliff, so overcome by the sight of the sea and the stirring poetry of the Roman writer Horace that he unzipped his flies and began to masturbate into the waters below. Professor Kenneth Dover could never be accused of inattention to detail.

While Dover was clearly no prude, he did, like many of his generation, find it hard to imagine adult men in serious and reciprocal homosexual relationships. His autobiography also includes a vivid recollection of the first time he experienced mutual masturbation with another boy, which makes it clear he felt such horseplay was a natural curiosity that you were meant to grow out of. It was this highly biased view which coloured his interpretation of the facts in his most famous work, *Greek Homosexuality* (published in 1978), one of the most influential works of classical scholarship ever written. Unfortunately, Dover's discussion of gay love in the book is portrayed as something hyper-sexualized and thoroughly unromantic; he seems incapable of understanding that anyone could ever enjoy receiving anal sex, or that an older man may be interested in being the passive partner. Dover paints an image of older men desperately trying to seduce younger boys, hanging out by the ancient gymnasia to ogle them and shower them with gifts. The young men were supposed to be coy and, if they relented, were not allowed to enjoy sex with the older man.

One of the stranger claims advanced by classicists in the wake of this book was that these relationships existed to strengthen the young man's virility.[6] The older man's semen – so they said – was a source of strength which flowed into the young man. The basis of these claims had nothing to do with ancient Greece, but was inspired by a practice commonplace among the Simbari people of Papua New Guinea. Even if the Simbari did perform a similar ceremony, and even if certain prurient elements have not been inferred by Western anthropologists ever on the hunt for the exotic,[7] the example offered by one single tribe cannot be enough to support its existence in ancient Greece unless the ancient Greeks tell us this themselves.

The only material that seems to discuss such a relationship is highly biased, coming from court cases against men accused of homosexuality in Athens and from ancient comedies. If it is true that the ancient Greeks *all* practised ritualized homosexuality, involving ejaculating into the mouths of younger boys to strengthen their virility, we would expect to hear a great deal more about it from serious sources like historians and tragic playwrights. Given ancient writers, as we will see, were far from shy about recording lurid gay love affairs between powerful men, their reticence in describing this ritualized sexual relationship between an older and a younger man is curious to say the least.

There were gay relationships in ancient Greece, some of equal age and some between men of different ages, we know that without a doubt. We also know that abusers took advantage of the power dynamics in a heavily hierarchical society to prey on young boys. It is probable that the sanctioned mentor-mentee systems were used as cover by some men to exercise their desires. At certain times, these may have been the only available structure through which homosexuality could express itself. But such exceptions do not tell us that *all* ancient Greek men had a bisexual predilection for younger boys. Distracted by an overly prurient interest in ritualized homosexuality, scholars have sometimes neglected the clear evidence for age-equal relationships, as well as relationships between a consenting younger adult and his older boyfriend. In other words, love.

HOW TO WRITE A QUEER HISTORY

Ancient history comes to us in broken sherds. Stories from here and there, whose authority cannot ever be vouched for: tiny pieces of vases; the flipsides of coins; scraps of parchment found in centuries-old libraries. Imagination is the glue which binds these tiny components together and so the wattle and daub of ancient history is composed of sundry fragments interspersed with conjecture and guesswork, which often say as much about our own times as they do about the ancient past.

It is a feature of fundamentalist thinking – common to the evangelism with which I was educated – to say that certain facts about Jesus' life were true, or that the sources which make them up are reliable. But it is exceptionally rare to find a solidly dependable fact from ancient history. We work with whispers and make what we can of them. For hundreds of years, writers claimed the lesbian poet Sappho had a *husband* called Kerkylas of Andros. Never questioning this information, they handed it down from generation to generation, depending upon it completely as a fact. That was until the 1850s, when William Mure was clever enough to point out that the name Kerkylas of Andros literally means 'Dick All-cock from [the isle of] MAN' and was almost certainly a joke.[8]

We face a problem with writing a history of queer life in the ancient world. We have artistic depictions of gay sex, snatches of songs about the joys of loving the same gender (both female to female, and male to male), ambiguous law codes and historical accounts told centuries later of institutions which seem analogous to same-sex marriage – and we have imagination. Dover, Wilde and von Gloeden came to their own conclusions about the nature of queer desire in the ancient world, and their conclusions became facts. We must be mindful of making the same mistake, though we should not allow that to deter us from the serious, scholarly business of trying – through little clues – to understand the ancient world and in turn to understand ourselves. I am fascinated not by love for men, but by how hatred – somehow – for something so innocent emerged. I am informed by my own past as an evangelical Christian, by my own present in one of the most extraordinary times to be gay in human history, by biological insights unavailable to those early pioneers and by emerging theories in modern politics.

Historians can make a choice when writing a history of sexuality. They can assume that sexuality is socially constructed. According to this theory, a desire for the same sex comes from power structures, and categories like 'homosexual' and 'heterosexual' were invented in the late 19th century. Although, as I will argue, the ancient Greeks were well aware of sexual orientation and even spoke of a *tropos* (literally 'orientation') towards people of the same sex.[9] Others might argue that even though society exerts a strong influence, homosexuality and gender identities are biological. They would point to the animal kingdom as well as genetic and hormonal data as evidence that sexual orientations have always existed. I take the view that neither side is completely right.

I think sexual orientation and gender identities must have a biological root cause but I don't believe something so complex and nuanced could ever be reduced solely to a biological drive. Different social conditions mean that desire expresses itself in different ways. In the modern world, love and sex are more liberated than they have been for most of human history. This is partly a consequence of birth-control and effective treatments for once-deadly venereal diseases. I think that some ancient Greek men and women were fundamentally attracted to their own gender, and the ancient Greeks responded to this desire in a very different way, heavily shaped by their much more patriarchal and hierarchical society.

Writers of queer histories, including Kenneth Dover, have often assumed that *any* mention of queerness is proof of its tolerance. These academics have used comedians mocking queer people, laws opposing queer people and speeches in political assemblies denouncing queer people as sources from which to extrapolate ideas about their lives. This is how conclusions have been drawn that lecherous, older gay men stalked gymnasia for young lovers in ancient Greece. I have taken the view that we are really looking at an early homophobic trope here, and not an accurate account of common practices.

While I am sceptical that the object of a man's attention was *always* a younger boy, it is vanishingly rare for ancient Greek writers to talk of love for another *man*, and it only happens after about the 3rd century BCE. Romans almost never describe it.[10] In over 1,000 years of literature, legal speeches, poems, graffiti, we hear of the idea a handful of times. But we do hear frequently of a 'man and boy' living together forever. We do hear of desiring a 'boy' even when he is an adult. We have vases and cups which show age-equal men having sex. What are we to make of this? How are we, then, to understand this word 'boy'?

Most of our translations were compiled by Victorians and – for the most part – we still rely on their industrious attempts to translate every Greek and Latin word today.[11] A key assumption made by these pioneers was that every word had one core definition. I do not think this can have been true: words have many different meanings and they are usually understood in context rather than in isolation. So we have another choice. Either we understand the word *boy* literally, and we assume that the reason there are so few sources that talk about loving *men* is because sex between two adult men did not exist. Or we assume that we have misunderstood the Greek and Latin words that we now translate as *boy* — we assume they did not literally mean to say a young lad. This seems overwhelmingly likely, since the words for *boy* can, for instance, be used to describe slaves of any age and other kinds of subordinate. Given that marriage between a man and a woman in ancient societies was, as a consequence of patriarchal values, between a superior male and a socially inferior female, it seems probable to me that the Greeks and Romans may have talked about same-sex desire using the same hierarchy. To do so, they invoked a word – which we translate as *boy* – because there had to be a superior and an inferior in a relationship. Once we allow for this cultural understanding of homosexuality, we put ourselves in a better position to understand its censorship and to track the political movements that came against it.

Ancient societies were as variegated, nuanced and complex as our own. Some histories of our queer past have assumed that some societies were tolerant or intolerant.[12] I tend to see tolerance as a graded spectrum. Even in ancient societies where laws were passed against queer people, like Byzantium, and executions took place, you see pockets of gay communities, tiny subcultures where people felt safe to be themselves. The question is always how large were those pockets, how accepted by mainstream society were they and how fierce were the criminal sanctions against queer people in the secular sphere.

Finally, it seems necessary to address a very dark side to ancient culture. Historians have been quick to read accounts of the rape of male slaves by their male masters as a sign of social acceptance, or to interpret vases from ancient Greece which show Greek soldiers raping their enemies similarly as evidence of open queer desire. It is my view that there is compelling evidence to suggest that when slave-owners raped their slaves, they did so to assert power and dominance over them.[13] This use of gay sex as a tool of repression does not necessarily make those slave-owners gay, but it does make them violent. To this day, rape is still perpetrated as a weapon of war by men against men. This does not make either party homosexual. Nor does it generally occur in societies that tolerate and accept same-sex desire – queer love between consenting adults is often banned in the same places where rape of men (and particularly of male slaves) is praised.

MEGARA

Archaic Greece, the common name given to the years before 500 BCE, comprises a history of shadows. We hear of clues, archaeological findings and inherited fragments from poems, and our task is to piece it all together into a history, while preserving a certain agnosticism about its absolute truth.

Of the few things we know for certain, we can say that – contrary to popular belief – ancient Athens was not the first Greek democracy. We do not know which of the many hundreds of small, independent city-states (for this was long before the days of a unified Greek nation state) that lay scattered across the plains and islands of ancient Greece really deserves that title, but we can be sure it was not Athens. We know this because when Athens was still a tyranny under the control of an elite band of aristocrats, a city which lay to its west – Megara – already had a functioning democracy.[14]

In the modern world, democracy is synonymous with equality and fairness. But our complex democratic ideals – the right to trial, equality before the law, freedom of the individual – took a long time to develop. Ancient democracy, for the most part, was dominated by mob-rule, terrifyingly populist and little more equitable than dictatorship. The Greek author Plutarch tells that 'having thrown out Theagenes the tyrant, the Megarians were self-controlled in their politics . . . but when the leaders of the democracy gave them unrestrained liberty, they became corrupted'.[15] We will use Plutarch a great deal as a source in this book, but we must do so cautiously: he was not a contemporary to these events, since he was writing under the Roman Empire between the 1st and 2nd centuries CE. However, he would have had access to many ancient sources that are now lost to us, and – in the absence of any other material – he is a useful source to consult.

At the time, Megara was riven with civil strife . A contemporary poet describes the 'mother of disorder' as one goddess: 'Poverty'.[16] Though Megara was a democracy with citizens participating in an assembly and drawing up its laws, aristocrats dominated the political landscape. To keep a cap on power, the rich Megarians continually bought off the poor with handouts and land. The super-rich of Megara paid for public festivals, for the sacrifices of animals and for the public's grain supply. This pseudo-benevolence was largesse with one singular purpose: to avert a bloody overthrow of the rich by the masses. As well as buying off the poorer people in society, the Megarian aristocracy used another tactic, which ended in disaster.

Demagogues from among the aristocrats increasingly used their rhetorical skills to see off their political enemies. Standing in the assembly in the midday heat, these men declared their political opponents enemies of the state, whipping up popular sentiment against them and driving them out of the city. The exiles were often rich and powerful, and, growing in number, they took up land outside Megara and ruminated bitterly on their fate. Growing all the time in size and strength, these men returned, and they did so with a hired army.[17] Seizing the city by force, democracy was toppled and tyranny restored.

The tyrant's name is lost to history, but we know he did a fair job of restoring order and peace to the city. The end of one of the earliest democracies in fact brought about a good deal of prosperity and levelled the gap between the rich and the poor that had destabilized Megara. A fountain house from the end of the 6th century BCE survives – a marvel of ancient engineering. It was open for public use, fresh water was accessible to all. The Megarians were deeply proud of their public building projects, and told a myth of a great builder named Skiron who helped to build their city walls (the Athenians, by contrast, never much liked Skiron, and told their own versions in which he was a wily murderer). These building projects are a sign that money was being spent on public facilities and not on private villas. In another marker of equality, most of the graves uncovered from this period contain very few artefacts. Unless the burial was for a child, the Megarians did not lavish their dead publicly with gifts. Outward displays of wealth were not tolerated. In contrast to the great tombs of ancient Egypt, whose nobility were laden with gold and silver and precious artefacts, even the most powerful people in Megara were seldom buried with more than a pot.[18]

Despite this, Megara was a rich city. It thrived as a major stop-off point on the trade sinews which snaked through the Greek countryside. All the houses in the city were well built with beautiful, high-quality stone, and over 100 surviving buildings contain the ancient equivalent of subterranean fridges, which may have been used to store food or to perform sacrifices to the gods. The city became synonymous with these underground larders – the Greek word being *megara*. It is very probable that these *megara* served to keep luxuries such as meat and wine from spoiling. Possibly, Megara was a city of wine-fridges.

There was one poet who was less than pleased with this new Megara. His name was Theognis, and like so many of the poets from the archaic period, we know almost nothing about him save what is contained in his poems. He complained of the common people's increasing ascendence into wealth and public life. Alongside his critique of social mobility, he also wrote about his love for other men.[19] He seemed to have been a member of the aristocratic class, and he certainly felt very free to sing of his proclivities. 'Happy is the man in love', Theognis sang phlegmatically, 'who works out at the gym and then comes home and sleeps all day with a beautiful boy'.[20]

In Greek, Theognis uses the word *pais* (often translated 'boy') to describe the lover with whom he slept.[21] In fact, the level of consent and sexual interest shown by his *pais* shows quite the reverse. The *pais* appears to have a ravenous sexual appetite: he wanders off with other men and only returns when he is 'sated with barley',[22] a thinly disguised metaphor that links grain with another type of seed. It means a male lover whose age is not specified, who is capable of sexual feelings and who can reciprocate. 'Boyfriend' or 'suitor' seems appropriate in translation. Theognis does not often specify the ages of his lovers, though he does seem to warn younger men against the pains of unrequited love.[23] It can be hard to piece together the exact age and nature of these relationships. Imagine a historian 2,500 years in the future studying 21st-century Britain, working only with the tiniest handful of texts between lovers, trying to figure out why 'girlfriend' or 'boyfriend' contain the words 'girl' and 'boy', and why they call each other 'babe' and 'baby', and what this suggests about their ages.

Ancient Greece was a highly hierarchical society. The ancient poet Hesiod conceived of a world order with the Olympian gods at the top, the titans just beneath, then monsters, then kings, then men, then slaves. A relationship between a man and a wife was not one of equals. The man was the controller of the household; his wife was his subordinate. We know almost nothing about women in archaic Greece, but it seems very likely that they were strictly confined to their houses. In queer relationships likewise, there had to be a dominant man and a subordinate – otherwise, it could not fit into the hierarchical world in which the Greeks believed. The term *pais* is often used to address *other adults* who are of lower or inferior status; much as the term 'sirrah' might be used in Shakespearean English. It is my belief that this is why ancient Greek writers – including Theognis – use the term. They are not saying their lovers are children.

In one poem, which would have been performed publicly to music, Theognis immortalizes the image of two men lying in bed, describing his *pais* as *kalós* ('beautiful'). It is a word used to capture the beauty of sculpture; poetry which moves its listener to tears; the perfect synchrony of dance; the changing harmonies of a song; the nobility of peace and justice. It is a word steeped in human creation and artifice. But Theognis was no chaste admirer of male bodies.

'Riding that horse sates your desires, but then you come back to my farmstead',[24] sings Theognis. The man he writes about is clearly something of a carnal connoisseur: sex will only sate his desires for a short time before he is off looking for more. The language of horse-riding is still with us today, it is the origin of the word 'bareback' among other innuendos. The Greek word for 'farmstead' (*stathmós*) here reveals another tongue-in-cheek double-entendre, as it also means 'a man's living quarters'. Far from slut-shaming, as some ancient poets partook in, Theognis celebrates the untrammelled libidinousness of his lovers.[25] The metaphors he uses, from everyday life, point to how commonly accepted same-sex desire was.

'You long for a noble charioteer, a beautiful paddock, a fresh spring, and a holy precinct,'[26] he continues. 'Holy precinct' is a playful euphemism – the thighs and firm bum of a male lover were often described as 'holy', so too was his penis. The 'holy precinct' in question is a not-so-subtle metaphor: a shrine everyone wants to visit, but only the most intimate of initiates may touch. Vases and drinking cups from nearby cities of the period preserve images of men gesturing with desire towards another man's behind.[27] Theognis' lover wants as much sex as he can get, but the poet did not always enjoy this level of success.

Theognis begs one of his love interests not to ignore him and threatens to kill himself.[28] He says the very sight of another makes him feel like he is placing his hands into a fire of vine leaves.[29] These leaves produced a fire which burned and crackled so hot that it melted metals. Theognis' poetry reveals the gamut of queer experience: from lying in bed with a lover, to sex, to chasing men you fancy, to rejection. It does so with a frank openness that implies a communal celebration of same-sex love. However, these later parts of Theognis' poetry – if they were by him (which is never totally certain with archaic poetry) – preserve forever his pain at loss and rejection. Having to live within the confines imposed by the standard heterosexual model (one superior man and one inferior woman) must have made his life very hard.[30]

The odd thing about these early signs of queer love in ancient Megara is how closely they are intertwined with the economic and political fortunes of the city-state. Theognis tells us about the beauty and sex-drive of his male lovers, as he tells us that aristocratic divides between classes were disappearing under the tyranny. 'A noble man who is not from a lower class does not mind marrying a lower-class woman,' he complains.[31] I don't want to misconstrue Megara as some sort of egalitarian paradise, life there would have been cruel and sometimes violent, and queer life there was certainly far from perfect, but it is in Megara, one of the earliest periods of recorded Greek history, that a fragile association may emerge between equality and tolerance for queer love. As much as Theognis might have preferred a return to the old status quo, it was as the boundaries between different societal groups weakened that queer desire could be celebrated.

LESBOS

When most people think of a queer ancient Greek society, they think not of Megara, but of Lesbos. The island lies closer to modern-day Turkey than it does to the Greek mainland and in the ancient world, Lesbos was a naturalist's paradise, a Garden of Eden. When he fell out with Plato, the philosopher Aristotle retreated to Lesbos for long periods to examine and categorize the flowers and trees, peering into tiny rock pools and surveying the critters whose entire world comprised barely enough water to fill a jam jar.³² But alongside its florae and faunae, the island, thanks to both its male and its female poets, was heavily associated with eroticism, even lending ancient Greek its word for fellatio, *lesbiazein*.

Like Theognis, Sappho of Lesbos was a lyric poet (akin to a singer-songwriter), and she lends her name and that of her island to queer women today.³³ Many of her songs were intended for wedding performances and private drinking parties. She was surrounded by a band of unmarried young women, and her poetry tells of her deep erotic attachment to some of them. Victorian scholars, deeply embarrassed by the idea that Sappho was into women, exerted a considerable amount of energy into claiming she was actually a schoolmistress.³⁴ She was famous in the ancient world and held up as an example of classic literature alongside the epic poets Homer and Hesiod and the tragic playwrights Sophocles, Aeschylus and Euripides, but – unlike her male counterparts – most of her poems have not survived into the modern world. In the few lines that have survived, she describes desire and same-sex love with an intensity few would dare to emulate today. 'When I look at you even for a second, it is impossible to speak . . . my tongue stiffens, and a soft fire runs all over my flesh . . . I am a coward – more pliable than grass,'³⁵ she sings.³⁶

In one fragment, Sappho celebrates the radiant beauty of a woman named Anactoria, and compares her to Helen of Troy,³⁷ whom Homer described as a goddess among mortals.³⁸ In another, Sappho prays to Aphrodite, asking her to have mercy for once again the poetess has fallen for an irresistibly beautiful woman.³⁹ The biographical tradition (which we must always take with a pinch of salt, since it commenced hundreds of years later) tells us that Sappho also had male lovers, among them a man named Phaon whom it was said Aphrodite had made especially handsome.

Mytilene – the capital city of Lesbos – was likely consumed by political infighting during Sappho's lifetime. Despite being a prosperous island, it seems that a series of attempts were made to overthrow the ruling parties and powers by various political factions. One key player was even said to be in love with Sappho, the poet Alcaeus. Alcaeus' poems are known for their bellicosity, some distance from the intensity and tenderness of Sappho's verses. Though the Roman lawyer Cicero – again, writing some centuries later – poured cold water over this notion, declaring that Alcaeus had been a writer '*de iuvenum amore*', 'on the love of young men'.[40] The Roman poet Horace also relates Alcaeus' verses on the 'dark-haired, dark-eyed' features of a handsome man called Lycus.[41] So, Lesbos was a place where Sappho was free to express her desire for other women and Alcaeus was possibly free to do the same for men.

Sappho is an incredibly precious find. Unfortunately, this early glimpse of women's sexuality was not to be replicated in later antiquity, and our vision is obscured by male voices determined to silence them.

BOEOTIA

To the north-west of ancient Athens lay a fertile, verdant landscape. This was not a place of towering temples but a land of simple farmers and shepherds. Cowherds roamed the fields, and agricultural workers gathered wheat for the harvest. As they tended their herds, Mount Helicon loomed in the distance, shrouded in myth and cloud. The ancients believed it was the muses' birthplace. A second mountain range towered to the south – Cithaeron, the mythical home of the god of wine, sex, theatre and, later, democracy: Dionysus. In this bucolic yet unremarkable region, called Boeotia (*Bee-oh-sha*), farmers went about their day-to-day lives much as they did all over Greece. But for the ancient Greeks, Boeotia was closely associated with same-sex love.[42]

Some scholars quote a writer living centuries later, an associate of the philosopher Socrates called Xenophon who wrote, 'The Boeotians live together – man and boyfriend – as if they are married'.[43] There is tantalizing material evidence corroborating Xenophon's claim. As archaeologists worked on a small site in Boeotia, something seemed to protrude out of the dirt and the mud. They knelt and began to brush carefully at it. It was a widemouthed cup, called a skyphos, which some thousands of years ago would have been used for drinking – possibly water, possibly wine – before it was lost to time. As the archaeologists extracted it and brushed it down, an image loomed into view.

On the cup, four young men stand tall with small, scratchy beards spread across their faces. They are fully grown, but not yet middle-aged. Two of the men, right in the centre, are wrapped together in the same cloak.[44] The cloak is a dark colour, decorated with swastikas – symbols of peace and life, long before the Nazis reappropriated them. The intricacy of this design points to a ceremony of tremendous importance. Some scholars have claimed that the cloak hides the two men as they have sex. This seems extremely unlikely – as we'll see later, there are plenty of drinking and mixing cups which pull no punches about their pornographic details. So, what was it for?

We know that cloaks were sometimes used in ancient marriage ceremonies, often with the bride wearing a man's cloak, as in Spartan weddings for instance.[45] Could it be that this innocuous drinking cup preserved for thousands of years the ritual Xenophon alludes to? The moment two men, their arms beneath the cloak, are joined to form one in a marriage-like bond – together forever as 'man and boyfriend'. If this is so, it is all the more remarkable that the two men at the centre of the skyphos seem to be the same age.[46]

A native Boeotian, Heracles was a legendary hero renowned for his ability to wrestle fire-breathing horses and kill many-headed hydras, as well as for his ambitious turns at engineering projects. As a young man, he was said to fall in love with a handsome youth called Iolaus, who became his closest companion and helped Heracles in many of his famous 12 labours. In many a children's storybook, he is remembered as Heracles' 'friend'. Heracles married women and he fathered children, but he was always said to retain a special affection for Iolaus. Their relationship was so close that when an army threatened Heracles' children – decades after their father's death – Iolaus rode into battle as an old man and miraculously transformed once more into a handsome youth.[47] According to Aristotle, young male lovers in ancient Boeotia would stand by the tomb of Iolaus and declare their love for each other.[48]

This tomb was a sacred site in Thebes, the Boeotian capital, a stone's throw from the gymnasium dedicated to Heracles. They were just as close in death as ever they had been in life.

ATHENS

In this period, Athens did not yet have her beautiful theatres, her marble statues or her glittering temple to Athena on the Acropolis. These would come later. They were the products of an expansive and greedy empire which Athens sucked dry for her own enrichment. Athens in this period was very much like other city-states: replete with a king, a few noble aristocrats and a vast population of serfs and slaves.

The rulers of Athens sprung from the nobility, from the leisure class. These men never worked for money a day in their lives. In fact, they would have regarded the very concept of work with terrible disdain. Instead, they spent most of their time training in the gym. Each member of the ruling families belonged to an *oikos* – a household. Their money came largely from huge farming estates worked by their serfs – the olive groves which dotted the surrounding area, as well as from mines. What they lacked in industry, they made up for in their canny ability to put down revolutions.

As in Megara, whenever the poor showed signs of revolt, the rich would, as if by magic, appear to pay for large, spectacular festivals. When a group of noble families approached Thespis, the most talented of Athens' festival choreographers, with a proposition, they wanted to pay him to combine the exquisite skill of his dancers with singing and storytelling to bring theatre to life. This – they hoped – would put an end to the pesky agitations of the *hoi polloi* (Greek for 'the many'). Ostensibly, these productions were performed under the auspices of the god Dionysus, but their true purpose was far less idealistic.

The poor were well fed at local temples, as aristocrats often competed with one another to provide the largest number of animals for slaughter. At the festival of Demeter, pork – a luxury for most people – was served, goat at the festival of Artemis.[49] The poor could expect to be wined and dined on holy days in return for their complicity in the rule of the aristocracy. The super-rich, in turn, were very careful in their own displays of wealth, and never had large, ostentatious houses.[50]

Some have mistaken this continuous redistribution of money for a kind of proto-communism, but aristocrats sat on a vast pile of cash, and only lifted a finger to redistribute a tiny fraction of it when they sensed rebellion in the air. The super-rich men of noble birth regarded everyone beneath them with snobbish disapproval – they nicknamed the poor the *kakoi*, or the 'evil ones'.

From time to time, the *kakoi* had had enough and not even a good show and some pork could satisfy them. Sometime around 700 BCE, they banded together to depose the kings of Athens. The elites responded by removing the king and installing not a democratic state, but a wider (though no less exclusive) circle of aristocrats. A complex system of government was devised which involved an *archon* (a ruler), a *polemarchos* (a warlord), a *basileus* (a religious leader) and six officials responsible for the administration of the city's affairs.[51] Anyone who worked for a living was excluded from political roles – which would remain for hundreds of years in the hands of those who were born into wealth.

In 594 BCE, a statesman called Solon was appointed *archon* (literally 'ruler'). At the time, the Athenian poor were heavily indebted to the rich, and he immediately set about reforming the constitution and passed sweeping reforms to forgive the debts of the poor.[52] He changed the value of the currency to make repayment of any outstanding debts much easier. He made debt slavery illegal, and he granted citizenship to huge numbers of serfs. Solon's new citizen criteria were based not on noble birth, but on how much land you owned. Those who had made their own money now had a stake in the city. As citizens, they now had the power to stand in the assembly and to help in the process of drawing up laws. Solon's masterstroke – or so he thought – was to give the wealthier members of the lower classes some stake in government and thus prevent revolution against the aristocrats forever. Solon was not just a politician, he was a poet. We have few surviving fragments of his writing, but one of them is especially revealing:

> Be one who loves boys in the flower of youth
> Desiring their thighs and their sweet mouths.[53]

Years later, Aristotle mentions a rumour that Solon was the mentor of the later tyrant of Athens, Peisistratus.[54] This word 'mentor' may have had erotic connotations, but Aristotle is quick to explain that they were not suitable ages and so they could never have been mentors. Even later writers claim that Solon 'was seized by erotic desire for Peisistratus'.[55] That writer also tells us that Solon 'was not secure against handsome men'.[56] Not only were there rumours around Solon and his love life, but he was able to write poetry openly and plainly praising queer desire. Could it be that Solon's reforms to wealth inequality had led to a rise in same-sex desire? Could it be that Solon himself was gay?

Solon was not the only Athenian inspired by queer love. Archaeologists have uncovered a large hoard of Athenian vases that display men having sex with each other in various positions. In one scene, a group of bearded men bend over a wine bowl. One man stands behind another and not-so-subtly slides into his partner (who is also bearded).[57] In another from 550 BCE, men exchange gifts, naked, while erect. They are of the same height and identical builds, though often one has a beard and the other does not.[58] On another pot, two men of identical age, who are both beardless, have sex, while the passive partner rests his arm lazily against the side of a pot. In addition to these pots, there is epigraphical evidence of same-sex desire in Athens. In graffiti from the 6th and 5th centuries BCE, fragments have been found scratched onto walls such as 'Lysitheus says that he loves Micion especially of the men in the city, for he is brave', as well as a catalogue of men's names who are all described as 'beautiful'.[59]

For the most part, there is evidence of a partial tolerance of same-sex love in Athens. But there were still laws that detailed who could and could not have gay sex. Solon is said to have written a law forbidding slaves from engaging in homosexuality, because he deemed them incapable of conducting themselves honourably.[60] This has traditionally been interpreted as evidence that homosexuality was for the elite only, but it could equally be understood as evidence that raping a slave was not – in this period – considered an honourable practice. The most acceptable time for these relationships to take place was when both men were still young. However, there can be no doubt from later sources that many of these youthful dalliances became life-long relationships, especially in Boeotia, as Xenophon suggests.

It is particularly noteworthy that this florescence of same-sex desire coincided with a period when some inequalities were levelled in the Athenian economy.

SPARTA

Archaic Sparta was at war with its neighbouring city-states from the earliest periods of recorded history. A rivalry with neighbouring Messenia fomented political infighting to the extent that it exploded onto the streets. This crisis left half the Spartan citizenry completely without land or money, while the other half was rich and prosperous.[61] The only solution – as it had been in Athens and in Megara – was a redistribution of wealth, but unfortunately, 'half-hearted' would be the best adjective to describe the Spartan approach to this unwelcome change in political affairs.

For centuries, the Spartans attributed the political changes during this dark time to one man: a politician named Lycourgos. Lycourgos is shrouded in mystery, and likely mythical; the laws that have been attributed to him were probably drawn up by a group of Spartan elders. Lycourgos was said to have abolished the use of silver and gold and to have forbidden extravagant burials and public displays of wealth. He also seized private property and carved it up, redistributing it among Spartan citizens. To this day, this mythology has a strong grip on our imaginations. Sparta is often portrayed as a heavily militaristic society of comrades in which few possessed any private wealth at all: the very meaning of the English word 'spartan'. But, as far as we can tell, the reality was somewhat different.

Sparta operated a system of equality in name only; whatever equality existed was highly performative.[62] Spartans met and dined in public mess halls, where the rich and the poor alike ate together. They also trained for war together – men trained with men, and women were also expected to be fighting-fit, as Lycourgos felt this physical fitness would prepare them for the trauma of childbirth. Yet we are told by 4th-century BCE sources that there was no shortage of private wealth.

In practice, wealth was the sole decider of Spartan class. Xenophon tells us that the rich in Sparta paid for the redistribution of bread to the poor, and the very rich made money by selling horses. Aristotle tells us, 'When some are excessively poor, others are excessively rich . . . this occurred during the Second Messenian War'.[63] Clearly, the image of Sparta as an egalitarian state was not one with which other ancient Greeks were familiar. To respond to these inequalities, Spartans developed a new system of politics.

One Spartan warrior, Aristodemus of Sparta (died 479 BCE), was reported to have said, 'A man is only what he owns'.[64] Their society superficially seemed to have equality, but in reality was highly competitive and individualistic. The Spartan political watchword was self-control. Preserve your own resources, and look after yourself and your family above all others. Sparta was a highly conservative society. This way you would have the money to pass down to your children. However, self-control as a political narrative extended far beyond financial resources. Xenophon tells us that one of Lycourgos' first acts was to encourage sexual shame among Spartan men.

'He laid down [a law] that a man should be ashamed to be seen entering or leaving his wife's quarters. By restricting sex, a man's desire for his wife was increased, their offspring would be stronger than had they been satisfied with one another'.⁶⁵ Conservatism was shown not just in Spartan approaches to the economy, but also in their approaches to sex. Financial self-restraint was mirrored by sexual self-restraint. Sexual desire became a weapon to be wielded by the state.

Not content with shaming heterosexuals into a frighteningly reductive relationship with sex, Lycourgos then turned his attention to queer people. In a dry passage from the *Spartan Lawcode*, all male homosexual activity was banned.⁶⁶ Men were to cultivate close, deep friendships, but anybody caught displaying 'outward desire' or consummating these deep friendships with sex was in violation of the law. This may come as a surprise to readers used to a later myth that ritualized homosexuality took place between warriors in Sparta; if it did, this ritualized bond between warriors must have been thoroughly Platonic in character. Interestingly, this may not have been true of female same-sex desire. The poetry of the Spartan singer Alcman – a lyric poet like Sappho and Theognis – preserves accounts of women giving erotic compliments to each other, and some scholars have speculated that Alcman's *First Maiden Song* may even contain a marriage-like ritual, which possibly had the aim of allowing unmarried women to live out their lives together.⁶⁷ It is possible that the emphasis on financial self-control and sexual self-restraint, at least in Sparta, was a masculine one.

The history of archaic Greece tells a story of two very different approaches to wealth inequality. In some cases, it was dealt with pragmatically: land was redistributed, and political equality was introduced. This system – though far from perfect – seems to have coincided with a flourishing of poetry and material culture celebrating same-sex desire.

In Sparta, however, wealth inequality may have been dealt with by a fetishization of self-discipline. Public displays of wealth were banned, but there seems to have been no effort to dislodge private wealth from the hands of a few. In addition, men were encouraged to believe that if they controlled their finances and desires they could hope to achieve high social status. Sex was shamed, and gay sex was forbidden.

ACHILLES AND PATROCLUS

The warlike Spartans might have enacted one of the first known homophobic laws in Greece, but among many other city-states there was a strong association between queer desire, military strength and legendary warriors. The *Iliad* by Homer is one of the oldest works of literature to survive from anywhere in the world. We don't know who Homer was, or even whether he was a real person, but after being passed down orally through the generations, the stories were finally written down some time in the 7th century BCE.[68] The *Iliad* tells the story of one of mythology's greatest warriors, Achilles, who was summoned alongside the whole of Greece in a mighty call to arms, and they sailed – under the command of Agamemnon, king of Mycenae – for Troy. Encamped around Troy's mighty walls, the Greeks waited for ten long years, fighting skirmishes on a near-daily basis with their Trojan foes.

Achilles had won many battles, and one of his spoils of war was Briseis, the daughter of a priest. But at the beginning of the *Iliad*, the enslaved Briseis is confiscated by the mighty Agamemnon. He takes Briseis as a show of his own strength and power, in part because he is intimidated by Achilles. Achilles is furious.

Achilles withdraws from battle while plague encircles the Greek camp, and he watches from the sidelines as his fellow soldiers are slaughtered in battle. One man stays by his side – Patroclus. Together, they play music, cook and eat, refusing to fight for their Greek allies in protest at Agamemnon's behaviour. They share the same quarters, though Homer boringly doesn't tell us whether they share a bed. The war ravages the Greek army, and they become desperate – they beg Achilles for his help and for the help of his army, the Myrmidons. But Achilles refuses to rejoin the battle.

Desperate, Patroclus begs Achilles to help. When Achilles refuses, Patroclus takes Achilles' helmet and armour and rides into battle. When they see Patroclus charging toward them, the Trojans scatter in terror – Achilles, so they think, has rejoined the fray. One man, Hector the prince of Troy, takes on Patroclus in one-to-one combat and cuts him down. Hours later, a messenger treads into Achilles' camp.

He stands before Achilles and his handmaidens and delivers the news that Patroclus – his dear friend – is dead. Achilles stood by as countless Greeks were killed, but in that moment of terrible grief, he reaches for the ashes of a nearby fire and smothers them over his face. He tears at his hair and screams into the sky. Hot tears gush down his face. In Greek culture, this was how a wife mourned her husband. Indeed, the words Homer uses at that point in the *Iliad* echo those he will use later when recounting how Andromache, princess of Troy, mourns the loss of her husband, Hector.

Homer is coy about the precise nature of the relationship between Achilles and Patroclus, and scholars have speculated that this can be attributed to the divided nature of Greek cities on the question of same-sex love. As we have seen, Athens, Megara and Boeotia were all in favour. But in Sparta, homosexual acts were illegal. Homer (or whoever first wrote the epics down) was a poet for all Greeks; his weary diplomacy goes a long way in explaining his silence. However, the intensity of their relationship and of Achilles' grief has made same-sex love a tempting inference for generations of readers. As time went on, the Greeks would look back on this relationship. Plato and future generations continued to question whether or not they were lovers. The Achilles and Patroclus story would become something of a bellwether of how far the Greeks were willing to tolerate queer love.

TWO

How Money Corrupted Love

> I put a stop to the bottoms, when I annihilated Gryttus!
> CLEON IN ARISTOPHANES, KNIGHTS 877

In 480 BCE, the Persians captured Athens. Fire raged and cries tore through the air as foreign soldiers in strange, woven fabrics charged into that ancient, hallowed city. The heads of gods were smashed off and rolled across the bloody ground as men, women and children fled for the hills and for the sea. That vast eastern shadow, the Persian Empire, had finally swooped to capture its prize. As the Persians razed the city, they were careful to erase every aspect of Athenian culture.

In the centre of the Athenian marketplace stood a bronze statue of two men. One reaches out to strike down some invisible enemy, while the other raises his hammer to the sky. Their names were Harmodius and Aristogeiton,[1] and they were famous in Athens for their role in the downfall of the last of Athens' tyrants. Doubtless, Persia – under the rule of the mighty monarch Xerxes – wished to dispose of such stirring anti-authoritarian iconography. But behind this statue lay another story.

Harmodius was a devastatingly handsome nobleman with important family connections. Like most other Greek aristocrats, he spent much of his time at the gym. He may have played with the discus, wrestled naked or lifted large, rectangular weights with handholds called *halteres*.[2] One day, he caught the eye of Aristogeiton, who unlike Harmodius was a member of Athens' new middle class, and had few family connections. It was an unlikely match between a mentor and a mentee, but they fell in love.[3,4]

The last tyrant of Athens was called Hippias. He had a brother, a proud man called Hipparchus, who in a twist of fate also lusted after the beautiful Harmodius. One day, at the gym, Hipparchus propositioned Harmodius and made it very clear that he intended to have sex with him, whether Harmodius was willing or not. This was not a harmless flirtation, it was a display of power, a threat of rape. When Harmodius declined, Hipparchus was furious. He made it clear that if Harmodius continued to refuse, he would sorely regret it.

Harmodius and Aristogeiton were uneasy. Aristogeiton did not have the power or the men to defend his boyfriend from the wrathful Hipparchus. So they resigned themselves to waiting to see what Hipparchus' next move would be and did their best to keep a low profile.

Weeks passed. Back at Harmodius' family home, his sister was preparing for her debut role in the year's festivities. Beaming with pride, the whole family walked out together into the street. It was then that Hipparchus struck. Shouting profanities at Harmodius' sister in front of all gathered there, he forbade her from joining in the festivities. Failure to attend ceremonies in Athens implied you had some kind of *miasma*, a malevolent force which surrounded you and risked polluting the sacred space in which the ceremony took place. Harmodius' whole family had been shunned and shamed by one of the most powerful men in Athens. Aristogeiton was enraged. The two lovers plotted revenge, both convinced this was only the beginning. They feared Hipparchus would stop at nothing to have Harmodius. He was – like his tyrant brother – a brutal man with a taste for violence and a whole gang of henchmen at his command.

The day of one of the most important festivals, the Panathenaia, dawned. Women and men lined the streets and a procession passed through the city from the Kerameikos district to the temple of Athena on the Acropolis.[5] A huge robe or *peplos* coloured a saffron-yellow was carried through the streets on a wagon built to resemble a ship, destined to adorn the great statue of Athena in the Erechtheum. Women sang and danced around the temple, and the air was rich with roasting meat to be distributed among the people as a sacrifice to Athena. Thucydides tells us that this was the only festival where men were allowed openly carry weapons around the city.[6] This small detail was essential to Harmodius and Aristogeiton's plan.

Arm in arm, they found Hipparchus in the crowd and stabbed him. His henchmen came running. Harmodius – that handsome man Hipparchus had so wanted – was killed instantly on the spot. Aristogeiton saw the life fade from his lover's eyes before he was dragged away, beaten and bloody, for questioning. Tossed into a dark prison, he was tortured for days while the tyrant Hippias orchestrated a brutal crackdown on the city. The horrors perpetrated by Hippias after his brother's murder spurred the Athenians (with a little help from Sparta) to free themselves from tyranny.

As Athens transitioned to a democratic state, the story of Harmodius and Aristogeiton was continuously retold. These were the men whose love was so strong that they stood up to a tyrant and in doing so precipitated the fall of his family from power. Hippias was, thanks to Harmodius and Aristogeiton, the last tyrant of Athens. During this early classical era, queer love was taking on a markedly different tone in the public imagination. It was less erotic, and more noble. These lovers were the men who made Athens into the city that we have immortalized ever since as the Western crucible of democracy and learning.

That is why the Persians, as they set Athens ablaze, made sure to remove the monument to Harmodius and Aristogeiton as they reduced the city's landmarks, including the temple to Athena on the Acropolis, to rubble. Tyrant-slayers could not be countenanced.[7]

THE RAPE OF EURYMEDON

Over a few decades, the Greeks successfully repelled Persia from their homeland. Strengthened by an alliance of Greek city-states and islands, the Athenian forces met the Persians at a large river called the Eurymedon, in modern-day southern Turkey. The victory was decisive. Back home in Greece, wine flowed and victory paeans were uproariously sung.

But there is a darker side to this story of military triumph. One Greek vase from the period depicts a disturbing scene. On one side, a Persian man clad in pyjama-like robes is bent over, his hands raised in the air in a gesture of surrender. Behind him stands a Greek warrior, naked but for a woollen cloak or *chlamys* fastened about his shoulders which does nothing to obscure his erection. He reaches out for the Persian with one hand. The other hand is grasped firmly around his penis. The meaning could not be clearer. As the defeated men ran for the hills, they were pursued by Greek forces intent on raping their vanquished enemies. The gory celebration of rape preserved on what has come to be known as the Eurymedon vase has been interpreted by some classicists as a sign of tolerance and acceptance of same-sex desire in the period. But is it really?

Rape, especially male-male rape, is used throughout the ancient world as a symbol of total defeat and humiliation. The coffin of one Egyptian warlord reads, perhaps prosaically, 'Atum has no power over me, for I fuck his buttocks'.[8] While Athens and other Greek city-states regarded same-sex desire as a power capable of destroying tyranny, this did not stop them from using rape on the battlefield as a means of cementing their own masculinity. It seems inevitable that returning Greek soldiers would associate anal sex with victory on the battlefield and, before long, Greek pottery began to celebrate these rape scenes. In fact, in the ancient Greek imagination, anal sex had far less to do with desire or love than with the grim business of war.

It is common, particularly in the study of ancient Rome, as we will see, to confuse frequent mentions of same-sex rape with a tolerance of homoeroticism. But a man who rapes another man or who uses sex as a means to express aggression is not the same as a man who desires other men. It may even be possible that the more a society associates homoeroticism with rape, the less likely it is to tolerate queer love.

Other stories would be told for many years around the Mediterranean that echoed the idea that same-sex love was antithetical to tyranny. The stories of gay men who fought and died together to protect their lovers would form the basis of many a tale of how tyrants came crashing down. Indeed, the writer Xenophon opined on the antithesis between tyrants and gay love:

> A tyrant is less well equipped to fall in love with boyfriends than he is to have children. Making love is by far the more pleasant if it is done with desire [rather than by necessity]. Desire always comes less naturally to a tyrant – Desire does not reach for attainable things, but the ones the Desirer hopes for.[9]

For Xenophon, same-sex love is antithetical to tyranny because it is primarily motivated by desire, not by the need to procreate.[10] If a tyrant wished to accrue more power and more status, they would forge an alliance and further their line through marriage with a woman – they wouldn't love another man, just for his own sake. Xenophon's views reflect a broader understanding once held by the democratic system of Athens – love between two men could act as a bulwark against dictatorship.

Harmodius and Aristogeiton were held up as exemplars of freedom because they could fall in love, because they could consent to love and because they died for love. When the Athenians regained control over their city, they rebuilt their statue. The Athenian statesman Pericles exhorted the Athenians to 'look upon Athens and become her lovers'.[11] It was a reminder to all: tyranny is not beaten by force in one fell swoop, it is eroded by one unstoppable power, a power which the tyrant cannot know – the power of love. For the Athenians, this love was – initially at least – quintessentially and unalterably the love of one man for another. It was queer love.

HOW QUEER WAS CLASSICAL ATHENS?

Scooped out of the earth on the south side of the highest hill in Athens, the Acropolis, lies a curious ruin. Steps cut into the rock reveal the outlines of rising rows of seats which fan out from a small, round, marble floor. To stand here and to look up at the towering acropolis, some 2,500 years later, is to stand on the spot where modern drama as we know it was born. Every performance from opera to late-night TV claims as ancestor the chiselled geography of this Greek hillside.

It was here that a hardened veteran of the Persian wars, thought to have been born during the reign of Hippias, came to stage his tragedies. Aeschylus was his name. Aeschylus was an accomplished innovator, and we think he wrote as many as 90 plays, though only a small handful survive. Arguably, his most famous is his depiction of the cycles of grief, mental disease and violence that could tear apart noble households in the *Oresteia*.

Aeschylus met his end when an eagle dropped a turtle upon his bald head, bludgeoning that poor genius to an instant death. Drama owes as much to Aeschylus as it does to Thespis. It was Aeschylus who reformed the musical accompaniment to plays, who instituted rules about the number of actors on stage and who crafted perennial tragedies that are still performed to this day. But it was also Aeschylus who, sometime between 470 and 450 BCE, staged a remarkable production in the history of queer theatre.

Achilles and Patroclus' love story was, as we've already seen, thinly disguised by Homer – the only clues in the text are Achilles' inconsolable grief and the advice his own mother gives him to find another lover after Patroclus' death. But that was more than enough for the Athenians, who were in no doubt that Achilles and Patroclus were among the greatest tragic lovers in history. There was even a rumour that Achilles and Patroclus' ashes were interred in the same grave. While ancient Greek librarians used to explain that for Homer to describe the relationship truly between Achilles and Patroclus, it wouldn't be *prepon* or 'proper',[12] this seems not to have troubled Aeschylus.

Aeschylus – the gruff and shaggy-bearded veteran-turned-playwright – staged a play entitled The *Myrmidons* (mur-mur-dons) centring on the death of Patroclus. The title came from the band of fighters who were Achilles' sworn men. Sometimes depicted in black armour, the battle-hungry Myrmidons were forced to sit and wait by the great Greek ships moored in deep trenches in the sand while Achilles refused to fight. When they returned to battle, the very sight of this elite fighting force, as they leapt over the Trojan palisade and charged at their enemy, was enough to make even the hardiest warriors turn and flee in terror. The *Myrmidons* survives only in fragments, but these fragments provide quite enough for us to reconstruct the events of the play.

A series of ambassadors pass over the threshold of Achilles' hut. They see him sitting inside, playing lazily with his lyre and singing to Patroclus. They beg him to return to battle, but Achilles – angry at King Agamemnon – stubbornly refuses. Agamemnon threatens him with stoning. Achilles reacts furiously. After everything he has done for the Greek army, they would tie him up at a post and pelt him with rocks?

Late at night, the Greeks are caught off-guard by a surprise attack. The Trojans set the entire Greek fleet ablaze. Ships in the ancient world often had wax figurines on the outside, and a wax cockerel on one of the Greek ships melts down the bow. The ambassadors return once more to beg Achilles' help. He refuses. It's at this point that Patroclus snaps and rides into battle wearing Achilles' armour – and is cut down.

After his death, the ghost of Patroclus returns to speak to Achilles, furious at the great warrior for abandoning him and the army. The language he uses leaves very little to the imagination:

It seems, Achilles, that you never appreciated the sacredness of my thighs,
You never were grateful for those countless kisses.[13]

Patroclus' ghost reminds Achilles of the love they shared, both physically and emotionally. Achilles is distraught. In one famous line, he tells another warrior, 'Pity the living, not the dead, Antilochus. Everything I had is gone'.[14] And unlike Aristogeiton, he had not been there for his lover's final moments. As Achilles himself says, 'There is a tale told among the Africans: one day an eagle soaring through the sky was struck by an arrow. He had seen the arrow was fashioned of eagle feathers, and he had said, "So I meet my end, not at another's hand, but at my own."'[15] Achilles laments the tragedy that he wrought himself: Patroclus died because of his own failure to act.

The extraordinary thing, from our perspective, is that this tale played out on the Athenian stage in front of thousands of audience members. Aeschylus even stages a scene where Achilles has sex with the dead body of his lover,[16] but the fact that the play was performed means that the subject matter was not considered obscene. There were severe consequences for producing a play that fell foul of public mores: one playwright, Phrynichus, was fined for a play depicting the capture of the city of Miletus in the 490s BCE. Aeschylus apparently received no such fine or disgrace. Tolerance (even celebration) of same-sex love was secure for now. However, it's hard to provide a date for this play's performance. It's thought to have been staged sometime between the years 470 and 456 BCE (after the time of the Persian invasion).[17]

The ancient world did not have magazines or the internet. But it did have pots. Pottery might seem an unlikely medium for pornography, but Athens had a thriving export industry sending images across the sea to modern-day Italy, where the Etruscan people – in particular – collected their pots enthusiastically. Etruria and its people had an unorthodox relationship to sexuality: unlike in the rest of the ancient world, marital sex was celebrated and the Etruscans both produced and bought art which showed off passionate sex between married people.[18]

This industry had begun in earnest in the 6th century BCE. One famous artist, now known as The Affecter, depicted men in varying states of undress. One Athenian pot that was dug up in Vulci, Italy, shows two naked older men. One is playing a pipe, and in front of him stands the other, pointing keenly at his own bum while looking back at the pipe-player with an expression of arrested supplication on his face. Other cups show younger couples without beards touching each other, each holding the other's penis. One shows a man standing behind his lover and reaching out a longing finger for his behind. A vase recovered from Orvieto shows an even racier set-up: four men stand patiently in line, waiting their turn to have sex with another man lying prone on the ground.

The porn pot industry tells us that this period in human history was remarkably tolerant of and very interested in same-sex desire. Combined with plays like the *Myrmidons*, a picture emerges of a culture in which queer imagery and storytelling was popular. But by the year 450 BCE, the gay porn pot industry had almost entirely stopped.[19] This was an ominous sign.

THE RICH GET RICHER, THE POOR GET POORER

Amid the ashes of the Persian wars, the Athenians saw an opportunity. They banded together a large number of smaller city-states and islands to form the Delian League, so called because of the island of Delos – where the league was sworn in at the sacred shrine of the muscly god of music, Apollo. Members of the league contributed money to a collective treasury, which was supposed to be used to build up armaments for mutual defence. For a few years, Delos was the home of this treasury, where it was carefully guarded by a select group of priests. Unfortunately for the priests, as the Persian threat subsided, Athens began to have other ideas.

The treasury was moved from the island of Delos to Athens, which, the Athenians felt, needed a bit of sprucing up. They had long nursed a desire for a salaried, standing army and a marble temple with an enormous bronze statue of Athena. In effect, this standing army of soldiers formed a new class of freemen with considerable disposable incomes. Fighting abroad in tiny skirmishes with neighbouring peasant villages was an incredibly lucrative business for the lower-middle-class men of Athens.

We have some idea of how lucrative. These soldiers were paid roughly one drachma per day,[20] but the cost of feeding a family was considerably less, at one obol per day (around one-sixth of a drachma). This meant there was suddenly a large proportion of the non-slave Athenian population with money to burn. Many more citizens could now afford luxuries. But it was not just soldiers who suddenly found themselves inundated with such riches. The artisans and labourers who built all of Athens' new monuments, from the Parthenon marbles to the City Dionysia Theatre, were given a similar wage. Athens had done what Nazi Germany would do in the 1930s: given its citizens exceptionally well-paid work to build infrastructure and maintain the standing army while enslaving large portions of the population. This influx of money freed those lucky enough to be Athenian citizens from having to work agricultural land, while for the many slaves life remained essentially unchanged.

Many of this new middle class bought up farms and land in the territory surrounding Athens, called Attica. Households were established. Little trinkets could be afforded. Wine shops opened. Recreational consumption was no longer just for the super-rich. Previously, Greeks had frowned upon public displays of wealth,[21] they had refrained from burying their dead with expensive items. Now, the economic situation was beginning to change.

Of course, all this money also made the rich even richer. As in previous times, their strategy was to keep the poor and the middle class from revolting by paying for ever more extravagant building and artistic projects. This became so common that a word for it was born: *leitourgia*. The *leitourgiai* (plural of *leitourgia*) comprised a list of projects that needed to be paid for, which the aristocracy was asked to contribute to in lieu of taxation. They – of course – had their preference for projects. It was a young noble called Pericles, for instance, who paid for Aeschylus to stage a play about the defeat of the Greeks' enemy, *Persians*. Less fortunate aristocrats would grumble about having to pay for warships. Presumably, a warship was less glamorous than a theatre, because theatres didn't tend to sink. The whole point in paying for extravagant projects was so the public could see your generosity and largesse, preserved in marble, or be entertained lavishly at your expense.

However, as the century drew on, the aristocrats were increasingly outgunned. A new generation of self-made super-rich individuals emerged. Their parents had started small-scale businesses which began to export across the wide, deep-blue seas. Soon they had so much money they could dwarf what many aristocrats could afford. Unfortunately for the poor, these self-made men were far less charitable. In fact, they often resented having to contribute at all.

Cleon son of Cleanetus was, by all accounts, an ugly man both in stature and temperament. Cleon was a member of Athens' nouveau riche. He had started life as a leather tanner, which may have been his father's profession too. He was also a gifted speaker, capable of whipping up a mob. Athens was a fully fledged democracy at the time – some may argue more democratic in the purest sense than anything that exists in the modern world. But by this time, almost all checks and balances had been removed from the assembly.[22] The thousands of citizens of Athens who gathered to debate motions and make decisions about key public affairs were little more than an unrestrained mob. Cleon was right at home.

It was said that when he first gained office, Cleon cut ties with all his friends so that he would never favour them over the city.[23] By the height of Cleon's influence, Athens was deep into a long and protracted war with Sparta. Once tentative allies in the face of the Persian threat, Sparta and Athens were now in perpetual conflict. Without fail, skirmishes would break out every summer, the ancient Greek fighting season. It was in the midst of this war that one island, Mytilene, chose – most unwisely – to revolt.

In 428 BCE, the small island city of Mytilene, located on Lesbos in the eastern Aegean, broke with Athens. Mytilene was not a democracy but a small oligarchy and always felt somewhat at odds with Athens' view of the world. In 428, they sent an embassy to the Spartans asking for their help. To say Athens was unhappy would put it mildly.

In the debate on Mytilene,[24] Cleon got to his feet. Addressing his powerful faction of self-made men, he made a statement that is familiar to us today. 'Men of Athens, a lack of learning, so long as it is accompanied with self-control is more useful than learned governance with *excess*. Those [of us] who are less well-born can manage the house of state far better than they can!'.[25] The elites – so Cleon says – may have their degrees, their intellectual ideas, but those of us who have made their own way in the world, without all that fancy learning, are the only ones who truly know how to run the state. Intelligence and academic advancement are unnecessary, useless and, even worse, a sign of excess.

Cleon argued for the total destruction of Mytilene and its people. He argued, in other words, for genocide. Whipping up the mob, he favoured sending an Athenian regiment to murder the men, women and children of the island. Mass butchery was, he claimed, the only way to teach the Mytileneans what befalls pride and arrogance. Cleon won. A huge warship set sail to put all the people of Mytilene to the sword. Only when the Athenian assembly met on the second day did a more reasoned side persuade the audience to relent. A second, faster vessel was sent to intercept the warship. It arrived just in time to stay the slaughter.

Cleon ultimately believed in one political narrative: *self-control*. He convinced himself and his followers that this was how he had obtained his vast wealth; his shrewd management of household finances extended to all his other activities in life. The verb which he used in the Mytilene debate, to describe how 'the less well-born can manage the house of state far better', was *oikousi*, from which the modern word 'economics' ultimately derives. The comparison of the affairs of the state to a household balance sheet was not invented in the 20th-century West. It is at least 2,500 years old. But – just as in the case of Margaret Thatcher and Ronald Reagan – this populist, household-centred view of the world ended in disaster for the queer people of ancient Athens.

It is in a satirical play by Aristophanes, who was certainly no fan of Cleon's, where we find the first clue about his behaviour. In a rant against Athens' ingratitude for his brilliance, Cleon, the protagonist, says, 'I put a stop to the *binoumenoi*, when I annihilated Gryttus!'[26]

The word *binoumenoi* comes from the verb *bineo*, which means 'I fuck', but it's in the passive. In English, it means something like 'the men who get fucked'; Greek as ever succeeds in fitting quite the mouthful of a phrase into a single, pithy word. Cleon is – in this play – boasting about having put a stop to a group of men who enjoyed getting fucked. He goes further; he describes his pleasure in wiping out a certain Gryttus. The verb he uses means to totally eradicate, to wipe from the face of a surface, to utterly erase. But who was this Gryttus?

Fortunately, a group of ancient Greeks used to write in the margins of play scripts to explain meanings at greater length. These highly useful historical commentaries are tricky to navigate: they are so compendious that nobody has ever translated them into English. They are called *scholia*. But one ancient Greek scholiast did write a *scholion* (the singular of *scholia*) to this line. He said, 'Of the many men who were calumnied for gay sex, one was Gryttus. A man who on account of his campness and being prone to pleasure used up all his time among male companions ... Cleon the demagogue sentenced him to death as a punishment'.[27] So, sometime in the 420s BCE, Athens made an example of this man, Gryttus. He died for the crime of having sex with other men.[28]

It is no coincidence that queer love in Athens came to be demonized around the same time that the politics of self-control was rising in popularity. Gay men became symbols of a depraved lack of self-control and abstinence. Athens had fallen. In the space of 100 years, Athens had gone from being a city known for its beautiful porn pots, a city where thousands enjoyed plays and stories about the power of gay love, to this – the forced execution of a man whose only crime seems to have been having sex with other men.

By this stage, a conspiracy of events precipitated by a rapid rise in wealth inequality had led to a politics of self-control. Cleon argued the people were better than the elites with their fancy theories, their fancy wines and their fancy parties. The trouble is that most of Cleon's audience probably also enjoyed spending their hard-earned cash on good wine imported from abroad. They would have all wanted a piece of the landed estates and the luxurious, extravagant houses of the super-rich. So Cleon found a different kind of extravagance to rail against.

Who better to attack than gay men? Gay sex was a symbol of stepping outside the boundaries of self-control, a symbol of extravagance and excess. To make matters worse, anal sex was increasingly seen as indissoluble from the theatre of war and the rape of enemy soldiers. Gay sex had the additional advantage of being an irreplaceable desire for only a very small fraction of the population. It became the perfect target. For the first time in the recorded history of Athens, men were put to death for the crime of gay sex.

A MAN'S WORLD

In ancient Greece – and later in Rome – to be *andreios*, or 'masculine', was to be perfect. It was to have attained the highest ideal of beauty. This is largely why Greek statues of men were naked, for the most part, and women were veiled or clothed. On the other hand, women were thought of as inferior creatures. Of course, ancient Greek education offered a confounding factor here. Women were barred from gymnasia, barred from most – if not all – athletic practices and barred from any form of serious education. We should always be wary of blanket rules and, to be sure, there were exceptions such as the socialite Aspasia who was said to have influenced the young Socrates.[29] But, in general, the average woman was believed to be much weaker, both physically and intellectually, than the average man.

It is not that women were considered an inferior and separate category of human being, but rather that womanhood was considered an inferior form of manhood. Gender was a spectrum, with virile, violent and beautiful men at the apex, less respectable men further down and women beneath them. Ancient Greek philosophy and medicine suggest that men and women, both dominant and subservient, could be shuffled up and down this spectrum and, in our terminology, change gender. However, this conception of gender as a spectrum rather than a binary did lead to some particularly odd ideas in the nascent discipline of ancient Greek medicine. Hippocrates was probably the first doctor in the West to apply something like the scientific method to healing. But in the matter of masculinity, he was just as strange as his fellow countrymen. He promoted the idea that the penis could shrivel and invert inside the body, leaving a vagina in its wake.

There is a small city on the island of Phaistos, which was home to a woman called Galatea.[30] Legend had it that her husband Lampros had told her to expose any female child she bore. The baby girl was to be taken to a mountainside and left for the wolves. Galatea became pregnant, and as her belly swelled, so did her fear. She gave birth in complete secret. All alone and terrified, she cradled her child. It was a girl. She struggled to stand and vowed that she would lie and pretend that her baby girl was in fact a boy.

Years passed, and Galatea dressed her daughter in boys' clothes, and she played and trained as any young man ought to. But eventually, Lampros grew suspicious. Petrified, Galatea took the child and sought sanctuary in a nearby temple. Under a high, vaulted ceiling, she begged the goddess Leto to save her baby girl. The goddess obliged. The girl was miraculously transformed into a boy. This story speaks to the sincere ancient Greek belief that girls *could* change into boys, and vice versa. The pathway was open for men – if they weren't sufficiently virile – to turn into women. They could, in ancient Greek terms, slip down the spectrum; they could become inferior. This story also speaks to a very different approach to trans people in the ancient world. Greeks were very familiar with the idea of gender fluidity, since they regarded gender as less a binary box and more a sliding scale. However, they still regarded the masculine as the peak of that scale and anything else as imperfect and frightening.

In addition, ancient Greek doctors held firm in their belief that women and not men were sexually promiscuous. This is why Greek sculpture always shows the penis as flaccid. The true, virile ancient Greek was supposed to be abstemious when it came to sex. Here again, self-control was always on display.

Passive male sexual partners were considered feminine and, according to doctors like Hippocrates, even stood the risk of becoming women. Hippocrates writes in one of his treatises on medicine about the case of the Scythian people. The Scythians were renowned as a race of archers, in fact, they were employed in the city of Athens as a kind of police force, with orders to shoot wrongdoers on sight. Hippocrates says they lived in a moist, humid climate, which led to them having less of the fire that constitutes masculinity. It made them weak and effeminate. Part of Cleon's argument against Gryttus had been that he too was 'moist', meaning camp or weak.[31] It was considered that a true man was 'dry' and capable of controlling himself from the wandering fancies induced by moisture which women, bottoms (men who prefer the passive role in gay sex) and Scythians were particularly vulnerable to. Cleon's anti-gay agenda and his obsession with self-control both show how queerphobia was mobilized to punish those who were perceived to be loose. Sex had become a crime and you could pay for it with your life.

REFUGEES

One of ancient Athens' greatest dramatists was a man named Euripides. Contemporaries joked that he was the middle-class son of a greengrocer, although many classicists think he came from a noble family. We are told by later Greeks that Euripides married, but did not enjoy being married to a woman. He, unlike his dramatist predecessors, had not been a noble warrior. Today, we would describe him as bookish – he was far more interested in philosophy and complex theories than war. Euripides is most famous for his *Medea*, which tells the tale of the sorceress and demi-goddess Medea who kills her own children to wreak vengeance on her husband, possibly inspired by Euripides' own difficult relationship with his wife.[32]

Euripides' other plays explored sexuality in an even more sensitive and nuanced way than Aeschylus' nearly half a century before.

In *Hippolytus*, a young man who abstains from sex receives a violent death at the machination of the gods. *Electra* and *Orestes* both explore the love between Orestes and his (boy)friend, Pylades. Euripides also adapted the Laius myth – where King Laius raped the son of the king of Pisa, Chrysippus – in a play which survives only in fragments.

Euripides' particular interest in queer love has its own autobiographical reasons. We are told by a later source that Euripides and Agathon, a celebrated tragic poet whose works have been lost, may have had an amorous liaison at the court of Macedon when the latter was 40 years old.[33] We are told in the same anecdote that when Archelaus saw this he was surprised: he expected Euripides to be attracted only to young men, but Euripides replied, 'it is not just spring that's the most beautiful, but autumn'.[34] Agathon certainly entered into a committed relationship with another man named Pausanias, but the three of them remained life-long friends. Unfortunately in Athens, Agathon was singled out for public humiliation.

In a play by the sharp-tongued Aristophanes, *The Women at the Thesmophoria*, Agathon appears dressed up as a woman. We are told that he walks like a female prostitute, waggling his bottom as if enticing someone to have sex with him.[35] Aristophanes was known for frequently lampooning political figures in his plays, but usually when he did so he gave them thinly disguised pseudonyms. Agathon's identity, however, was never protected.

As Aristophanes' career progressed, it seemed impossible for him to stage a play without a passing threat of same-sex sexual violence.[36] He attacked political enemies for their love of taking a cock.[37] He looks back at the period in Athens' past when men were free to love other men without being punished or mocked for it, and he laughs:

> It used to be necessary for lads sitting in the gym to wipe out the marks left in the sand by their thighs,
>
> So they would not show any trace of indecency.[38]

Here Aristophanes makes a joke about predatory older men desperate to see young men's buttocks in the sand. In another play, he describes a pair of men – Pisthetaerus and Euelpides – who run away from Athens to found an ideal city. Euelpides describes just what sort of city he'd like to found:

> I want a town where the father of a hot boy will approach me as if I have done him a great wrong:
> Ah, Stilbonides, is this right?
> You met my son at the gym, but you didn't kiss him, you didn't speak to him,
> You didn't take him with you, and you didn't even cop a feel of his balls?[39]

Aristophanes characterizes queer desire as predatory, making cheap jokes about the supposed perversions of older gay men. It was against this background that Agathon was trying to live out a peaceful life in Athens with his long-term partner, Pausanias. They are recorded in Plato's *Symposium* as cohabiting and deeply in love with one another.

As the century drew to a close, these three queer men at the centre of Athenian cultural life – Agathon, Pausanias and Euripides – packed their bags and left Athens.[40] They went north, crossing the Attica border, into an emerging kingdom – the kingdom of Macedon. They did so at the invitation of King Archelaus, who offered to pay them a considerable sum to live at his court and compose there. Archelaus, king of a thriving, prosperous nation, was considerably more relaxed about same-sex desire than the politicians of Athens.[41] He welcomed queer artists and poets from numerous more repressive Greek states, and, as time went on, Macedon became the place of queer legend. Stories of its lively sex parties and the lascivious behaviour of its ruling elite reached the Athenians, who turned their noses up in distaste. But no power on earth could check the mighty rise of Macedon which bore down like a tiger on Athens, once more cowering in the shadows of the Peloponnese.

One of the gay refugees in Macedon was the epic poet Choerilus of Samos. An ancient text tells us that he had once been a lover of the historian Herodotus, who had made Choerilus his *paidika* (another term, closely related to *pais*, for a same-sex lover).[42] As we have seen earlier, this implies that Choerilus was the bottom in this relationship. The same text tells us that Choerilus never returned to Athens and died in Macedon, as did Agathon and Euripides. Even the great philosopher Socrates was invited to Macedon, but unfortunately he chose to remain in Athens – where he was subsequently put on trial and executed for 'corrupting the youth'.

THREE

Queer as Macedon

> Though they were man-killers, they behaved like man-whores.
>
> FRAGMENT 115 F225A

Once the most powerful city in the region, Athens was fast becoming a minor backwater. The city had lost so many men in its drawn-out and bloody conflict with Sparta, known as the Peloponnesian War, that the Athenians had been forced to turn to their slaves for help.[1] The slaves were promised that if they could just temporarily forget about their brutal treatment and fight for their oppressors then they *might* be granted status as freedmen (with no money, no land and few voting powers).[2]

A small number of slaves did agree to these terms and at the Battle of Arginusae in 406 BCE they donned oars and manned the great wooden benches of the battleships, filling in the gaps where citizens were missing. Surprisingly, these untrained slaves were victorious against the Spartans — and yet the battle itself was still regarded a colossal failure. A sudden storm allowed the defeated Spartans to flee and prevented the Athenians from rescuing their own sailors. Many perished, and although the generals managed to find their way back to Athens safely, the bodies that washed up on the beaches after the battle were left there to rot.

Back in Athens, the people were appalled to hear that the generals had abandoned their sailors. A populist wing led by a man named Theramenes entered the legislative assembly with shaven heads dressed in black robes.[3] They claimed to be in mourning for the Athenian dead, who should have been carried back to their homeland and buried with all the appropriate rites. Theramenes insisted that the generals had to pay for their failure.

They were beheaded. This unique motivational strategy seems, unsurprisingly, to have yielded poor results. Shortly after Arginusae, Athens lost its war with Sparta. For a time, it even lost its democracy altogether. Given that this democracy had a penchant for show-trials and executions, this probably was no bad thing. The oligarchy the Spartans installed lasted only about a year, however, before the Athenians successfully overthrew it and returned themselves triumphantly to mob rule.

By contrast, Macedon was on the rise. Macedon had benefited from Athens' decline around the final years of the Peloponnesian War and its attacks on its queer community. Euripides' last play, the *Bacchae*, is an indictment of the homophobic politics of self-control that had gripped his old home.

The *Bacchae* begins when a god makes an appearance among the mortals. He is the god of communion, of sex, of wine, of theatre; he is the god of nature, of growth – he is the antithesis of the individual.[4] His name is Dionysus, and he is heading for Thebes. Thebes, however, is ruled by a tyrant called Pentheus. He is a young, ambitious king who wants glory for himself and his regime at any cost, and he refuses to believe that Dionysus is a real god. He thinks he's too foreign and soft, with feminine features, robes, scent and hair. Much like the Athenian politicians in Euripides' day, Pentheus is a paragon of self-control and masculinity – how could it be that a god, a being even superior to a king, could be so effeminate?

Dionysus is understandably offended by Pentheus. He whips up his supporters among the women of the city, who join in his rites in a Bacchic frenzy. Intoxicated with drink and possibly drugs,[5] the Theban women run to the hills to take part in unearthly collective rituals. They defy their husbands, abandon their duty to their households and have sex with men on the open rocks beneath fir trees. Irate, Pentheus has Dionysus thrown in a dungeon. But the god conjures an earthquake and escapes to rejoin his followers.

Pentheus, curious to know more about this god who seems to defy all his ideas about what makes a man powerful and strong, goes to the mountainside to spy on Dionysus. He climbs a tree to observe the followers from on high. He sees miraculous things: women drawing milk from the ground and bending trees into impossible positions. But he is spotted. The bacchants rip him down from the tree where he is hiding, and his own mother Agave tears him limb from limb. The other women join in too, clawing at his flesh, ripping off his limbs and severing his head. In the mayhem, Thebes' entire ruling family literally tears itself apart.

We do not see Pentheus' bloody end. A messenger walks on stage to inform us, in grim detail, of his death. The messenger in Greek tragedy is a 'stock' character, which is to say that nearly every ancient tragedy has one. It is the messenger who tells us how Oedipus gouged out his own eyes; how Hercules was burned alive by his wife's poisoned cloak; how Medea killed the princess Glauce. These actions were not shown on the stage, not out of reluctance to show gore – most in the audience would at one stage or another have played their part in the theatre of war – but because horror for its own sake had no meaning in ancient drama. Violence was an inescapable feature of daily life. The messenger was there to interpret these murders and mutilations for the audience, to explain why they happened and how they could be avoided. He tells us:

> It's best to have a prudent mind revering
> Divine affairs. I think it's wisest counsel
> For mortals sorely need this thing.[6]

The messenger – in an ironic twist – says that for all Pentheus' distaste for sex, cross-dressing, wine and ritual parties, he still came to a bitter end because he was not 'prudent'. The phrase 'a prudent mind' points to a middle way between rigidly policed masculinity and the rabid excesses of drunken, Bacchic orgies. In an earlier speech, the messenger praises light enjoyment of the finer things in life:

> Without some wine there's no desire or joy,
> No pleasant pleasures for our mortal flesh.[7]

Euripides acknowledges that self-discipline can be a beautiful thing. But he spies a problem – self-control can also become excessive. Denying all pleasure and seeking to control everything will only tear you apart.

Euripides never saw the *Bacchae* performed. It was, apparently on his instruction, only staged in Athens shortly after his death.[8] His desire to keep the play quiet during his lifetime reflects the controversy at its heart. Euripides, a queer man who lived out his last years in exile, knew all too well that the shift in cultural values towards self-control coincided with a precipitous decline in tolerance for same-sex love. But in his writing, he imagined a world in which a king, who values restraint above all else, is punished for attempting to repress the erotic impulses of his people.

PHILIP OF MACEDON

Philip II of Macedon rose to power at the age of 24 in the year 359 BCE.[9] He never met Euripides or the other Athenians who fled to Macedon – they had died decades before he was born – but their cultural legacy on the court he grew up in was not so quick to fade. Philip was a deft political strategist and a brilliant general loved by his soldiers and his people. He insisted on riding at the vanguard of his army, putting himself in grievous peril. Only a few years into his reign, he even lost an eye as he charged into battle at the last Athenian stronghold of Methone in the Thermaic Gulf. Despite his gruff exterior, however, the king of Macedon also enjoyed the softer side of life.

Macedon's capital at Aegae to this day hosts the ruins of a vast, sprawling palace that once sat atop a raised terrace.[10] This impressive structure was three times the size of the Parthenon temple in Athens. It was on this site where – if certain ancient sources are credible – the king of Macedon resided,[11] surrounded by a large contingent of young men called the Royal Pages.[12] There could have been as many as 85 pages and all of them were from influential, neighbouring families. It is not clear how many of them were kept at court as quasi-hostages to ensure their families' good behaviour and how many were there for the honour and the thrill. In time, however, the stories of what these men and Philip did in the bedroom would become legendary.

Much of what we know about the royal pages comes from an ancient Greek historian called Theopompus who lived during Philip's reign and kept a close eye on Macedon's growing power. Although Theopompus' descriptions of Philip and the ruling elite of Macedonia give us a valuable impression of life there, in general, he disapproved of the Macedonians and so his writing has to be taken with a pinch of salt. Like many of his day, he was more of a rhetorician than what we'd think of as a modern historian – in other words, a columnist rather than a news anchor.[13]

Theopompus objects in the strongest possible terms to anyone seen to be having a good time, most especially kings. In general, he disapproved of any Greek king who was seen to show a lack of self-discipline as such excess would – so he believed – bring about a decline in the state. Pompous Theopompus complained, for instance, that the king of Syracuse, Nysaius, 'wore elaborate clothing, ate too much, drank too much, and engaged in outrageous sex with both men and women'.[14] But like many prudes, there seems to be nothing Theopompus loved more than a lurid tale. He also narrated a story about a prostitute who was viciously dismembered by the priests of Apollo. He denounced the Pharsalians (living in modern-day Thessaly, Greece) as 'the laziest and most extravagant' of people.[15] He often protested that 'overeating and eating meat take away rational thought and make the soul slower'.[16] He did, however, reserve effusive praise for the Spartan kings Agesilaus and Lysander, who – in Theopompus' exacting eyes – had lived an ordered life.

It is from Theopompus that we learn that Philip's royal pages were elite soldiers, probably in their 20s, with ripped torsos who shaved all their body hair. They had sex with the king whenever he requested, and they were also happy to have sex with each other. Philip was even said to have retained the legal power to whip the pages whenever he saw fit – only he had this power. With a colourful flourish, Theopompus finishes his description by telling us that although the royal pages 'were man-killers, they behaved like man-whores'.[17] Unfortunately for Philip, this would prove all too true.

THE BURNING OF OLYNTHUS

The ancient town of Olynthus is now a small archaeological site at the end of a winding, sandy track. Just over 2,350 years ago, Philip II laid siege to it. His soldiers ransacked the place, burning its buildings and seizing its men, women and children. All Olynthus' people, including some Athenians guarding the town, were sold into slavery. This was meted out as vengeance because Olynthus had betrayed Macedon and sought an allegiance with Athens. The destruction of this small city shows the brutality Philip was willing to wield against anyone who stood in his path. But by burning that city to the ground, the Macedonians also inadvertently preserved for us a picture of what ancient Greek city-states had looked like just before economic inequality really took off.

All that remains of Olynthus today are ankle-high walls. But they reveal a story about how the people of Olynthus lived – the walls trace the skeletons of houses, all of which have a nearly identical framework. We know there were prominent figures in Olynthian society (Philip II enslaved them, along with everyone else), and, usually, we might expect them to be wealthier and live in bigger houses. But all the houses in Olynthus are roughly the same size, suggesting everyone had similar levels of wealth.[18] It seems to have been a relatively egalitarian place when they were constructed in the middle of the 5th century BCE.[19]

In the Athens of the 5th century BCE, private wealth was not an honourable thing to possess. There is a reason that the most extraordinary buildings we have inherited from this period – like the Parthenon on the Athenian Acropolis – are all public buildings, not stately homes or royal tombs. Even in the 4th century BCE, Athenians had a strong sense of their history as a relatively equal city. The Athenian politician and statesman Demosthenes, a contemporary of Philip II, opines in a speech *about the burning of Olynthus* that in past generations the wealthy were modest, and generous in giving to the public. 'The houses of Miltiades and Aristides (famous Athenian generals) were no more splendid than their neighbours'.[20] Even the most powerful men in Athens' past were said to have lived in relatively normal houses like those built at Olynthus, but by the time of Demosthenes and Philip II this was starting to change.

At the height of its power, much of Athens' wealth came from Laurion, a rocky outcrop outside the city that contained a rich supply of silver ore. Slaves ordered into the mines faced brutal conditions. Cramped in tiny, dark, damp spaces, they hammered at the rock for hours on end. The Athenian economy was built on an expansive population of enslaved human beings. They were expendable; if they died, you bought another. Or, you captured a nearby town and enslaved the entire population.

Surprisingly, though, the bones dug up of slaves from the 5th century BCE suggest they were relatively well fed. Isotopic analyses show traces of a high-protein diet, rich in fibrous cereals – a sign of excellent nutrition. They were not fed luxurious foods, but nor were they starved. But as time goes on, this begins to change. From the beginning of the 4th century BCE, the quality of nutrition drops dramatically.[21]

This pattern is echoed across nearly all the grave sites in ancient Athens. Food inequality emerges. The graves of the richest are untouched by these dietary shifts; they eat as they always have. But the diet of the poor begins to suffer. The community had broken down, the individual and his household had become the main unit of society. The temples were no longer being given money by the rich to redistribute food to the poor. The rich were getting much richer, and they were starting to show off their wealth for the first time in Athenian history – and the poorer were no longer being cared for.

In the early 5th century BCE, just as in archaic Megara, most graves in Athens were identical in size and shape. A hundred years later, that picture had changed. In 409 BCE (around four years before Euripides wrote the *Bacchae* in Macedon), a rich Athenian named Diogeiton spent a ridiculous 5,000 drachmas on his brother's tomb.[22] This was an enormous sum, nearly 14 years' pay for a soldier or skilled labourer, for a single tomb. The funeral may have cost even more. The appearance of these extravagant burials and tombs points to a noticeable widening of inequalities. At the same time, as the grave analyses show, diet of the poor became more meagre and less nutritional.

The household was a powerful unit for the economic advancement of certain citizens, but it left others behind, malnourished and poor. Diogeiton's brother's tomb was part of the changing political landscape, which ancient comedians were starting to draw attention to. In 388 BCE, Aristophanes staged a play entitled *Wealth*. A man who has not enjoyed the best of financial luck encounters a blind god who can barely find his way. This god is Wealth. Welcoming Wealth into his crumbling, humble little home, the poor Athenian – whose name is Chremylos – tries to cure Wealth of his blindness. That way, he remarks merrily, Wealth will be able to see again and redirect all his money more equally.

Lying on a bed, Wealth responds well to the gentle ministrations of Chremylos' slave Cario. His sight miraculously returns, and he sees the crumbled old ruin belonging to the man by whom he has been so expertly and generously cared for. He sees the impoverished people all around him, and the vast wealth hoarded by the rich, and he grows restless. Wealth decides to redistribute money equally. For Aristophanes, this leads to chaos: luxuries are banned, slaves – shockingly to the ancient Athenians – are freed, a rich old woman loses her concubine who has only been sleeping with her for her money. The other gods are furious. The newfound interest in worshipping Wealth has deprived them of their sacrifices.

The play offers an important insight into what happened at the dawn of the 4th century BCE. Although Aristophanes derides the idea of wealth redistribution, the whole premise of the comedy rests on the huge divide between the rich and the poor, and the fact that this divide is not based on virtue or merit, but on chance and greed.

Fifty years after Diogeiton buried his brother, another Athenian spent over 12,000 drachmas on a tomb in 349 BCE. Though it cost well over double that of Diogeiton's tomb, it was not constructed to honour a dearly beloved relative. It was for a mistress. In Athens, where adultery was a sensitive topic often discussed in courts of law, this was deeply shocking.[23] By the mid-4th century BCE, rich Athenians had so much disposable cash that they were willing to pay an entire lifetime's wages for the average skilled labourer on the tomb of a mistress.

MORE ATHENIAN HOMOPHOBIA

The Athenian politician Demosthenes lived and died as Athens' power dwindled and Macedon rose. A ruthless lawyer who decimated his opponents in the law courts, his many successes on behalf of the super-rich of Athens had led him to wield great influence. But this man – skilled orator though he was – famously shunned the Athenian gymnasium. He would have been wily with words and wiry in form.

An eccentric outsider, he honed his craft with ruthless self-discipline and relentless vocal training. Standing on top of a cliff by the sea, he bellowed to be heard over the crashing of the rocks. At home, he would practise every day with pebbles in his mouth. He even refused to drink wine, sticking to water. Unlike most Athenians, he had almost no private tutelage and was a life-long autodidact. This also fitted into his narrative that while other men were extravagant, he was abstemious and careful with his money.[24]

Demosthenes had a bitter enemy in the public arena, a fellow orator by the name of Aeschines. Aeschines was well built – unlike Demosthenes – with curly hair. He and Demosthenes came to blows over their differing views of Macedon. After Philip II laid waste to Olynthus, directly threatening Athenian territory, Aeschines was sent in an embassy to negotiate. After meeting with

Philip, breaking bread and returning home, Aeschines stood up in the Athenian assembly and proclaimed that Philip II was a Greek just like them. He argued for peace between the two warring states, and that Athens should extend the hand of friendship to Macedon. He urged the thousands of Athenians gathered in the assembly not to stand up to Macedon, but to stand with them. Demosthenes, given the merciless violence Philip had just meted out to Athenian allies, was incandescent. He also nursed a deep prejudice that Athens was superior in every way to Macedon. He thought Athenians more cultured, more austere, more hardy and more masculine than the Macedonians.

No lawyer was more prodigious than Demosthenes, he possessed an incisive gift with words and Aeschines was no match for him. He issued a prosecution against Aeschines to have him expelled from the city, arguing that his fraternization with Philip had been an unforgiveable betrayal of Athens. In a seemingly bizarre twist, he even accused Aeschines of giving oral sex to Philip.

Aeschines struck back and laid waste to Demosthenes' character in turn. He accused him of taking on expensive clients and prostituting himself for money. Demosthenes was nothing more, Aeschines said, than a sex slave, a *kinaidos*, with a dirty body (*kinaidia* had been the charge brought against Gryttus and the other gay men by Cleon).[25] He mocked Demosthenes' lisp, implying it was a sign that he liked to give blowjobs. He described Demosthenes' speaking style as if he were camply pirouetting around the courtroom.[26] With a final flourish, Aeschines accused Demosthenes of 'making himself a boy' (*paidopoiia*).[27]

Demosthenes responded in kind. He mercilessly mocked Aeschines' family history and the fact that he had once trained as an actor. Demosthenes painted this as effete and levelled the euphemistic charge that Aeschines loved to sell his body, and particularly his mouth, for money. Both Demosthenes and Aeschines stirred the homophobic prejudices of their Athenian audience to destroy each other, prejudices well entrenched since the populist policies of Cleon nearly a century earlier.

Though they may seem puerile attacks, these political debates mark another sea-change in attitudes to gay love and sex in Athens. Three hundred years before, the lawmaker Solon had publicly praised the delights of boys' bodies and Athenian pottery had celebrated gay love and sex. One hundred years before, plays had been performed celebrating the lives of queer heroes like Achilles and Patroclus. Now, two politicians were tussling like lions and hurling homophobic insults at one another. And they wielded homosexuality as a weapon because it worked.[28]

Aeschines had even worse up his sleeve. When one of Demosthenes' friends, Timarchus, also started to attack Aeschines for his appeasement of Philip of Macedon, Aeschines struck back hard. In his youth, Aeschines said, Timarchus had received money for having sex with men at the house of a famous doctor (amusingly named Euthydicus). In addition, Aeschines alleged many other men had paid for Timarchus' services, in particular a man named Misgolas who held extravagant parties with flute players and vast quantities of drink.

As fun as these parties may sound, Aeschines was deeply unimpressed. He implied that what Timarchus had done was illegal. It is unclear what law Timarchus was supposed to have broken, whether it was having sex with men or being paid to have sex,[29] but the ambiguity around the legal status of homosexuality was significant in itself. Timarchus was expelled from the city of Athens.

Despite pillorying Timarchus for his alleged past as a high-class male prostitute, Aeschines did say that homosexuality could be noble. He argued that in days of old, the gymnasium was the proper and right place for gay love and that the love of Athens' noble figures Aristogeiton and Harmodius had brought down a tyrant. He eulogized the 'noble' aspects of gay love permissible in Athens: 'On the one hand, you have desirable men who exercise self-restraint, and on the other you have those who harm themselves.'[30] It was fine for Timarchus to be beautiful, it was fine for him to be gay, but he should never have *acted* on his desires.

A new ideology was being born in Athens. Same-sex desire was acknowledged as something that some people felt, but it was inadvisable to act upon it. Aeschines argued that queer sex was evil but that a loving, chaste, mentor-like relationship was acceptable. Provided that homosexuality was bleached of any intimacy and purely thought of as an almost spiritual bond, it could be countenanced. The pain imposed by this doctrine on the queer people of ancient Athens – a people who had contributed to the city's poetry, its laws and the establishment of its democracy – continues its dire legacy today. Queer people are still told to exercise restraint over their desires; in our professional lives and in our personal lives, we are asked not to perform homosexuality. Religions demand our chastity and order us to surrender one of the most fulfilling and beautiful moments our body can give us – sex with a person we love.

In Athenian courts, one could hire a speechwriter, but – unlike in modern courts with barristers and advocates – a defendant was expected to speak for himself. In a speech by a writer called Lysias, composed for a client to deliver in a court of law, the speaker openly describes the same-sex attraction for which he is on trial. He pleads with the audience, 'I beg you do not think worse of me, since you know that all men experience desire. The best and most self-controlled man is he who can bear his misfortunes in the most orderly way.'[31]

Athenians understood that same-sex desire was part of life, but now they thought it was a sign of one's personal fortitude and masculinity to resist these tempting desires. It is probably no coincidence that Greek sources on Macedon are at such pains to tell us that Philip was sexually involved with men. For the Greeks, this was proof that Philip was excessive, depraved and incapable of the restraint required for political office.

THE DEFEAT OF ATHENS

At Chaeronea in the Peloponnese, the forces of the Greek city-states clashed with those of Macedon and lost. From a few sources, we can piece together a scene from the aftermath of the battle. Amid the blood and mud, the thousands of mangled corpses, the discarded javelins, fallen daggers and shattered remains of shields, there walked a solitary figure. His robe trailed behind him mingling with the filth. He paused and fixed his single remaining eye on two bodies of his vanquished opponents that lay before him.

One lay with his head lolling back, his dark-blond curls arranged like a loose halo, resting on the shoulder of another man. Both soldiers must have clutched each other as they died. All this power, all this might – Philip II had finally subdued Greece, Athens finally had been brought to heel, and what had he won? Brave men indeed, he thought. From far off, the attendants watched on anxiously as their king knelt before these warriors and tears streamed down his cheeks. With one hand, he touched the two men. 'Anyone who thinks these men did or suffered anything of disgrace', he said (according to Plutarch), 'will die in agony.'[32]

Philip II had seen the price of war. The 300 men who lay strewn on the right flank of the battlefield of Chaeronea were the Sacred Band of Thebes. Philip thought they were an army composed of gay men; each couple he found dead in each other's arms, he assumed, were boyfriends sworn to protect each other. His reaction suggests that for many of the Greek city-states fighting against him, homosexuality would have been a cause of immense embarrassment. Why else would he have had cause to defend them? The Sacred Band of Thebes made up less than 1 per cent of the overall Greek fighting force, yet Philip reserved especial reverence for them. To his mind, perhaps, these men had died to defend a land that hated their way of life.[33] Archaeologists working at the battle site found a burial mound where 254 skeletons lay side by side, arm in arm, in seven separate rows.[34]

While Athenians exercised a politics of moderation and self-restraint, Philip was a prolific polygamist. He seems to have used marriage primarily as a political tool – a means to bind families and cement alliances. Although he did his duty and had children, it did not seem to have prevented him from enjoying sex with men. Like the Sacred Band of Thebes, he maintained strong personal bonds with many of them.[35] One of the 'man-whores' – as Theopompus colourfully described the Royal Pages – was a soldier called Pausanias (no relation to Agathon's lover of the same name). Pausanias was extraordinarily beautiful and when he appeared at court, he quickly drew Philip's attention. In time, he was invited into the king's private apartments.

According to a later source, composed on the island of Sicily in the Roman era,[36] Philip wined and dined this handsome man and they soon became inseparable at court. It may not have been uncommon to hear, wandering down a royal corridor, the sound of Pausanias and Philip at it again. Ancient sources encourage us to imagine that Pausanias was always the passive partner; the king maintaining his rightful dominance between the sheets. Naturally, it was impossible for even the most diligent and well-researched historian to know which position Philip preferred but such conjecture speaks to an increasing association in ancient Greek minds between sexual domination and power.

Sadly for Pausanias there was no shortage of other pretty men at court and Philip soon had eyes on someone else. When he discovered that Philip's attentions had been captivated by an equally handsome, athletic young man, he marched furiously up to his rival. Scandalously, and with no hint of hypocrisy, Pausanias publicly denounced Philip's new lover as a catamite who enjoyed nothing better than being railed by the king every night in the bedroom. Pausanias demanded that this young man prove his masculinity. Not long after, in a fearsome battle against the Illyrians (a tribe living in the Balkans), Philip's new boyfriend charged rashly against his enemy. He was rewarded for his bravery and his loyalty to Macedon with a spear plunged straight through his heart. Philip was consumed with grief. He laid on a lavish funeral, but the friends and allies of his dead lover had other ideas. One of them, Attalus, laid the blame squarely at Pausanias' feet.

Attalus challenged Pausanias to a drinking competition one night and got him so drunk that he could barely stand. Pausanias was gently persuaded to walk into a room where a group of men were waiting for him. These men looked after the king's mules, they were from a much lower rank than a favoured royal page.

Pausanias – powerless – was held down as the muleteers raped him. When he awoke the next day in agony and covered in dung, he ran to King Philip, desperately seeking justice. He wanted Attalus dead.

Philip was conflicted. If he helped Pausanias it would risk open rebellion at court – the royal pages held delicate diplomatic positions. Insulting or attacking any one of them risked rebellion from one of Philip's allies and so he deliberated for days, while Pausanias lay in bed, ruminating and plotting revenge. A few days later, Pausanias returned to Philip and asked him once again to have Attalus killed. This time, Philip outright refused.

In the great theatre at Aegae, King Philip attended the wedding of his daughter Cleopatra to King Alexander of Epirus. The theatre still stands today, a great round dome with grass undulating where seats once stood. It was here, in the centre of the theatre, where Pausanias stabbed Philip in the chest. So fell one of the ancient world's most powerful men, killed not by an army but allegedly by a scorned lover. News of Philip's assassination spread far and wide. Word quickly reached Athens that the king of Macedon had been stabbed. It was said that Demosthenes – upon hearing the news – paraded around the streets of Athens wearing a garland and an elaborately decorated robe.

It is historical consensus that Pausanias of Orestis assassinated Philip II at his daughter's wedding,[37] and we have two main sources for gay antics at the court of Macedon under Philip's reign. The first is the near-contemporary Theopompus, who nursed a particular hatred for Philip; the second is the much later Diodorus Siculus, who was possibly more concerned with collecting salacious rumours than with establishing historical fact. Historians have also long speculated that Philip's son Alexander the Great, or his mother, may have been somehow involved in persuading Pausanias to bring that king's reign to an untimely end. We will never know the truth. But the story of Pausanias' feud with his king is an important one: whatever its historicity, other ancient sources considered Philip's homosexuality to be so great a weakness that it brought about his ruin. By this period in Greek history, homosexuality was firmly something effeminate, soft and weak; it was frequently used to attack those in power from a position of jealousy. The absolute facts about whether Philip was or was not killed by his gay lover are less important than the broader social climate which had moved firmly against gay sex.

FOUR

Plato and the Philosophy of the Closet

> Everyone was in love with him, struck and confounded by him.
>
> PLATO, CHARMIDES 154C

In 348 BCE, ten years before Philip II of Macedon was murdered, an old Athenian man with a wiry, grey beard, and brow furrowed with deep lines of thought, lay in an austere bed. He was wrapped in linen and his chest rattled with his last breaths on earth. The air was thick with cicada-song, and a girl stood by his bedside playing the flute. With one final gasp, Plato was dead.[1]

He died where he had been happiest. The Academy which he had founded was a sprawling institution – part boarding house and part university – for the cleverest minds of the day, drawn from all over Greece by his teachings.[2] In a small clearing at the back of the Academy, a group of young men gathered to bury their teacher in the Garden of the Muses. In the centre stood a shrine to the muses underscoring the blurred boundary in Plato's thought between divine inspiration and works of art. In his long life, Plato wrought the foundations of Western politics, religion and philosophy. But alongside these extraordinary contributions, he nursed a strong discomfort about queer desire – and yet queer sex and desire in Plato's works are not just occasionally mentioned (as they would be in the works of later philosophers), they are front and centre of his discussion about passion. Plato's obsession with gay desire begs many questions, not least whether he felt attracted to other men himself.

PLATO'S YOUTH

Great men in the ancient world are often associated with miraculous births,[3] and so it was with Plato. The philosopher's mother Perictione was from an important Athenian family and his father was called Ariston of Collytus. However, later biographers took seriously the maxim that one should never let the truth get in the way of a good myth, and a story went around that Plato's father was in fact the god Apollo. This was not the only myth to swirl around the baby Plato. Bees from Mount Hymettus were said to have flown down and dripped honey into his open mouth. Such attempts to mythologize the lives of great minds are commonplace in the philosophical canon.

As a teenager, Plato witnessed the calamitous fall of Athenian power during the Peloponnesian War against Sparta. In 411 BCE, Athens fell to a violent coup. The 400 oligarchs at its head used their army to parade through the city, torturing and murdering any detractors. The democracy that Athens had established was temporarily destroyed. Even some of Plato's own relatives were brutally put to the sword. Barely 14 when the 400 tyrants were overthrown, Plato was introduced to an old man with a reputation as a great teacher who idled his days wandering around Athens in filthy clothes with a battered walking stick. The old man's name was Socrates, and he claimed to be able to teach 'the love of wisdom', or 'philosophy'. Regrettably, Socrates' teachings were not revered by all.

In 399 BCE, when Plato was still in his 20s, Socrates found himself on trial. Dragged before a grand jury of citizens, all peering down at him from raised seats, he was charged with 'not honouring the City's gods' and with 'corrupting young men'.[4] The meaning of the second charge is something of a riddle. We know Socrates' defence hinged on his firm belief in the divine, which suggests that the first of the two charges was for atheism (an offence in Athens).[5] But as for the second charge, it is quite possible that Socrates was accused of seducing some young men for whose education he was responsible.[6] It is a friend of Socrates' called Xenophon who inadvertently reveals the true meaning of the charge which brought Socrates to his death:

> 'It is truly strange to me that some were persuaded that Socrates corrupted the young. Firstly, Socrates was the most self-continent, in matters of sex and the stomach, of all men . . .'[7]

The jury, however, were unconvinced. Socrates lost the trial and died in a prison cell surrounded by a group of young men, having dismissed his wife Xanthippe[8] for being too emotional about his impending forced suicide. This is characteristic of the rising emphasis on self-control; contain your emotions and condemn the emotions of others. Xanthippe, holding a baby in her arms, was not allowed to stand alongside Socrates and cry. In the text recounting Socrates' suicide, Plato's *Phaedo*, when the men then begin to weep at his approaching death, Socrates admonishes them, 'for goodness' sake, what are you doing? I only just sent away the women so they wouldn't disturb this perfect moment; I heard one should die in silence.'[9] Even when dying, Socrates is portrayed as implausibly unemotional. We are told that he lay on a bed, drank the poison hemlock from a cup and gradually fell asleep in the sweetest possible manner. The reality of hemlock poisoning is about the furthest thing from a sweet departure we can imagine. Before death, it causes vomiting, spasms, seizures and tremors. Socrates' final moments, if this is indeed how he died, would have been violent and distressing for all to witness.

Plato would have been almost 30 when Socrates died, and yet he was unmarried. This was unusual. By the age of 30, ancient Greek men were expected to marry. Their wives would have been young teenagers, who had recently had their first period. In a lavish wedding ceremony, the bride would be showered with symbols of fertility by young boys and led into the bed chamber. Here, she would be taken to bed by her husband as much as twice her age. He would have been expected to grow a beard and have a hairy chest; she would be barely pubescent. She would have been expected to have sex with him that night and immediately assume her wifely duties in the household, which included having children. He probably would already be sexually experienced with slaves, and possibly with men.

Even men for whom we have evidence of queer love affairs, like Euripides, married. Euripides had two notoriously unsuccessful marriages, and he was said to hate all women.[10] For a man not to marry was deeply suspicious to a society now built primarily on the unit of the household.

One possible explanation for Plato's bachelorhood is his preoccupation with same-sex desire, though he generally considered it an unhealthy impulse, to be resisted. It is possible that having witnessed the prosecution of Socrates and many Athenian homosexuals, Plato nursed a strong, internalized homophobia.

Disenchanted with Athens, the philosopher left the city in pursuit of a different life when he was around 40 years old. He sailed across the Mediterranean and eventually made his way west to Sicily where he found himself at the court of an eccentric king. The great palace of Dionysius I, king of Syracuse, was a seat of luxury unlike anything Plato would have witnessed in Athens. Dionysius, like Philip II of Macedon, lived the high life. The stories of Plato's time there come to us from Diogenes Laertius' *Lives of Eminent Philosophers*. This text was written centuries after Plato's death; however, it's likely Diogenes Laertius was writing from earlier sources that are now lost to us.

King Dionysius, however, had a turbulent history with outspoken thinkers. Once, he had invited the poet Philoxenus to his court. The banquet was sumptuous, great wooden tables groaned with wine and local delicacies. The king became drunk and, according to Diogenes Laertius, decided to recite some poems of his own composition. When Philoxenus dared to critique them, the poor poet was thrown in prison. It wasn't long before Plato met the same fate.

King Dionysius, displeased with Plato's rude critiques of the excess of the Syracusan court, was said to have sold the philosopher into slavery for 20 minas. Plato was clapped in irons and led to the slave market where, had it not been for the timely intervention of a powerful friend, he may well have died deep down a dark mine, excavating silver for a rich lord. Plato vowed to repay his friend Anniceris of Cyrene upon his return to Athens, but Anniceris refused. 'Go and found a school of philosophy instead,' he said, and Plato did just that.

It is possible that Plato ended up at the court of Dionysius I because he was searching for more information about an obscure cult, whose views and habits had a profound impact on his philosophy. He may already have encountered them at Athens, but their origins lay to the west, in modern-day Italy. The cult was steeped in mystery, ritual and austerity, and they shared many ideas with the early Christians who appeared centuries later. They were called the Pythagoreans.

Led by Pythagoras,[11] the cult of the Pythagoreans had been established some centuries before Plato was born. Many have heard of the Pythagorean theorem, which although not invented by Pythagoras (there is good evidence the Babylonians had already been using the theorem for centuries before his birth)[12] is closely associated with him. In one apocryphal story, we are told that once Pythagoras had computed the theorem, he ran straight to a local temple, pulling behind him a very fat and recalcitrant ox. When he eventually managed to drag the ox up the temple steps, he pulled out a knife and slit its throat in celebration of his mathematical discovery. It seems unlikely that Pythagoras did do this (it bears a remarkable similarity to a tale about the mathematician Thales),[13] since of the fragments of Pythagoras' life we know, one thing is certain – his opposition to the mistreatment of animals.

There is another story about Pythagoras that seems more likely to have been based on his genuine philosophy, even if it has been exaggerated by the tradition. One day, on his native island of Samos, Pythagoras encountered a man beating a helpless dog with a stick. Pythagoras ran forwards and wrenched the stick from the man. 'STOP!' he shouted. 'That's my friend! I recognize his voice!'

This story was written down by the ancient philosopher Xenophanes, who was sceptical of Pythagoras' ideas, but it reveals a maxim of Pythagorean thinking. Pythagoras and his disciples believed firmly in the principle of metempsychosis – the transmigration of souls. Indeed, Pythagoras claimed to have had many lives himself, as did other Pythagoreans. According to a – likely fabricated – tale that illustrates his philosophy, he once walked into the Temple of Apollo at Didyma, where a shield was on display. He exclaimed that it was his shield, but the temple attendants said it was not – it had belonged to the legendary hero of the Trojan War Euphorbus, whose name was written on the back.[14] Pythagoras insisted it had been his in a previous life, and that he was in fact descended from Euphorbus.

There is another story about life after death in which one of Pythagoras' slaves, a man called Salmoxis who became incredibly rich upon being freed, plays a starring role.[15] Back in his native Thrace, he would invite people into his great banqueting hall where he would tell them that if they followed him and the Pythagorean laws, not only would they live a happy life, but when they died, they would go to a place of eternal good things. Many of the laws that Salmoxis told his followers to adhere to (the *akousmata*, or 'the things to be listened to') were Pythagoras' laws – some were reasonably sensible, others were deeply odd.

Salmoxis went to extraordinary lengths to prove that he had the power to return from the dead. Little did his guests know that beneath the stone floor of his banqueting hall lay a secret underground cave. One day, Salmoxis vanished. Presumably, he left a note to say he had died, but there was no trace of his body. Everyone believed he was dead until three years later, when he returned magically to life. He claimed upon his return that he was back from the dead, but perhaps he had run out of food and decided now was the time to re-emerge from his underground chamber.

The Pythagoreans were not dissimilar to some schools of Buddhism, given that they thought the right conduct in life would enable one to eventually escape the process of the transmigration of souls into other animals. They seem to have believed in paradise, and they believed in following very strict rules to get there.

The Pythagoreans were commanded never to wear rings that showed divine imagery[16] or to keep birds in the house, they were also told they had to roll up their bedclothes to prevent their imprint being left. Shoes must be placed on the right foot first, and Pythagoreans were never allowed to urinate facing the sun. Finally, they were strictly commanded to have children and not to have sex for any other purpose.[17] There may have been a logic to these rules, but their overriding purpose was to create uniformity in the community and a strict obedience to rules. Like so many of the Pythagorean *akousmata*, their main functions were to create camaraderie and teach self-control.

The story about Pythagoras and the ox holds a glimmer of truth. The Pythagoreans were fascinated by the study of mathematics. They believed that the universe was perfectly ordered according to a hidden design.[18] By learning the language of this design, mathematics, they hoped to uncover not only the secrets of the world, but the secret of living a truly ordered life.

Many ancient philosophers thought that the universe contained a secret, mysterious order. The pin-prick stars in the inky black of the night sky were arranged in heaven according to shapes and categories. The movement of the heavens was thought to be like the movement of trees or of animals, and seen as a sign that the whole cosmos – like them – breathed with life. These thinkers even wondered whether the planets each had a 'soul'. When a pattern was discovered in the universe, much as in music, it was said to be a thing of beauty – it was called a 'harmony'. These patterns were sacred to the Pythagoreans, who marvelled that there were seven Pleiades in the sky, seven vowels (in Greek) and seven heroes who attacked Thebes;[19] this was how the number seven came to be significant. The fact that musical harmony is providentially mathematical, and could produce such beautiful, stimulating sounds intrigued them still further. One Pythagorean, living in a similar time to Plato, wrote that it was impossible to understand anything without numbers.[20] Mathematics, with its patterns and orders, was thought to be the purest form of harmony.

Indeed, the Pythagoreans even believed mathematics handed them the power to perform miracles. After his death, it was said that Pythagoras himself had been a miracle-worker.[21] Out walking one day, crossing a dusty path, he encountered a serpent which reared back, hissing furiously. He knew the snake was deadly poisonous, but before the snake could sink its fangs into Pythagoras, he knelt down and bit it and it died instantly on the ground. It was said that as he passed rivers, they said hello to him. It was also said that his thigh was made of gold, and that he could appear in two places at the same time.

THE LITTLE GROVE

To the north-west of Athens, outside the cemetery dedicated to the war-dead, stood a towering two-doored gate. The wood was fixed into huge stone foundations and the gate lay open during the day. If you passed through it, you would find yourself on a road stretching out into a green grove of trees. Lining the route were monuments to the great Athenian dead and on either side were flourishing gardens – the homes of the rich and successful. Beyond the road stood a high wall which enclosed a different kind of idyll.

Plato chose this sacred spot for his Academy – a grove dedicated to Athena, goddess of knowledge, wisdom, war and Athens herself.[22] The beginners he taught in the gymnasium, beneath a portico which opened on one side. He would stand while his eager students settled on benches. He taught them about the universe and about ethics, learning from his Pythagorean contacts what it took to be an ordered, good person. His more advanced students – like Aristotle – he is said to have taught from his own house.

Plato's house, the place where he died, was a small one-roomed building. Here, he kept his manuscripts in a library of scrolls nestled on shelves from floor to ceiling. There was a whiteboard (called a *leukōma* in Greek), maps and a globe, and even an alarm-clock of Plato's very own design.[23] On the side of one of the walls, hung a painting which depicted the very last moments of his teacher, Socrates, drinking poison.

Socrates himself – like Jesus – did not write down his teachings. He believed that writing did not have the same living quality as speech.[24] What was written was set in stone; what was spoken was adaptable. This made him convenient – like Jesus – for other, later writers to use to propose their own ideas. Plato certainly used Socrates as a character in his own philosophical writings, as did Xenophon, another friend of Socrates who wrote down his sayings after he died.

Socrates was a soldier in the army when the Athenians clashed with the Corinthians in the early stages of the Peloponnesian War, and he was in the thick of the fighting. As spears rained down on the Athenian forces, the soldiers locked their shields together and marched slowly forwards.[25] Without warning, a man to Socrates' left charged towards the enemy. Alcibiades, his face alive with a berserk fury, broke the wall and threw himself at the Corinthians. Socrates followed fast and seized Alcibiades, dragging him back away from the fray. Exhausted, with every muscle aching, they survived the battle and made their way back to Athens.

Alcibiades, like Socrates, is given a voice in one of Plato's dialogues. Still a handsome young man, he bursts into a drinking party. 'I'm a little tipsy,' he confesses while he plies Socrates with compliments.[26] He recounts to the assembled men how he used to think Socrates fancied handsome men, and that he was very eager to learn from Socrates; if Socrates wanted to enjoy Alcibiades' body in return, he was content with that.[27] But in fact, Alcibiades says, Socrates is full of self-control – and he employs the same word that Euripides uses of Pentheus in the *Bacchae*, the same word that Cleon uses to explain the only behaviour that's important to him.[28] Much as in Plato's characterization of Socrates' death, Socrates is able to control himself. Plato reveres his mentor's ability to resist his sexual interest in handsome young men.

The wrestling school at Taureas is lost to history, but we do know it was a private training ground for the richest and fittest Athenian men.[29] There would have been an open, grassy area where men competed and wrestled, and all around ran a stone colonnade. At the opening of one of Plato's dialogues, Socrates had just arrived at this famous wrestling school fresh from the battle of Potidaea.[30] The men cluster around him, begging for stories of the battle, until Socrates catches sight of one young man.

> This young man seemed a marvel to me, he was tall and handsome. Everyone was in love with him, struck and confounded by him. A number of admirers[31] followed behind him. This did not especially surprise either me or any of the other men, but I noticed that the attendants[32] were captivated too, since not one of them looked at anyone else . . . they all admired him like the statue of a god.[33]

After striking a conversation with the young Charmides, Socrates became very excited. 'I was aflame,' he says in the dialogue.[34] This flame was ignited when Charmides shifted in his seat and his cloak, tied loosely about his chest and legs, slipped and revealed something which Plato does not quite divulge – whatever it was, Socrates could hardly contain his excitement.

Unfortunately, instead of pursuing a passionate love affair with Charmides, Socrates decides to lecture him: 'The self-governed man knows what he knows and what he does not know . . . and it is in this way that a household be well governed by self-control, a city well ruled, and might not self-control rule over everything?'[35]

Socrates, or at least the Socrates written by Plato, does not act on his desire. He controls his emotions. There are other passages from Plato's dialogues where Socrates shows some enthusiasm for same-sex love. A desperate man described as mad with love, Hippothales, asks Socrates for his advice on what to do about his desire for a younger man.[36] When one of the men he fancied left the gym, Hippothales pursued him, following him all the way home, singing a song of his own composition about this young man's beauty and charms.

The *Lysis* dialogue, which this scene comes from, presents a fascinating problem for scholars. Throughout the rest of the work,

Socrates uses this story of obsession as a jumping-off point for a discussion about the true nature of friendship – does that mean that Plato has written a manifesto for equality in same-sex relationships?[37] Or is Plato warning us that friendship can become infected with erotic desire, which has a contaminating, maddening effect?[38]

Part of the difficulty of getting to the root of any problem in Greek philosophy is that serious work in parsing out the meanings of ancient Greek words is still underway. Much of our understanding is based on highly biased Victorian translations.[39] Whether Plato's use of Greek vocabulary is erotic or refers to a friendship or to a mentoring system which we have not fully understood in the modern world requires a thoroughly detailed survey of every use of the words, which has yet to be undertaken.

But there is a mercurial element to Plato's writing too. While Plato wrote of the difficulties of experiencing sexual desire, politicians – like Demosthenes and Aeschines – attacked one another viciously using blunt homophobic slurs. It is possible his mentor Socrates had been persecuted for queer desire and it is also true that Timarchus had recently been expelled from Athens after being accused of accepting money for queer sex. So perhaps the ongoing debate in modern scholarship is a product of Plato's own deliberate ambiguity. In fact, there is one poem, possibly written by Plato,[40] upon the death of his friend Dion, Dionysius I's brother-in-law, that suggests Plato was no stranger to queer desire.[41] The epigram ends:

O, [how][42] Dion maddened my soul with desire.[43]

In earlier lines, Plato compares the loss of Dion to Hecuba Queen of Troy weeping for her destroyed city. The metaphor seems apt. Troy was destroyed by fire, a metaphor which Plato and other Greek writers often use to describe how desire consumes the body. The use of the verb 'maddened' is emphatic too – Plato seems to fear how Dion affected him. The poem and the *Lysis* tell us that Plato likely understood what it felt like to desire another man, but he also wrote extensively about controlling these desires.

RESISTING LOVE

Plato's Socrates puts forth a metaphor to explain the workings of the mind in which he describes thought as a charioteer mastering two horses. The charioteer's job is to steer the horses in the right direction, but there is a pliant horse and a disobedient horse. These two horses provided the inspiration for Freud's *id* (the unrestrained, animalistic part of our souls) and *super-ego* (the voice of society). For Socrates, the first horse (the good) is perfectly white, large and beautifully proportioned, and obeys only reason; it needs no whip. The second horse is black, fat and poorly formed, with a thick neck and misty-grey eyes; he barely obeys the whip.

> When the charioteer sees a face that fills him with love, you will feel your whole soul is warmed, you will be filled by the tickling desire of goads. The horse which is obedient, always hemmed in by modesty, controls itself so as not to charge upon the beloved (written in the masculine gender). But the other does not obey the whip and leaps forward forcefully . . . both the charioteer and the good horse will not be compelled to do unlawful things . . . they come to the beloved boy and remember the joy of Aphrodite . . .[44]

Here, the charioteer recalls an image of the goddess of Beauty, who sits chastely, and he pulls up short. He falls backwards, dragging the reins with him. For Socrates, thoughts of a pure, true form of beauty inspire us to withdraw. In comparison, he realizes the boy is something less than true. He is able to maintain his self-control. Homosexual desire is portrayed by Plato as something ugly, tempting, but nothing like true beauty.

In Plato's dialogue *Gorgias*, Socrates sits with the hedonistic philosopher Callicles at a dinner party. It is here, surrounded by food and drink, with slaves coming to-and-fro bringing new dishes, that Socrates turns to Callicles and asks him, earnestly and with concern, whether the life of a homosexual can be fulfilling:

'Isn't the life of same-sex male lovers fearful and shameful and pitiable? Would you call these men happy when they have their desires in plenty?'

'Are you not ashamed to raise this, Socrates?'

'Are you saying that pleasure and good are the same thing? Or is there some pleasure which is not good?'[45]

Here he is asking a similar question asked by evangelical Christians: whether something is actually good just because it feels good. In fact, Socrates sounds evangelical because it's a line of questioning inherited by later Christian teaching.[46]

There is only one way for such pleasure to be seen as a good, as Socrates says in the *Symposium*. In the *Symposium*, drinkers lay in pairs on raised beds. In the dim glow of the candlelight, their heads were garlanded with ivy – symbol of the wine god Dionysus – and a large mixing bowl stood between them, black and red, possibly showing the story of the great lovers Achilles and Patroclus.[47] They were all drunk, with the exception of Socrates who sat soberly watching them all.[48]

While one of the slaves danced and played the flute, Agathon and Pausanias lay one in front of the other and watched. Plato set the dialogue around 416 BCE, a little time before Agathon and Pausanias fled north to Macedon. Here they were in their own home where they lived together as partners, hosting other luminaries of this illustrious period in the life of Athens. While Cleon may have already issued his attacks on certain queer men, they remained for the time being in the city. A famous doctor Eryximachus directs conversation onto the topic at hand: 'we should all give as good a speech in praise of Love as we can,' he says.[49]

Throughout the dialogue, Plato uses various queer voices (including Pausanias, Agathon and Socrates) to expound upon his own theory that there are two types of love. On the one hand, you have Heavenly love. This is the love of poetry, of music, of intellect, of friendship; it is pure and chaste and free from sex. On the other hand, you have Common love, which is sexual, base and somehow rough and uncultured.

Gradually, through the dialogue, Plato distinguishes more and more between Heavenly love and Common love. He ends with Socrates describing how first one sees physical beauty and then one can understand intellectual beauty.[50] He does seem to believe that queer desire, unconsummated, can be the basis for a strong intellect, but Socrates never says that sexual consummation is acceptable at any stage. He says, 'whenever someone through the correct way to admire a boy's beauty and begins to look upon it, he is almost able to reach the final secret'.[51] The language Plato uses emphasizes the tortured self-restraint of looking but never indulging. He believes this grants the man who experiences same-sex desire the ability to know the true form of beauty. But his comments in the *Gorgias* make it quite clear that he believes this should never be a sexual relationship. Xenophon even tells us separately that people used to visit Socrates for advice on how to cure their same-sex attractions.[52]

HOMOPHOBIA'S DEBT TO ECONOMICS

We will never know for sure whether Plato himself was anti-gay sex or in favour of it. But it is clear that the climate in Athens at the time was opposed to it. As well as the role of growing inequalities and monetization in forming the household and promoting self-restraint as a desirable behaviour, there was another problem stalking Athens in the 4th century BCE. That problem was debt.[53]

In the 32 speeches of Demosthenes, debt is mentioned 150 times. A number of legal cases in Athens at the time were based on a failure to meet credit obligations. A student of Socrates, Aeschines of Sphettos, was brought before a court at the very beginning of the 4th century BCE and charged with living a luxurious lifestyle, spending his money on perfumes and not meeting his obligations to his bankers.[54] The interest Aeschines was being charged, however, may well raise some eyebrows. At 3 per cent per month (this equates to around 42 per cent per annum),[55] the bankers stood to make a fortune. From the 4th century BCE in Athens alone, there are 16 different surviving pieces of legislation relating to debt. It was a big business. But debt in the ancient world was far riskier than today.

Xenophon tells us that when farmers had had a particularly good yield for a number of years, they often used their extra cash to set up a business to grow their money still further. They would set up a little shop, go into business as a merchant or, according to Xenophon, set up a loan company.[56] If true, this would have meant a large number of unregulated loan sharks circling in ancient society seeking to make a quick buck.

Plato and his student Aristotle fiercely discuss the evils of debt. Plato claims that the greed that leads to debt is the reason democracy came to be (Plato is no fan of democracy in many of his works).[57] For Plato, debt is about living beyond one's means and therefore exhibits a lack of self-control. In Athens, most people would have used their property as collateral. We are told by Demosthenes that some people used jewellery,[58] copper[59] or even a gold crown[60] to secure their loans. People could also use their houses or their land. Of course, a whole tranche of Athenian society had neither property nor possessions, and as wealth inequality increased, this group got even larger. These people were the ptochoi (often translated 'beggars', but really they were a class of people without fixed assets and the translation 'beggar' does not quite do them justice).[61] Ptochoi had existed hundreds of years before since Homer's day, indeed Odysseus disguises himself as one when he returns to Ithaca.

Odysseus disguises himself to spy on the men who have taken control of his palace. Homer goes out of his way to show the barbarity of these suitors: they have sex with the women of the household and jeer about it, and they throw out Odysseus who they believe is a ptochos. This shows their barbarity because in early Greece, a ptochos with no fixed assets could expect to be cared for by his city. This had changed radically by the time of Plato. You might think, then, the ptochos had no grounds to be lent to whatever. In this, you would be mistaken.

It seems strange to us to lend money to a beggar, but in Athens it was perfectly routine. The reason for this has a very dark side.

The *ptochos* (singular of *ptochoi*) could be lent money, but in the absence of any property or possessions to secure his loan, he would be required to offer up his own body. He could be sold into slavery at any moment to repay his debt. For Plato, who may have been sold into slavery by Dionysius, the idea of borrowing money was simply too risky. Plato was never a rich man, he relied on his friends to fund the Academy. He had very little to give to secure a loan, and so had to cultivate a fierce sense of independence.

It should come as little surprise that such an unequal, debt-ridden, individualistic society as this would invent the study of economics. We know that Aristotle wrote a treatise on the topic, though not much of it survives. The complete text of Xenophon's *Oeconomicus*, however, we do have and it provides one of the most revealing pictures of Athens during this time.

The *Oeconomicus* tells us about a farming family with slaves who manage their affairs neatly and orderly. The husband is named Ischomachus – we are not told his wife's name. As a result, they succeed in increasing the wealth of their household. In one passage, Ischomachus explains how he and his wife were taught to run it:

> 'My mother told me that my task is to use self-control,' [my wife told me]. 'Yes, by Zeus,' I said, 'and my father said the same to me. Self-control is the task of both a man and a woman, so the property might become better and matters grow from beauty and justice.'[62]

This couple describe how self-restraint will lead to the accumulation of household wealth. Much as in archaic Sparta, where self-restraint was used to justify why some men had more money than others, there are signs it was becoming an object of fixation in ancient Athens. The puritanical husband-and-wife team in this treatise even extend their love of self-restraint to their long-suffering slaves: 'And when we appointed a housekeeper, we looked hard for a woman who seemed to us to be most self-restrained in matters of the stomach, of wine, of sleep, and of relations with men.'[63]

The connection between self-restraint in bodily desires and shrewd accumulation of wealth is explicit. It should come as no surprise then to find the *Oeconomicus* raging against another issue:

> I do think that those who fall head-over-heels in love cannot give much attention to anything except the object of their desire. It is no easy thing to find a hope or preoccupation sweeter than queer love.[64] Indeed, when things need to get done, there can be no harder price than prevention of being with those you love.[65]

Ischomachus thinks that queer people cannot be trusted with money. The ancient logic here is that queer people experience excessive desire. Since excess desire reveals a lack of self-control, they could never be trusted with the running of the household. This quiet picture of suburban family life is easy to overlook and has often been assumed to be rather dull by classicists, but it provides important clues about how the zeal for economic management coincided with a rising homophobia.

The *Oeconomicus* preserves an ancient idea that still exists in the modern world: amid scarce resources, wealth is generated through self-control. In Australia, a multi-millionaire made headlines all over the world when he suggested young people should stop spending their money on avocado-on-toast and save for a deposit for a house instead.[66] The argument that everyone could be rich if only they would exercise enough restraint in expenditure is still around today.

Towards the end of Plato's life, he was thinking more and more about self-governance and how the state itself should become – like the household – subject to restraint. He began to argue increasingly that certain behaviours ran contrary to a natural order, an idea he surely inherited from the Pythagoreans, and that restraint must be exercised to keep unnatural desires and excessive behaviours from destroying the state.

Despite his appalling treatment at the hands of Dionysius I, Plato returned to Sicily in 366 BCE. He did so once Dionysius I was safely dead, and only at the request of his friend Dion, a relative of the new king Dionysius II. We have a detailed letter from Plato, by this time in his 70s, explaining what he intended to teach the young Dionysius II: 'If he pursues the course I am describing, if he is educated in thoughtfulness and self-control . . . he may well double his father's empire.'[67]

Perhaps this trip inspired Plato to think more about his own ideal state, a concept he explores at length in many of his works. One of the last things Plato wrote was his *Laws*, a series of prescriptions and proscriptions which a city should follow if it is to live in harmony with the natural order. His utopian city is presided over by a philosopher-king, who is unelected but derives his right to rule from his great intellect.

In one passage, Plato makes the gays' place in his kingdom very clear: 'the pleasure of reproduction is part of the nature of the coming together of man and woman and is owed to nature, but the coming together (i.e. sex) of men to men or women to women is against nature.'[68] Inherited from the Pythagoreans, Plato believed that nature had a coherent design and that everything natural had a purpose, a role to play in the grand order. That's why, at the end of his life, Plato believed that same-sex desire, which cannot be for reproduction, was unnatural.

The idea that there *was* a design, a secret order to all the chaos, may have been especially seductive during a time in which war, slavery, debt and economic insecurity all conspired to make the lives of Plato's contemporaries frightening. But the cost of this was to reduce sex to a single function. It was to deny that sex can perform many functions and that pleasure and love are reasons enough in themselves.

FIVE

Alexander the Straight?

> Such men [who have sex with men] are sick because of nurture.
>
> ARISTOTLE, NICOMACHAEAN ETHICS 1148B

Plato died in 348 BCE, a decade before the Battle of Chaeronea (338 BCE) when Athens and her allies were soundly defeated by Philip II of Macedon. Two years later, Philip himself was assassinated and the fledgling Macedonian empire was left to Alexander, his heir. Alexander of Macedon, later Alexander the Great, took advantage of Philip's enrichment of Macedon and defeat of the Greek city-states, as well as the weak position of Persia in the East. He conquered Persia, marched down into Egypt and may even have reached as far east as modern-day Pakistan. With Alexander came what ancient historians call the Hellenistic period, when Greek philosophy and money flooded the Mediterranean and Asia in the wake of Alexander's unstoppable armies.

Alexander the Great, from his teenage years, was famously handsome. He had beautiful hair, was lean and muscular, and all about him – according to one source – was a pleasant scent which made men and women all around him swoon with desire.[1] It was said, however, that the Athenian politician Demosthenes belittled Alexander the Great in private, calling him a '*pais*'.[2] The term 'boy', as we have seen, is often used for gay lovers in the ancient world. As well as describing Alexander as a 'boy', Demosthenes also referred to Alexander as '*Margites*', the protagonist of an ancient burlesque poem, meaning 'lustful man'. It is far from certain, but Demosthenes' private references to Alexander imply that this most extraordinary general was a lascivious queer.

At the court of his father Philip II, Alexander received the very best education that anybody in the ancient world could ask for. Philip sent for none other than Aristotle – an erstwhile pupil of Plato and one of the world's greatest thinkers – to come to Mieza (the shrine of the nymphs in Macedon) when Alexander was still a teenager. Here, Alexander and Aristotle would sit in the garden, and Alexander was schooled not just in military strategy and political theory, but in matters that are far more mysterious.[3]

We are told by Plutarch that Aristotle sought to impart on his young charge the secret mysteries of acroamatic and epoptic reasoning. We do not know exactly what this involved. It seems likely that in that garden, Alexander was taught advanced rhetoric and the power to subdue his opponents not by the sword, but with the word. His teacher was a master of this art: we are told that Plato refused to teach the subject at his Academy, delegating the task to Aristotle.[4] Alexander adored literature of all sorts, and devoured Aristotle's very own edition of Homer's *Iliad*.[5] According to legend, he slept with this revised edition under a pillow next to a knife with which to dispose of any nighttime assassins.[6] Alexander also shared Aristotle's fascination with medicine and the healing arts.

One text attributed to Aristotle betrays a fervent dislike of camp, gay men. Though we cannot be certain who wrote it, the text lays bare the worsening attitudes to queer and camp individuals in the Hellenistic period of Greek history.

> The sign of the *kinaidos* (a man who enjoys sex with men) is a weepy eye, and a knocking together of the knees. The head is held to the right on the shoulder. The hands are turned upside down and move freely through the air. There are glances of the eyes, like those of Dionysius the Sophist.[7]

Aristotle (or perhaps one of his disciples) attempts to diagnose what a gay man looks like and how he behaves. By this time, a prevailing idea in philosophy claimed that how a person looked betrayed information about their character and inner behaviour. The lax hand gestures and incline of the head were taken to be the signs of an evil person. This is the beginning of a long tradition of the characterization of camp people as sinister.

In another text, which we are sure was written by Aristotle, he describes men who are by nature homosexual as 'sick' and goes further than any other ancient commentators in diagnosing a new cause of same-sex desire.[8] Aristotle argues that while some men desire other men because it's their nature,

> in other cases, it arises from nurture. The latter is the case – for example – for those among boys who were raped. When nature is the cause, no one can say these men lack self-control, just as one would not say it of women who have sex. According to the same logic, it can be said that some men are sick by nature.[9]

Aristotle's claim is still with us centuries later. Either gay people are sick or they are victims, evangelicals tell us. The fact that Aristotle uses the medical language of sickness and disease to discuss homosexuality shows just how far homophobia had spread. However, he does note that some forms of same-sex desire have nothing to do with a lack of self-control. This idea was not completely new. Xenophon talked some decades before Aristotle about how some men may have a natural *tropos* ('orientation') towards other men.[10]

As Alexander grew older, he became more and more interested in sex and relationships with men. He grew estranged from Aristotle and turned to drink.[11] Despite all his power, it's said he became deeply ashamed in later life. In his youth, however, the ancient historian Plutarch tells us, Alexander was a model of self-restraint. He never had sex with women until he married with the sole exception of a woman called Barsine,[12] although he would go on to have many affairs with women and wed multiple wives. Even when he captured many cities, he did not rape the women he captured which was apparently rare enough to be worthy of comment. It is said of the Persian women he captured that he admired their stature, but passed them with all the interest of a man looking at statues.[13]

Alexander, or at least the Alexander that Plutarch conveys, spent the early part of his life demonstrating his extraordinary self-control. He was sitting at his desk on campaign, perusing various tightly bound letters that were brought to him and scribbling careful responses, when a messenger arrived and Alexander bid him come forward. It was a letter from Philoxenus, who was probably (though we are not certain) Alexander's commander of the seas of Greece and Asia Minor. The letter contained various details of campaigns and attempts to subdue rebellious seamen. It was only when Alexander reached the end of the letter that things began to get interesting. There was a little postscript from Philoxenus that should Alexander be interested, a man named Theodorus of Tarentum was very eager to sell him 'two boys of surpassing beauty'. Alexander replied. He commanded Philoxenus to sentence Theodorus to a horrific death; the instruction had a melodramatic flourish: 'to dispatch him into complete destruction'.[14] Clearly, this offer touched a nerve.

The young Alexander, at least as presented by Plutarch, went out of his way to show his complete disinterest in all sex. Plutarch tells us, 'Sleep and sex made him aware he was mortal, since pleasure and tiredness originate from the same weakness of nature'.[15] It was said that when exotic fruits, fish and food were brought to him, Alexander gave them to his companions instead. This habit, however, seems to have eroded as life went on; towards the end of his life, Alexander is reported to have spent as much as 10,000 drachmas on a single meal.[16] It seems that the fruits of self-control appealed less to the most powerful man who had ever lived. One imagines he wondered what the point had been in conquering the known world, if he wasn't allowed a few indulgences.

ALEXANDER THE CONQUEROR

While his father had subdued Greece, Alexander set about conquering Asia. It's true that the old superpowers of Egypt and Persia were waning in their influence, but there can be no doubt about Alexander's extraordinary gift for military command and his charismatic ability to woo the inhabitants of every country he came to.

Having marched his armies into Balochistan, Alexander stopped to rest in Gedrosia where, one evening, he watched a play in the theatre.[17] As the aulos players emerged on the stage, Alexander took his seat in marble at the very front of the audience. The king looked on expectantly at the stage, at its exquisitely painted backdrop, depicting the wild, untameable sea of Troy. A young man hurried into the seat directly next to Alexander. Alexander leaned in to kiss him, and the entire crowd cheered and applauded. The lover's name was Bagoas, and he was far from the only man Alexander ever kissed. The most famous of his lovers, a man Alexander had known since he was a young teenager under the tutelage of Aristotle, was Hephaestion.

When Alexander took the ancient and hallowed city of Troy, his army set up camp. In the early evening, the waning sun gilded that fabled grassy plain where Achilles and Hector struggled and died. Alexander and Hephaestion, accompanied by a small procession, set out on foot for a small tomb outside the ancient citadel. They knelt before the tomb, placing their interlocked hands upon it. It was believed to be the burial ground of the warriors Achilles and Patroclus, the two great lovers of the Trojan War. Alexander placed a crown of flowers on Achilles' side of the tomb, and Hephaestion did the same on Patroclus'.[18]

Modern historians are often very reticent to claim Alexander and Hephaestion had sex. Personally, I cannot imagine a world in which they did not. Nor apparently, could ancient historians. Curtius, writing about Alexander, explains that he was possessed of 'restraint in unrestrained desires, an indulgence of desire within limits'.[19] This implies Alexander had a reputation for a highly selective, careful attitude to sex. With those he loved, sex was fine; but, as we know, he was enraged by the idea that he would ever pay for sex with boy-slaves. As his tutor Aristotle had pointed out, some men are by nature queer, and it seems Alexander was one of them. Hephaestion was also the same age as Alexander,[20] defying the age-unequal model of same-sex relationships which has long been assumed by classicists to have been the only model of Greek homosexuality.

It was said that Hephaestion became ill at Ecbatana in modern-day Iran. A doctor called Glaucias attended urgently to him and reports were sent to Alexander as often as there were developments, but nothing could be done. Eventually, after many hours, Glaucias knelt before Alexander and told him that his beloved Hephaestion, with whom he had spent his entire adult life and in whom he had trusted command of his armies, was dead.

Alexander, said to be a great healer himself, commanded Glaucias be hanged at the gates of Ecbatana for his failure. He then turned to his engineers and ordered that they strip the city of its defences. He sent a messenger to a priest in Egypt, commanding him to deify Hephaestion.

Outside Ecbatana, an enormous pyre (said to be over 250 feet tall) was constructed.[21] Hephaestion's body was placed at the top, surveying the city where he had died. Alexander loaded between 10,000 and 12,000 talents of gold on the pyre, so that it shone in the setting sun. As the red and orange flames consumed the pyre, people for miles around must have seen the smoke rising into the sky. Alexander was inconsolable.

There were other loves in Alexander's life, but none who meant so much to him as Hephaestion.[22]

DIOGENES THE CYNIC

Wherever Alexander conquered, he brought the Greek and Macedonian economies and their ways of handling transactions in money with him.[23] In Egypt, salt-makers, beekeepers and peasants were subjected to cash taxes. A failure to pay led to immediate imprisonment. Worse treatment could be meted out still. In one fragment, a local ruler Apollonios commands his tax collector either to make up deficient tax himself or to flay alive the poor men who could not pay it.[24] There is another papyrus document that shows proof of the arrest of a humble salt-worker for the failure to pay a very small amount of tax.

Beekeepers in ancient Egypt's Alexandria found themselves faced with a new form of market economy. Wealthy Greek men bought up huge numbers of beehives, as many as 1,000, and rented them out to the peasants. The keepers would also have to pay the rent for a donkey to transport their hives across Egypt, for they were constantly on the move to ensure the best honey they could make. If these beekeepers strayed into a different district, they would be punished with another tax. Failure to pay in cash on the spot meant the beekeepers would be arrested.

This small snapshot of 4th and 3rd century BCE Alexandria shows the financial pains that additional taxes had brought to ordinary people. From the reign of Ptolemy III Euergetes, who ruled Egypt around 70 years after the death of Alexander, we possess a stash of documents that show local farmers signing contracts with each other for sureties in case they were targeted. These contracts are all for very modest sums indeed. The economy in which ordinary people lived was highly dependent on debt, and tax collectors were predatory and rife. It is no surprise that in such a high-tax, debt-ridden market economy, philosophies sprang up that treated desire and excess of any sort with suspicion. In a tragic turn of events, it was the rule of a man known for his love of other men, Alexander the Great, that led to a precarious economic situation in which homophobia grew.

The philosopher Diogenes of Sinope had a few run-ins with the Macedonians. At the Battle of Chaeronea, it was said he was captured by Philip II. Upon being brought before the king, he eyed him beadily, and said, 'I am a spy of your gluttony'.[25] Diogenes, when released and returned to Athens, appeared to have little respect for Alexander either. Alexander, who was always interested in philosophy, encountered Diogenes in Athens early in his reign. He attempted to engage the philosopher in conversation, to which Diogenes replied, 'would you mind moving out of the way? You are blocking the sun'.[26]

He showed utter contempt for the fine things in life. He spent much of his life as an itinerant in Athens, wandering the streets in filthy, sodden rags. When he was not wandering around asking people questions, Diogenes could be found sitting in a large wine-jar, though it seems unlikely he was responsible for having finished off its contents. He derived his joy not from wine, but from upsetting as many people as he could.

Whenever he found a particularly large throng of people, he walked into their midst and farted. He enjoyed farting so much that he is said to have written an entire treatise on the matter, pithily called *On Farting*. When one passing young man cried out in rage at the philosopher for letting out a particularly whiffy fart, Diogenes jabbed him with his stick: 'the sin, fool, is not the fart, but in failing to understand that farts are natural!' he cried.[27] But farting was far from the limit of what Diogenes was prepared to do in public. Diogenes also loved to find a group of haughty-looking men, position himself in front of them, and masturbate vigorously while grinning at them. We're told he did this for two reasons: firstly, to demonstrate how ridiculous it is to pay a sex worker to relieve you,[28] and secondly, to point out that being horny was a natural feeling and it was only natural to relieve it.

Diogenes' philosophy was not difficult to understand: just as Plato and the Pythagoreans had pioneered the idea of natural order, so Diogenes believed anything that was natural should be encouraged. Apparently though, this did not extend to everything natural. Perhaps in the marketplace amid the sellers and shoppers, Diogenes caught sight of a fellow Athenian parading through the cobbled street. They were dressed in women's clothes, adorned in make-up and perfume. Diogenes pushed past a throng before him and tapped his target annoyingly on the shoulder with his stick. 'You,' he shouted, 'are you not ashamed? You should be ashamed for being worse than nature intended you, for she made you a man but you force yourself to become a woman!'[29] We are not told whether his victim shouted back or what happened next, but the episode is revealing. It tells us that Diogenes believed firmly in the 'natural' categories of man and woman and viewed the transgression of this border to be an offence against nature (since, in his view, women were 'naturally' inferior to men). Whether this incident actually took place in a city as hostile to queer behaviour as Athens remains unclear, but the anecdote — told centuries after Diogenes' death — leaves no doubt about his views on queer identities.

In Cynic philosophy, the school which Diogenes founded, the natural form of man does have desires which should be conservatively managed through masturbation; love and sex, he thought, were unnecessary attempts to reach pleasure. He used to say of men in love that they were reaching for unattainable pleasure.[30] Diogenes, who fetishized poverty, did not believe that desire of any sort for another person was natural.

We possess a fragment of a letter allegedly written by Diogenes to Alexander the Great.[31] In it, this beggar-philosopher, so obsessed with poverty and conservative simplicity, told the great king that there was no way he could become a respectable man, 'for you are controlled by Hephaestion's thighs'.[32] For Diogenes, Alexander's same-sex love — however controlled — was a sign of his inability to adhere to nature, and therefore he could never be a respected and good king. Apparently, Alexander's ability to subdue the known world to his command was not sufficient evidence to the philosopher that he was a strong and powerful monarch.

Copycat versions of Diogenes sprung up all over the Greek world, and he appears to have generated something of a cult following. Like monks in the modern world, Diogenes and his followers rejected the complexities of society and embraced a simpler way of living. They embraced poverty. They looked to simple categories in the world like male and female, and held to a belief in nature, decrying the complexities of custom and society. They eschewed all forms of pleasure. Even though they came from natural sources, Diogenes was equally opposed to drug-taking.

In Xenophon's *Oeconomicus*, the ideal husband-and-wife team develop rigorous self-discipline to build up their wealth. Apart from being heavily selective in the people they employ, not drinking too much and never having anything to do with the sort of unbridled person who dares to fall in love with someone of the same sex, they avoid another terrible source of poor self-discipline. Henbane,[33] a poisonous plant in the nightshade family, is to be abandoned they say because it brings about pleasure.[34] There can be no doubt that henbane, a highly toxic plant, is a dangerous substance, but it is interesting that they ban it not because it is poisonous, but because it is pleasurable. In very light doses, henbane likely did bring on a high; like many mind-altering substances – such as alcohol – too much of it was highly toxic.

Diogenes the Cynic is said to have railed against a 'drug-dealer' named Lysias, possibly because drugs are said to bring about unnatural states of mind. If a much later writer, Julius Pollux, can be relied upon, Lysias sold drugs that resulted in abortions.[35] It is probable that Diogenes is not just railing against the abortive feature of these pharmaceuticals, mainly because one of the many things Diogenes is said to have opposed is procreation in the first place. Recreational drugs in the ancient world often overlapped with contraceptive drugs, henbane being one such example, as well as the opium poppy which was widely crushed up and pressed into tablets, consumed recreationally in both the Hellenistic and the Roman world.[36]

A SHIPWRECKED PHILOSOPHER

Zeno checked the inventory of his ship one last time. Satisfied, he rolled up his scroll, sighed and boarded the vessel. Trips to Athens were always expensive: the port, Piraeus, charged a tax on all goods that came in. It's thought that in the late 400s BCE, it had been 5 per cent, but by Zeno's time – in the late 300s BCE, shortly after the death of Alexander – it had risen to as much as 50 per cent (depending on what was being transported).[37] Unlike with modern taxation, the tax was levied on the cost of the whole product, not on the profits made.[38] Zeno was not a rich man, and had likely taken out a loan to start his business ferrying wares across the rippling waters which girt the continents of Europe and Asia.

The ship, curved and long, made its way across the deep. Land appeared in the distance, just as Zeno spied a great, black cloud amassing. Suddenly, a lightning bolt shot from the blackened sky and lit the waters. The boat lurched. Zeno flew through the air, holding onto the rigging for dear life. Men screamed, flinging themselves into the sea as the ship rammed into the rocks.

When Zeno awoke, he felt the sand warm and wet beneath his cheek. He found, to his surprise, that he could stand, and he began to make his way slowly along the beach. His clothes began to dry in the sun as he went, which infused him with more vigour. Nature always provided, he may have thought. It was as Zeno walked that he became conscious of what he had lost. Nature had taken from him his ship, his money, his livelihood; and yet what had he retained? He had his life. He was still breathing, still had sight and thought. There were things, he may have noted, you could control, and there were things you could not. In the end, all you had were your wits.

As luck would have it, Zeno's ship had been wrecked not far from Athens, his original destination. That very day, he found himself in a bookshop surrounded by scrolls stored like wine bottles in a wicker rack. It was here that he picked up Xenophon's *Memorabilia*, which contained the story of Socrates' life. Zeno was enchanted. Eventually the bookseller approached and asked Zeno what he was looking for. He replied that he didn't know.

'I think,' said the bookseller, 'you might follow that man over there,' and he pointed just outside the bookshop to where Crates, unshaven, hirsute, and smelling strongly of fish was shouting at some poor unfortunate soul who had dared to take a little more care in his appearance.[39]

Crates was a pupil of Diogenes, although he was not as implacably opposed to marriage as his mentor had been.[40] His wife, the beautiful Hipparchia of Maroneia, was a famous philosopher in her own right. When they married, surrounded by their friends in the middle of the street, they kissed and amid the garlands and well-wishers, Crates and Hipparchia were drawn to the floor in a passionate embrace. It was here in public that they consummated their marriage.[41] Diogenes likely would have approved of the fact that Crates, who was a wealthy man, sold all his possessions to live a life of poverty. But he may have found it harder to credit Crates' enthusiastic embrace of sex.

Zeno, having lost everything, began to beg in the fashion of the Cynics. He listened to teachings from a variety of philosophical schools, until eventually he felt able to contribute something of his own.

At the entrance to the marketplace in Athens stood a gleaming bronze statue of Hermes, the god of commerce, holding a wand. Men and women seeking to buy or sell passed by Hermes every day. Just behind the statue was a marble portico painted with interwoven scenes from myth and history. It was called the painted Stoa.[42] The first panel – according to the ancient Greek Pausanias, who wrote one of the world's first guidebooks (*A Description of Greece*)[43] – showed the Athenian army battling against the Spartans. The wall in the middle showed Theseus, the legendary first king of Athens, fighting with the Amazons, a race of warrior women. On the other side, a circle of kings stood in terrible judgement over Ajax son of Oileus in Troy. Ajax had dragged the princess and seer Cassandra from her sanctuary in the temple of Athena and raped her.[44] Though the painting did not depict it, Ajax was sentenced to be stoned to death outside the walls of the vanquished city.

It was in front of these murals that Zeno stood and taught his students, wearing a thin cloak, which he never changed all year round.[45] The philosophy that he taught, apparently while scowling continuously,[46] was a blend of Cynicism, Platonism and his own ideas about the world. It came to be known as Stoicism, after the painted Stoa. The day Zeno's ship was wrecked, the world changed forever. For without Zeno and his tutelage at Crates' hand, there could have been no Christianity.[47] For it was on the bedrock of Zeno's ideas that the Church would reform the mission of Christ to appeal to the Greek and wider Roman world.

Zeno had nearly died, but by embracing poverty and begging on the streets of Athens, he had learned the true value of life. His rejection of money and excess clearly struck a chord with many in ancient Greece. But Stoic philosophy was not just about the rejection of money. It was about seeking control in a world that felt adrift.

The Stoics divided phenomena into things that were under our control (eph'ēmin) and things that were not under our control (ouk eph'ēmin). Stoics were advised by Zeno to disregard those things beyond our control: the weather, the behaviours of friends, the vagaries of illness and disease. In a sense, Stoicism was a subtler form of Pythagoreanism, which had sought mastery over the whole universe. Stoics sought only to control what they could in their lives.

Anything within the body, and most particularly emotions, the Stoics believed lay within our control. Emotions, according to Stoic thought, arose because a person had on some level decided to feel that way; love was a choice, desire was a choice, avarice was a choice. By carefully contemplating and meditating on emotions, Zeno taught, one could learn to be free of them. The most dangerous of the emotions, for the Stoics, was pleasure. As Zeno wrote in a letter to King Antigonus, 'A man yearning for philosophy turns away from notorious pleasure which renders womanly[48] the minds of young men, it is obvious that we lean to good form not just by nature, but also by choice.'[49]

Pleasure here means anything from giddy delight to a passing fancy. It means a glass of wine, watching the sunset, kissing the most beautiful person in the room. Pleasure, for the Stoics, is characterized by ephemerality. It has been fashionable to assume that ancient Stoics were against short-term pleasure and in favour of long-term ones. While there is some reason to believe this was true of the later Roman Stoics,[50] Zeno was in favour of a life of rigorous self-discipline and total rejection of pleasure of all sorts.

For Zeno, the pursuit of profit nearly cost him his life. He would have looked all around him at the marketplace and seen people scrabbling to make enough to pay off their debts and feed their families. Amidst this world of bustling commerce and merciless mercantilism, Zeno did not see that pleasure was a goal worth working for. His strict emphasis on self-discipline and poverty coincided with the economic uncertainties, indebtedness, wealth inequality and tax burdens of the age. Alongside his works Republic and On Emotions, we are told that Zeno wrote a lost manuscript called The Art of Love. We don't know what it contained but, like

Plato and possibly Socrates before him, Zeno nursed an interest in men which caused him no little personal embarrassment.

Nearly 500 years later, in the early 3rd century CE, a writer named Athenaeus wrote a book about a dinner party held for a group of highly eccentric scholars. At the party, the guests compete with one another to cite the most tangential and abstruse fragments of philosophical or poetic texts that they have stored in their memory. The work is called *Deipnosophistae*, which most scholars translate as the *Dinner Sophists*, but could be translated as something like the *Clever Diners*. The *Clever Diners* preserves thousands of fragments of ancient philosophy, aphorisms and ideas that would otherwise be completely lost to us. It is from *Clever Diners* Book 13 that a segment comes about Zeno the Stoic. We are told that a contemporary of his, Antigonus of Carystus wrote a biography of Zeno in which he claims Zeno was attracted *exclusively* to men.[51]

A later Stoic, Cleanthes, tells us that Zeno also believed it possible – like Aristotle – to tell someone's character from their appearance.[52] Touting this supposed connection between physical beauty and moral virtue, he apparently chased handsome young men until they agreed to let him 'teach them philosophy'.[53] They were at most, later Stoics tell us, 28 years old. They were on the cusp of married life and adulthood, in peak physical fitness and possessed of commensurately strong mental powers. By teaching them virtue, perhaps Zeno was ennobling his erotic interest. To have sex would have been to succumb to the emotion of *eros* and therefore to participate in pleasure – it could not be countenanced.[54]

At the age of 98, Zeno tripped in the Stoa and fell, breaking his toe. Rather than get up, the philosopher held his breath and died some minutes later. This likely apocryphal story was designed to highlight the man's self-control: he could even resist the will to live. But ancient Stoicism did not die with him.

HOW TO PLEASURE YOURSELF

Of all the people in the ancient world, few have been so maligned as Epicurus of Samos. Even Shakespeare refers to idlers and those enslaved to sexual passions as 'epicures'.[55] This may have been because

Epicurus himself had a vicious tongue: he once accused his near-contemporary Aristotle of being a drug-peddler. Epicurus was born on the island of Samos in the year 341 BCE, the son of an Athenian schoolmaster called Neocles. Naturally, given his father's profession, Epicurus was given the best education his parents could provide. At school, he would have learned grammar, music, rhetoric and the theology of the ancient Greek pantheon. Sitting with a wax tablet on his lap, he learned to write, and his schoolmaster dictated knowledge for him to memorize. But it seems he was not an easy pupil.

When Epicurus was being taught about the foundations of the universe, his teacher droned on about how Hesiod, an ancient poet, speculated that the first god was Chaos, and that it was Chaos who made everything come into being. After Chaos came 'wide-bosomed Earth' and after 'wide-bosomed Earth' came the Olympians (Zeus, Hera, Aphrodite, etc.) and with them came Desire. It was at this point that the schoolteacher became conscious that his less-than-zealous charge had not copied down a single word. Upon the schoolteacher inquiring as to the reason for Epicurus' intransigence, he was told, 'I am confused, Sir, for who made Chaos?'[56]

This problem seems to have vexed the adult Epicurus too. Who created the original god and what were the consequences of belief in all the gods? One of the key tenets of Epicurus' philosophy was a studied scepticism of religion. There were unanswered questions about the gods, as far as he was concerned. It was a dangerous opinion to have in ancient Greece. Long before Epicurus made his first journey to Athens, the city already had a reputation for violence towards atheists – a reputation well-earned when, for instance, they executed Socrates on two charges: atheism and seducing young men. At the turn of the 5th century BCE, Theodorus of Cyrene was also put to death by the state for expressing scepticism about the gods.

The stories told about Epicurus suggest he was sceptical about the existence of the gods. The traditional Greek explanation was rooted in the hierarchical nature of Greek society. Since there are noble things and noble people, the reasoning went, there must be a noblest, best thing, and that must be the divine. This argument is now known as *e gradibus entium* in Latin, or 'from the steps of being'. However, Epicurus imagined a radically different sort of hierarchy. Rather than arguing for a hierarchy of nobility, Epicurus argued there was a hierarchy of pleasure. He argued that if there are good, pleasant things in the world, there must be a best, most pleasant thing, and that best thing must be pleasure itself rather than God.[57] He surmised that, since we are all mortal, all we can do in life is seek out the maximal pleasure that we can.

At the age of 18, Epicurus had already spent a year doing military service in the city and bought a plot of land. Here he planted a garden where he could teach his students how to pursue pleasure. For Epicurus, the end goal of life was to have experienced as much pleasure as possible; of course, sometimes this meant foregoing short-term pleasures. However, his views on sex were perfectly plain: 'They say sex is never profitable, but [I say] it is lovely unless it's harmful.'[58] To avoid the risks of harm and enhance the potential for pleasure, Epicurus accordingly gave advice on how to have the best sex: 'If you remove the chance to see, talk, and spend time with the one you love, then sexual passion is dissolved'.[59] Epicurus' shocking proposition, in a philosophical world dominated by Stoicism and Platonism, was that enjoying sex could be part of a good, moral life. 'I cannot think of good without the pleasure of sex', he wrote.[60]

Throughout his life, Epicurus was mocked and attacked for his love of pleasure. In a fragment of a comic play, a schoolteacher abandons traditional teaching and decides to impart Epicureanism to his young student.[61] Accordingly, the student gets uproariously drunk, eating far too much and spending lots of money. A contemporary from the rival Sceptic school of philosophy (which encouraged its proponents to abandon definite beliefs about anything) described Epicurus as 'taking pleasure in his tummy, than which there is nothing more greedy'.[62] Popular comics and philosophers despised Epicurus because he did not advocate abstinence from pleasure.

It is hard to know much more about Epicurus' ideas, and the little we do know comes as much from his critics as from his followers.

Buried beneath metres of ash and sediment from the eruption of Vesuvius in Italy is a beautiful holiday home that may have once belonged to a relative of Julius Caesar. The library is known to contain a treasure trove of Epicurean texts, both written by later philosophers and possibly by Epicurus himself. Archaeologists were able to access the library of the so-called Villa of the Papyri some time ago, and in the process extracted several charred scrolls. Because the scrolls were written in metallic ink, they can be read using X-rays. This technique is still being perfected, and at the time of writing the reading is not complete. The mathematical conundrum is how to flatten a tightly furled scroll, which at present remains a fiendishly difficult and unsolved problem. However, when the breakthrough occurs, it is highly likely that we will get to read full manuscripts by Epicurus. His ideas about the world and what he really thought could then be much clearer to all of us. Was he really gay, or was this merely an accusation designed to highlight his love of excess? Did he really believe pleasure was the highest good? Was his philosophy around sex more abstemious than we imagine?

By the time Epicurus died in 270 BCE, the effects of Alexander the Great's conquest of much of North Africa, the Mediterranean and Asia Minor were well entrenched. The snaking trade networks ferried goods to and fro, as well as ideas and philosophies. After Alexander the Great transformed Greece's neighbours into its subordinates, a definitive change in culture and economies was brought about. People's relationship with money changed, and kings were favoured over democracies, reflecting the inequalities in the economy. People in the Hellenistic period were, as we observed in a previous chapter, less well fed than in classical times and they were taxed more.[63] Attitudes to queer desire were, as we would expect, becoming increasingly hostile.

A WISTFUL LOVE FOR MEN

Ptolemy III Euergetes ruled Egypt as pharaoh from 246 BCE. He waged a series of bloody campaigns across the Alexandrian sands. But his interest was not solely in matters of the sword. Euergetes was a devoted lover of literature. His greatest obsession was with Greek tragedy – the pain and emotional turmoil of the Greek stage, and the great works of Sophocles, Euripides and Aeschylus.

The trouble was there existed only one original copy of these plays anywhere in the world – at Athens. Accordingly, he sent ambassadors to Athens by boat. They petitioned the Athenians for original copies of the plays of Aeschylus, Sophocles and Euripides. For the price of 15 talents of gold (just over half a tonne), the Athenians agreed to lend the original copies of these plays to the Alexandrians. When his ambassadors returned to the baking heat of Egypt through the wide mouth of the Nile, Euergetes looked upon these treasures reverentially. He ordered them to be copied out post-haste by the scholars of the Great Library of Alexandria. Once the copies were ready, he held on to the originals and sent the copies back in their stead to a furious Athens.

But from that moment on, Alexandria maintained the only original copies in the world of those plays. Sadly for us, not all of them survived the tribulations of the centuries. In 48 BCE, Julius Caesar's forces burned the library to the ground; even if those great works of literature did survive that siege, they could not have survived another burning by Christian extremists several centuries later.[64]

Alexandria was the Oxford or Harvard of its day – a hive of bustling scholarly activity. Its library was not organized according to the sophisticated referencing systems we have become used to today. Instead, as you walked down the marbled aisles, past shelf after wooden shelf, you encountered miniature statues of various literary giants. If you turned right at the bust of a scowling Plato, you would find arranged alphabetically all his scrolls. Scholars today have speculated that this arrangement is the basis for the ancient and medieval 'memory palace' techniques (whereby people remember details, by placing them in an imaginary building – a palace or a library).[65]

One of the library's scholars was a man named Herondas, who preserves for us a curious story about the behaviour of the women of Alexandria.[66] In his tale, two women – Metro and Koritto

– discuss a magical object made of wood, covered in beautiful leather, with two dangling straps.[67] The Dildo of Alexandria, as it is called, was apparently passed from woman to woman, so magical were its powers. Metro tells Koritto that she got it from a woman named Nossis, who in turn had it passed to her from Eubole.[68] According to their description of this magical, shared dildo, it was made by a craftsman named Kerdon. 'Kerdon', in Greek, means 'profit'. A small community of married women in Alexandria – Herondas excitedly relates – were passing around this dildo, which was closely associated with success and financial gain. Koritto says she has heard that there could be a second dildo, and she would do anything to get her hands on it – save, she admits, having sex with the maker Kerdon.

The story of the Dildo of Alexandria is generally thought to be a fantasy.[69] But this small anecdote does illustrate how Greek-speaking women in Alexandria in this period of history were feared – how their association with sex and the fear of same-sex desire was closely associated in the mind of Herondas and other Greek writers with the breakdown of the family, by now the most important unit in the Hellenistic economy.

Theocritus, a Greek scholar and writer who lived in Alexandria, discusses a melancholy love for men openly in his work. In one of his poems, a middle-aged man pines desperately for a younger man:

There was no remedy to love's fires, no flashing smile
On his lips, no bright glance from his eyes, no red blush on his
    cheek,
No speech, not even a kiss that would make this desire bearable.
He looked askance at his lover like a beast does his hunters.[70]

This older man is obsessed with the beloved's beauty. He idolizes him and begs for a sign of reciprocation. In the end, the obsessed and distressed admirer resolves to hang himself and bring an end to his misery. He begs that this at least will see his lover acknowledge him:

> When you see my pained body hanging from the doorframe,
> Don't ignore me, stand and weep a while.[71]

The beloved does not pay him the slightest attention even when he dies. It is only later that in a bath house, the god of love surprises the young man and slams a rock over his head. The beloved dies in a pool of blood.

Theocritus does not paint a positive picture of queer desire,[72] describing it as a condition that brings such pain it ends in death.[73] There are stories from Theocritus of equal-age lovers too. The affection between these two men is described in arcane vocabulary from a blend of different ancient dialects not common in Alexandria.[74] It is like a modern writer consciously choosing to write in Shakespeare's language.

> Would that it be that Love gave breath to us equally,
> And we would become a song to future lovers,
> ...They loved each other equally under one yoke,
> These were men of the golden age when the beloved returned
>   his love[75]

Here the poet conjures an image of a lost paradise, in a bygone language, in which love between men was equal and reciprocal. It is made explicitly clear to the reader that this age is now at an end. Why would it be that amid such hostility to queer desire, with philosophers denouncing it and laws attacking it, a writer like Theocritus would dare even address the topic? Theocritus was likely writing as a member of a cloistered scholarly community partially insulated from the rest of the secular world. It is possible that this left him freer to explore his ideas. Such communities, as the Church and the theatre would in later times, may have appealed to individuals who did not quite fit the family model. This is pure speculation, but it could be that the academic environment provided a kind of refuge for discussion of queer desire. Both the story of the Dildo of Alexandria and the wistful tales of gay men killing themselves point to a markedly different relationship with sexuality in ancient Alexandria.

The ideas forged in the world Alexander conquered, of Stoicism and self-control, are direct products of a high-tax, trade-focused economy where the individual and his family were the only insurance against poverty and slavery. These ideas would form the bedrock of Christianity and Western thinking, but it is only half of the story of how the West came to think about queer sex. To understand the other half, we need to travel north-east, to the land of ancient Judea. We also need to turn back the clock some centuries to see how ancient Jewish law came to categorize the male and the female, and how horrific societal upheavals conditioned homophobia there too.

SIX

Love in the Time of the Old Testament

(1300 BCE – 100 CE)

> Jonathan's soul was bound to David, and he loved him as himself.
>
> 1 SAM. 18.1–3

Far to Greece's east lies a land whose empires and battles fill the pages of the Old Testament. Between two vast rivers, the Tigris and the Euphrates, the rich land of Mesopotamia (now Iraq) was home to some of the world's oldest cities. The Sumerians, thought to be one of the earliest peoples to develop writing, are remembered today for their colossal ziggurats (a huge tower constructed of a series of successively smaller layers one on top of the other) and the epic tale of their warrior-king Gilgamesh. But they were just one of many powerful Mesopotamian civilizations, all of which form the historical and cultural background of the Bible. Thousands of years before the Peloponnesian War, the civilizations of Sumer (5th–4th millennia BCE), Assyria (2nd millennium BCE) and Babylon (2nd–1st millennia BCE) thrived and fought.

Myth has it that the shining, glazed-brick walls of Babylon were adorned with ledges filled with lush, exotic plants. This greenery, creeping over the city's fortifications, gave the illusion that the city of Babylon was garlanded with hundreds of gardens hanging in mid-air. They were said to have been added by King

Nebuchadnezzar II (neh-boo-kad-nezz-ar), though there's neither archaeological nor textual evidence that they ever existed.[1] Very likely, this wonder of the ancient world remained in the popular imagination as a symbol of Nebuchadnezzar's great legacy as the king who transformed Babylon from a trading town to a great metropolis.

Following the defeat of the neighbouring Assyrian Empire, Nebuchadnezzar's father Nabopolassar was the first to begin extending the walls of the city, but Nebuchadnezzar exceeded even his father's ambitions and began a building project of colossal expense. Unearthed between 1899 and 1917, the great main gate was decorated with yellow lions set against a sky-blue backdrop, finished in glazed brick.[2] These lions, symbolic guardians of Babylon, represented the goddess of sex and war – Ishtar. Within this temple lived diverse groups of people who did not conform to traditional genders. The *assinnus* and the *kalûs* were often cross-dressers, eunuchs or homosexuals and were given protection by Ishtar.[3]

Travellers to the city, after passing through the gates under the watchful gaze of its armed sentries, would be confronted by the fortress-like temple of Ninmah.[4] Elsewhere in Babylon stood the great temple of Etemenanki, a ziggurat reaching so high its tip was said to touch the clouds.[5] It was built in honour of the god Marduk, the chief god of the Babylonians, who in an epic struggle with chaos had brought order to the primordial world and founded a race of men.[6]

Those who had an audience with the king would have stood before his throne in the great royal chamber decorated with lions and palm trees. Babylon's wealth was without equal. Archaeological reports show that over half the population lived on more than 10 hectares of land.[7] At this time, when wealth inequality was low, queerness appears to have gone unpunished. Indeed, it was a celebrated part of Ishtar's cult and there is evidence this celebration was no fad. In one of the oldest texts to survive from anywhere in the world, the Sumerian *Hymn to Inanna* references the power of the goddess Inanna (the

Sumerian counterpart to Ishtar) to transform man into woman and woman into man. Babylonian law codes do not – unlike some other Mesopotamian societies – have any penalty against same-sex love.[8]

The source of Babylon's great wealth and growing empire was its extraordinarily disciplined army, which under the reign of Nebuchadnezzar II marched all across the ancient Levant, bringing a small city called Jerusalem within its compass.

Babylon was not the only power that threatened Jerusalem. To the south-west stalked another superpower. Egypt controlled most of north-east Africa and made frequent forays into the Levant. After the Israelites[9] – whom legend has it were led by Moses in the Old Testament[10] – crossed the Red Sea, they eventually rebuilt Jerusalem. Since this period in history lacks the detailed historical tradition of the Greek city-states, there is considerably more guesswork involved in blending together legend, Biblical tales and archaeological findings.[11] But from the little we can tell based on cross-referencing the Bible, the Chronicle of Babylon, Egyptian writings and the work of much later Greek historians, this was far from a peaceful period. Jerusalem was continually harassed on all sides by competing powers leading to a state of prolonged insecurity.

In 609 BCE, Syria and Palestine were seized by Egypt.[12] Just five years later, when he was still a prince, Nebuchadnezzar waged a campaign against Egypt and won Syria and the Palestinian Hills for himself. The following year King Jehoiakim of Judah submitted to Babylon, and Nebuchadnezzar accepted the terms of surrender.

With two wolfish forces prowling on either side of his kingdom, Jehoiakim lived in a perpetual state of anxiety. If he made one wrong move, he would lose his throne, and his people could be sold into slavery. When Babylon's campaign to push against the Egyptian frontier failed a few years later, King Jehoiakim sensed a shift in power and asked for Egypt's protection. This state of affairs lasted for several years with Judah pivoting towards a different power whenever its survival required it. Eventually, Jehoiakim died and his son took the throne. Unfortunately for the new king, the

Babylonian forces marched straight for Jerusalem and on 1 March 597 BCE,[13] the city was seized.

The new king was dragged out of the city and taken to Babylon where he would live out his days as a hostage. Nebuchadnezzar gave orders to install Mattatiah – the deposed king's uncle – on the throne as a servant of Babylon. But history was destined to repeat itself: the stooge king, renamed Zedekiah upon his coronation, rebelled against Babylon after encouragement from the Egyptian Pharaoh Psamtik II. The sudden lurches in allegiance, the quick succession of different kings, all amounted to a deeply precarious situation.

On 18 July 586 BCE,[14] the Babylonian army retook Jerusalem. Zedekiah was pulled through the city in chains. His people lined the streets to witness his punishment. Just in front of him were his sons, forced into a kneeling position. Two soldiers held Zedekiah in place and pinned his eyes open as both his sons were stabbed. He was forced to watch his children die before, on Nebuchadnezzar's orders, the soldiers took a knife and blinded Zedekiah so that the last thing he saw on earth was his sons' murder. This was the ultimate price of betrayal.[15]

The people of Jerusalem were hounded out of their city. Husbands and wives were separated, children taken screaming from their parents. As these refugee-slaves were forcibly marched down through the Palestinian Hills, they turned back to see their home set ablaze. Nebuchadnezzar had given orders that the city be torched and its temple ransacked. A series of priceless treasures were taken to Babylon where they remained in the royal vault, a symbol of the capitulation of Judah, and Prince Belshazzar hosted an uproarious party for his friends.[16] Judah's king had failed to appease both Egypt and Babylon, and now the Judaean people were homeless and without a ruler, wandering in the desert or else held captive and forced to do the bidding of some new master.

LEVITICUS

The torment of Jerusalem's capture galvanized the Judaeans. Without a city and without a ruler, they became dependent on their religious identity which helped them through some of the darkest days their people had faced. Historians believe it was in this period that much of what we now call the Bible was written. This includes some passages still printed in Bibles that condemn homosexuality. As many know, the Christian Bible is divided into the Old and the New Testament. The Old Testament was written in Hebrew and describes the rise of the kingdom of Judah; the New Testament was written in ancient Greek and describes the life of Jesus Christ and the message of his followers. Some ancient texts – especially those written in classical Greece and later in Rome – can be traced to a precise year because of meticulous contemporary record-keeping. But this is not the case with the Hebrew Old Testament. Indeed, we are lucky if we can pin down the century *by which* a text from the Bible was written (what scholars call the *terminus ante quem*).

Leviticus, one of the Hebrew books of the Old Testament, is exceptionally hard to date. Many modern believers claim that this ancient text's murky origins prove it to be a real font of true, divine law.[17] The more obscure a text's origins, apparently, the more burnished its divine credentials. Nonetheless, it is the job of historians and philologists to ask how a text has come to us, who wrote it, and why.

Most of Leviticus is thought to have been written sometime around a period of significant political upheaval,[18] very possibly the invasion of Jerusalem by Nebuchadnezzar II. The text we have inherited contains mixed orders on how to live a clean and pure life: what to eat, how to sacrifice, how to live. Despite this clarity within the text, we are far from sure when or why it was written. Providing an exact date for ancient texts composed in such febrile times is a very difficult business. To date a text, scholars often rely on careful analysis of vocabulary and writing styles, but it is far from foolproof. This book's editor, for example, informed me in an early edit, that I overuse the word 'halcyon' and has taken steps to address this extravagance. Had these steps not been taken, however, it may be possible to tell my writing apart from others' by the frequency of that word. Such tell-tale signs can be picked up by computers and human scholars and used to speculate on which parts of the text were written by the same person. Increasingly, computational approaches are becoming more common, as AI is able to group different patterns of text faster than humans. Another way scholars identify who wrote a passage relies on more subjective opinions about literary style and arguments about the ideas in the texts. Where a text contains contradictory ideas or major variations in style, scholars may assume that it was written by different people and possibly in different time periods. However, such approaches work under the assumption that texts are logically coherent, which is not necessarily a secure assumption. Because we very seldom have access to the original manuscripts, scholars often rely on themes or specific mentions of events in texts to date them too.

On the basis of vocabulary, style and theology,[19] Leviticus can be divided into two sections. The older section 'P' for Priestly Source (Chapters 1–16) and a newer section 'H' for Holiness Source (Chapters 17–27),[20] though the precise division into these two neat categories is still being debated. The Priestly parts of Leviticus talk about the slaughter of animals and the role of priests in determining the pure from the impure in matters of food; the Holiness code is a more scattered series of commandments on what is pure or impure and may (though nothing is certain) refer more to ordinary people than to priests.[21] What unites both texts, however, is a preoccupation with the identity of the Jews and the security of their homeland, which seems at constant risk of loss.

In Lev. 18.24, God warns the Judaeans, 'Do not defile yourselves in any of these ways, because this is how the nations that I am going to drive out before you became defiled'. A second passage commands that if its laws are not kept, the land of Judah will 'vomit out' its inhabitants.[22] Given the immense political insecurity in the region, the preoccupation with God expelling his chosen people from the land of Judah is understandable. Some scholars have suggested Leviticus was written as much as a century after the invasion of Jerusalem by Nebuchadnezzar,[23] but others have suggested it may be before the exile from Jerusalem.[24] Coming down on one side or the other without controversy is difficult.

In the modern world, Leviticus has been used in the highest courts to uphold deeply unjust laws despite the trouble of establishing its provenance and ascertaining its meaning. Among its many purity codes, it includes what appears to be a ban on queer sex. Incredibly, it was cited by the US Supreme Court Chief Justice Warren Burger as late as 1986 in his decision 'to hold that the act of homosexual sodomy is somehow protected as a fundamental right would be to cast aside millennia of moral teaching'.[25] Sadly, Burger seems to have been ignorant of the far older Sumerian and Babylonian texts which celebrate queer identities. In the British House of Lords, Lord Arran sought to decriminalize consensual homosexual activity between two adults in 1966. This was met with consternation and horror by certain people-of-letters among the British public. In the House of Lords, Lord Arran related that these letters 'are full of the most fearful condemnation', and 'that curiously enough, they all seem to quote Deuteronomy and Leviticus'.[26]

Thankfully, Lord Arran was unmoved by these frantic pleas to heed the moral warnings of this mysterious ancient document. He was not, it seems, gay himself, but he was a deeply humane man with the heart to be moved by the testimony of gay men and their families who suffered every day. He stood in the Upper Chamber to enlighten his audience, reading from one letter penned by a desperate father:

> We, that is my wife and I, are particularly anxious that this Bill shall become law because our son is, most unfortunately, a homosexual. Naturally we are very concerned, worried and terrified lest he gets into serious trouble as a result. Recently I had a friendly talk with him on his behaviour and the appalling consequences should he get found out. To my horror he replied, 'Don't worry, Dad, if we get found out there will be no disgrace, I shall quietly snuff it.'[27]

These parents faced losing their son to suicide if criminal penalties for same-sex desire were not repealed. The justification for these shameful episodes in our history lies not in evidence of harm, but in these old laws from the Old Testament – even as I write this, many colonial era laws are still in force.[28]

The law cited most often in these cases was Lev. 18.22. Strange then that, contrary to what evangelical preachers may say, modern scholarship is at a loss to say what precisely it means. It's not even unanimous that it is a law against homosexuality. But before we dive into the details of the state of play, this is the verse as it appears in a standard Biblical translation today: 'You shall not lie with a man as with woman; it is an abomination.' This translation gives the impression of a clear and straightforward meaning. But while working out the meanings of words in ancient languages is always a difficult business, it is especially so with Hebrew. Usually, scholars will look at all the uses of the word and attempt to describe the context-dependent nuances of its meaning. Any one word has all sorts of different interpretations, none of which can be said to be completely right. It is much easier to conduct this research when a scholar can analyse many different uses of a word. But the corpus of Biblical Hebrew is much smaller than those of other ancient languages. Biblical Hebrew is also a language of religion, which exacerbates the ferocity of debate.

Consequently, you have some scholars who believe that Lev. 18.22 is a ban on incestuous sex and so does not condemn consensual same-sex activity between unrelated partners at all. Others argue the passage condemns sex with married men.[29] There are those who think that it bans all non-procreative sex, and this is why homosexuality comes under attack.[30] If the law even is about consensual homosexuality, it is still not entirely clear what is being banned. Does the writer of Leviticus oppose an active or a passive role in gay sex (topping or bottoming)? Who is the sinner, or are they both? On this question too, there is no academic consensus. Some think that only topping is banned.[31] Others have argued by comparison with similar passages that the sinner is in fact the bottom.[32] And still others argue the law is about maintaining the purity of the male sex.[33] This array of different readings proves that the only thing we can say about this ancient text is that we are not sure when it was written, by whom or what it means. It is part of our continuous interrogation of our past that we ask these questions, but we can rarely come to any solid answers.

I know the pain of discovering those simple words printed with such authority in the Bible. Part of me wishes I could say that this text has nothing to do with homosexuality, as many writers have tried to do. But what I would say is that these texts are fraught with complexity, and nobody has the authority to tell you with any certainty what they mean. And they certainly do not have the right to deny you the freedom to love on such fragile authority.

EVEN OLDER HOMOPHOBIA

The Babylonian law codes do not mention same-sex sexual activity, the Sumerians actively encouraged it. The Hittite laws are also silent on the issue, though they do forbid both incest and bestiality as Leviticus does.[34] Both were probably written much earlier than Leviticus. On the other hand, the law code of Middle Assyria (around 1000 BCE) reserved a particular punishment for buggery, one which the modern world has not taken up with quite as much enthusiasm as Leviticus.

According to Middle Assyrian Law Code A20, if a man is found to have had sex with his comrade,[35] the whole group must gang-rape and castrate him. This is found alongside other eccentric laws like: 'if a woman crushes a man's testicles in a fight, she shall have her finger cut off. If the other testicle becomes infected, she will have her eyes gouged out'.[36] Scholars think that offences against male citizens were punished much more harshly than those against slaves or women.[37]

Middle Assyria had complex rules surrounding debt and no mechanisms for its forgiveness. To secure a debt, a debtor could use his assets such as his house, or he could pledge his son or daughter as collateral; if the loan was not repaid on time, they would be sold into slavery.[38] The existence of these complex debt laws points to a society where debt was commonplace, and the consequences for getting it wrong were severe.

Archaeologists examined grave goods from the Late Bronze Age (before the Middle Assyrian law codes) and the Iron Age (around the time the Middle Assyrian law codes were written) and rated the contents of each grave on a value scale of 0–10. They concluded that the graves of the Late Bronze Age were more egalitarian (with fewer graves containing low value items), and in the Iron Age, there was a more skewed distribution in high-value grave goods.[39] This could be taken as evidence that wealth inequality was on the rise by the time of the Middle Assyrian law codes.[40] By contrast, the Babylonian laws regulated debt interest and promoted fairness in pricing.[41] We know that distressed individuals were also liberated from their debts at regular periods.[42]

STAYING PURE

> You shall not do as they do in Egypt, where once you dwelt, nor shall you do as they do in the land of Canaan to which I am bringing you, you shall not conform to their institutions.[43]

Leviticus' panic about queer sex follows on from the text above, which is a panic about the identity of Judaeans wandering in the desert. Leviticus famously contains many rules for daily life, for instance prohibiting its adherents from eating shellfish or pork and from mixing seeds of different sorts. For many centuries, writers assumed there had – at some stage – been practical reasons for these rules. Perhaps pork goes rancid faster than other meats; shellfish is notorious for expiring quickly in hot weather, after all. It was not, however, until the work of one revolutionary anthropologist that a better explanation for Leviticus' rules was formulated.

Mary Margaret Douglas (née Tew) was born in March 1921.[44] Her parents had been holidaying in San Remo, Italy, on a return trip from their colonial posting in British-occupied Burma, when she came into the world. Her mother and father were both academically gifted and had a great influence on her early life; as did Mary's eccentric Great Aunt Ethel who lived in a caravan, wore home-knitted bright-coloured garments, ate only nuts and fruit and tended to her angora rabbits. Between both influences, Mary learned academic discipline and bohemian antinomianism.

Tragedy struck the family when Mary's mother was diagnosed with cancer and died, and her father succumbed to ill-health. She was sent to a Catholic convent, where every moment of every day she was subjected to rules and rituals. Baths were taken like clockwork twice a week in freezing-cold water, with the girls wearing calico cloaks so they would never be naked, even when they washed. Pink ribbons were handed out to pupils who had behaved impeccably for eight weeks, and each activity ended with the sound of a bell ringing. It was a regimented life, but it seems Mary thrived in an environment that was strict but loving and she learned early on how order and structure can do much to rescue one from pain and loss.[45] It was against this backdrop that Mary Douglas developed into the formidable academic she would later become, and it also provided some inspiration for her work. Her books entitled Purity and Danger, Rules and Meanings and How Institutions Think seem to owe something to her experiences in the convent.

It was in Purity and Danger that Douglas advanced her groundbreaking explanation for why the Leviticus law codes have such rigid rules. This explanation is now widely accepted. She argued there that shellfish were not considered proper fish. Real fish, in Jewish thinking, were defined as sea-dwelling and did not live on land. Shellfish often live in liminal areas such as rockpools. They were inconvenient, in between categories; as if they could not quite make up their mind on whether to be fish or land animals. Likewise, proper land animals had cloven hoofs and chewed the cud – for example, sheep and cows. Pigs, exhibiting a naughtily rebellious streak, have cloven hoofs but do not chew the cud. Thus, Douglas argued, Leviticus proscribes them as unholy, since they do not fit into the neat categories that the law codes impose on nature. The Leviticus law codes offered structure in a changing, insecure, anxious world, they were about instilling discipline and self-control. As she put it, 'holiness is exemplified by completeness'.[46]

In ancient Judah, man and woman (like fish and cows) were defined clearly and separately.[47] The inconvenience to the religion posed by trans and queer people (like shellfish and pigs) in many ways mirrors the inconvenience of mixing of seeds and fabrics, as they hover between these artificially constructed categories. As I have already shown, it is not true to say that gender has always been regarded as a binary. The existence of the *assinnus* and the *kalûs* in Babylonian religion points to the fact that the Jewish law codes represented something of a novelty in the region. The writing of Gen. 1–3 redefined gender as bounded between male and female. Where religion and the region's temples had been sacred spaces for queer people in times gone by, the Leviticus law codes banned such dangerous, transgressive identities.

The panicked insistence that trans and non-binary people should fit into 'natural' male and female categories is better understood as a cultural phenomenon that has arisen at specific moments in history rather than a reflection of some eternal truth about human nature. It would be easy for trans people to conform, it would make their lives infinitely simpler. Their resistance alone shows that their gender identity is worth fighting for, worth losing out economically, worth being marginalized. Despite the opaque history of the text, Leviticus continues to be used throughout the world to justify hatred of queer people. But it is far from alone in being the only Bible passage summoned in defence of bigotry.

HAM AND NOAH

After the great flood, Noah and his three sons set about cultivating the land. His sons were Shem (the ancestor of the Israelites and the Arameans), Ham (ancestor of the Canaanites) and Japheth (ancestor of the Greeks and Asia Minor). One of the crops Noah cultivated was grapes, which spiralled outwards and twisted into vineyards. Noah tended to these crops and picked the ripe fruits, transforming them into wine.

One night, as the dusk set in, Noah drank so much of his new concoction that he became drunk. It must have been a hot evening, because he stumbled to his tent and sprawled inside naked after ordering two of his sons to guard the entrance. We aren't told precisely what happened next, but in the following text Noah curses his son the ancestor of the Canaanites: 'Cursed be Canaan!

The lowest of slaves he will be to his brothers!'[48] The question that has gripped both priests and scholars ever since is, why did Noah curse Canaan?

One interpretation is that Noah was using wine to increase his libido and that Ham had entered his father's tent and seen him having sex with a woman.[49] Noah, furious at Ham for his discovery, condemned all his descendants through his curse on Ham's son Canaan. A later Rabbinic tradition holds that Ham castrated Noah, and this was the reason for his curse upon Canaan. In a heated discussion in the Babylonian Talmud,[50] two rabbis argue this out. One – Rav – posits that castration made the most sense because why else would Canaan be cursed? The other – Samuel – argues for the interpretation commonly found in evangelical circles: Ham didn't castrate his father, he raped him. There are tenuous linguistic reasons to suppose that some sort of sexual act was involved, but it is far from clear what sort and who was doing it.[51]

Whether Ham raped Noah is not a question that is likely to be resolved. Like most Biblical passages, the myriad possible interpretations are part of the appeal of the text: it can be used to justify nearly any view from a ban on castration to support for slavery. Like prophecy, Biblical texts rely on variable interpretations to enhance their appeal to as wide an audience as possible. This is why we must be very cautious in using them to justify our own views on morality. At the height of the transatlantic slave trade it was used to support the enslavement of Africans, who were cast as Ham's descendants.[52] Such reprehensible uses of the text to justify evil are part of the danger of Biblical passages, so mercurial are their origins. The most infamous story of the Old Testament, whose name came to be associated so closely with queer desire, is no exception to this rule.

SODOM[53]

On a hilltop stood a tent of woven goat's hair. By its entrance, a man of impossible age sat in thought watching three figures walking towards him. As they approached, Abraham hurried painfully to his feet, he knew who they were – angels, servants of the Lord. He shouted to his wife, Sarah, to bring water so the angels could bathe their feet. They rested beneath a great tree and Abraham asked Sarah to make as much bread as she could, while he hurried off to a nearby pen. He took a fat, young calf, slit its throat and roasted the fresh meat. Then he opened a wooden barrel of curds and milk and brought it all before his supernatural guests. They ate gratefully. Presently, one of them looked up. 'Where is Sarah?' he asked. 'Sarah? She is in the tent,' replied Abraham. 'I will be back in one year, or thereabouts,' the angel said, 'and by that time, she will have a child, I promise you.' From inside the tent came an amused mutter. 'I am worn out, and Abraham is old. Will this really happen?'[54] 'Why did Sarah laugh?' the angel asked. 'Surely she does not think there is anything too hard for the Lord to accomplish?'[55]

This story of hospitality and its rewards (Sarah does indeed have a son, Isaac, even if at one point her husband comes very close to sacrificing him)[56] is from Gen. 18. Abraham was a nomad driving a flock across the plains and hills of the Levant when the angels came and repaid his generosity with a child, despite Abraham and Sarah's geriatric ages (Abraham is said to be 99 at the time). But not everyone in the book of Genesis was quite so hospitable as Abraham.

After finishing their meal, the angels looked down from the hill to see the city of Sodom like a blot on the horizon. As they walked together across the hilltop, God spoke to Abraham of his intention to take vengeance on the city of Sodom. Abraham pleaded with God not to destroy the city, that there may be good men in there, and so God resolved to send his angels down to investigate.

Two figures arrived at Sodom's gates just as the sun sank in the west. A man, Lot, was sitting by the city's gateway.[57] When Lot saw them, he – like Abraham – recognized instantly who they were and bowed his face to the ground.[58] Lot bid the strangers wash their feet at his house. He offered them bread and they ate at his table, but then they were disturbed by the sound of doors slamming and men shouting. Then, a loud knock at the door.

Outside stood a huge throng. 'Come out!' cried the group's leader. 'And bring the men who came with you tonight! We're going to rape them right here in front of your house.'

Lot pleaded with the man, 'They're my guests, they have done no wrong. Do not take them. Don't do this wicked, wicked thing. I have two daughters instead, two virgins who've never known a man, and you can do whatever you like with them, but don't harm these two men.'

At this, the mob's leader lurched forward. He smashed open the door, seized Lot and threw him backwards. Behind Lot, the two angels in cloaks arose as one from their seats and pointed their hands at the intruders. At once, the attacker's eyes became milky-white, clouded over. He staggered back, blind. The whole throng likewise blinded stumbled through the streets. Lot and his family fled Sodom with the angels into the night. As the sun rose the next day, God rained fire down on the city.

In Genesis, the story of Sodom follows on straight after the tale of Abraham's hospitality, suggesting that we are meant to contrast Abraham and Lot's hospitality with the inhospitable, cruel people of Sodom. Like many ancient texts that were orally performed, phrases and words and gestures are often recycled in similar scenes. The language and formulas used in both are nearly identical in the early stages: Abraham sits at the front of his tent; Lot sits at the front of the city. Abraham bows his face to the ground, so does Lot. Abraham washes the angels' feet first, so does Lot. Abraham offers the angels freshly baked bread, so does Lot. But Sodom's inhabitants wanted to commit the ultimate act of inhospitality, they intended to rape the two angels. This was proof of God's view that the city deserved annihilation.

For hundreds of years, this text was taken to be a simple tale about the importance of hospitality. This was how it was understood by the early Christians; the Gospel of Matthew suggests that Sodom was a place of inhospitality rather than homosexuality.[59] Ezekiel, a Jewish priest exiled from Jerusalem by Nebuchadnezzar II, attributes the fall of Sodom to their pride, excess and gluttony – not to homosexuality.[60] Lot's offering up his own daughters is appalling, but it underscores his primary goal: to protect his guests. Lot's story isn't the only example in the Old Testament of someone protecting their guests from a rapacious mob. A similar passage exists in Judges where the guests are this time a Levite and his mortal wife. In that instance, the mortal wife is not endowed with the power to strike blind the hoard of rapists and is raped so brutally that she dies of her injuries.[61] A harrowing civil war ensues over her death.[62]

Sodom represents a moment when the greatest fear of the people of Judah came true: a city was destroyed because it did not follow the rules. When Abraham obeyed the rules of hospitality a line was fathered which led to the kings of Israel. In the next tale, however, Sodom was razed because its inhabitants violently flouted the rules of hospitality. Over the centuries, Christians began to blame homosexuality and excessive sexual desire – not inhospitality or gluttony – when a city was plagued with natural disasters or diseases they feared were sent from God. The story of Sodom became so closely linked with sex that any kind of deviant sexual act (from a woman being on top to oral and queer sex) came to be known as sodomy.[63] A gradual drift took place in the story's meaning: initially, Sodom was associated with selfishness and greed, then with homosexuality. They are linked, in ancient thought, by a connection between greed and excessive desire. Much like Leviticus and the story of Ham and Noah, the history of the homophobia in these texts has as much (if not more) to do with how they've been read and interpreted over the years as how they were written.

TWO GAY LOVERS

At his trial, Oscar Wilde praised two men from the Old Testament, David and Jonathan, as examples of 'such great affection of an elder for a younger man'. Assuming the Biblical passages, which (as we shall see) are far from consistent, are correct, David would indeed have been younger than Jonathan by some margin. But was Wilde right to say that they were lovers?

For centuries, commentators went out of their way to show that David and Jonathan *could not* have been lovers – it was, they said, obvious that no such relationship could ever have been intended in the text.[64] Their reasoning ranged from the ban on homosexuality in Lev. 18:22 to the extreme lengths to which David later went to marry the beautiful Bathsheba, including having her husband Uriah killed. But the authors of Leviticus were not necessarily the same as those of the David and Jonathan story, and Oscar Wilde, of course, was married too. However, if it is so obvious that there is nothing queer to see here, why has so much effort been expended in denying it?

The Old Testament contains two differing accounts of how the future king of the Israelites David first came to the court of King Saul (possibly around the turn of the 1st millennium BCE).[65] In the first, Saul is tormented by an evil spirit and David is brought in to comfort him and play music.[66] In the second, more dramatic account, David – an unknown shepherd's boy – singlehandedly slays the giant Goliath and brings his severed head before the king. Saul receives David at his camp, and the shepherd boy bows. Beside Saul stood his son, the prince, Jonathan.

> After David had spoken with Saul, Jonathan's soul was bound to David, and he loved him as himself. From then on, Saul took David and did not allow him to return to his family. Jonathan formed a covenant with David because he loved him as himself.[67]

Jonathan's reaction to David has been passed off by many as a very good friendship.[68] This, I think, is overly cautious. In the case of the phrase 'Jonathan's soul was bound to David' it is possible to read a little further into the Hebrew. The word for 'soul', *nephesh*, is very often found in phrases associated with craving, notably sexual craving.[69] The groom in the erotic *Song of Songs* describes his bride as 'the woman whom my *nephesh* loves'.[70] This bond is deeper, it is more loving. The verb for 'loved' in this case is less straightforward: *āhēb* in Hebrew can often be used for the formation of political agreements and carries much less romantic force than the English word (a commonly misunderstood phrase is when the same verb is used of God's 'love', which carries much more of a sense of God's 'agreement' or 'approval' than his affection).[71] But the love between the two men is also described as 'surpassing the love of women'.[72]

After some time, Saul grows concerned about the relationship between his son and David. He tries to have David assassinated in his own bed, and it is Jonathan who intervenes and helps David into exile. When Jonathan dies, David's mourning song is a haunting send-off to a man whom he loved. So there are certainly grounds to consider the relationship between these two men as homoerotic.[73] They even enter a 'covenant', a běrît, which some scholars have suggested may have been a sort of marital ceremony.[74] Jonathan immediately strips off his cloak and his armour and gives them to David as gifts.

The question of whether David and Jonathan were lovers is of course purely academic since they are characters in a literary history written centuries after the events supposedly took place. But if the writers of this passage intended its readers to see a homoerotic liaison between one of the founding kings of Israel, from whom Jesus himself claimed descent, and the incumbent prince, there must have been a reason. There are two plausible explanations for the less-than-subtle hints. The first is that they help to make sense of a humble shepherd boy's rapid rise to power. In order to legitimize David's reign, he needed a connection to a strong ruling family such as tutelage at the hand of his older lover, Jonathan. The story of love may also have served to prevent any reader imagining that David was a usurper who murdered Jonathan and gained his rise illegitimately.

It is also possible that the two men had a very intense and formalized friendship, one which we find hard to imagine in the modern world. Conservative thinkers have always been keen on this more Platonic interpretation and ask repeatedly the same reductive question: is there any evidence the two men ever had sex? Explicit proof is impossible for obvious reasons, so the question will always remain open.

But another explanation for the romantic intimacy between David and Jonathan, however, lies in an ancient and mysterious Mesopotamian epic that inspired many of the tales and themes of the Bible. To explore this, we have to go back in time once more and return to ancient Babylon.

GILGAMESH AND ENKIDU

The Epic of Gilgamesh is one of the oldest literary texts in the world. Preserved on fragmented tablets in the Great Library of King Ashurbanipal (669–631 BCE) in the city of Nineveh (as well as other cities and libraries scattered throughout Mesopotamia), the poem tells the story of how the Sumerian king, Gilgamesh of Uruk, met his match. When the epic was discovered in the 19th century, scholars found some parts of it surprisingly familiar. It appeared that much of the Old Testament echoed the Epic of Gilgamesh, and Genesis in particular bears some remarkable resemblances to the poem.[75] Gilgamesh, who was possibly a real king but whose history is shrouded in myth and legend, laboured day and night to build up the walls around the fortress city of Uruk. But for all his extraordinary qualities as a builder, Gilgamesh had a flaw.

The text of the epic recounts how the young, restless king terrorized the entire population. Coming home from a successful day's building, Gilgamesh looked to find a young woman to ravage. The text describes how the people lived in terror that he would prey on their families. No one was safe – he was indiscriminate in his sexual tastes, a sign of his unabating appetite, taking young women from their husbands. He is also described as tiring out all the young men of the city with endless ball games.

A delegation of the people of Uruk prayed to the fertility goddess Aruru. Aruru responded by bringing to life a half-giant with long tresses adorned with elaborate and feminine decorations. This man's name was Enkidu. Unfortunately, he was also insatiable and seemed a terror to the local people, so they asked for the help of a prostitute named Shamhat. Shamhat, one of the most beautiful and sensual women in the land, found Enkidu and had sex with him for six days and seven nights. Finally, Shamhat decides she's had enough sex and leaves Enkidu, but not before she has told him of the powers of Gilgamesh. Naturally enough, Enkidu wanted nothing more than to fight Gilgamesh. But Shamhat encouraged him to think differently. The implication is that Enkidu should consider having sex with the king instead.

That night, Gilgamesh lay asleep in the palace and dreamt of an axe falling from the sky into the streets of Uruk. In the dream, he married the axe and took it as a wife – and even his mother loved the axe and wanted him to be with it. There is a play on words here: 'axe' in Sumerian can suggest meanings like 'female impersonator'.[76] When he awoke, Gilgamesh told his mother about his dream and asked her what it meant. She told him it signified that he would find a friend whom he will love as a wife, a friend who would come to save his life.

The next day, Gilgamesh rushed to the small house of a pair of newlyweds, intending to take the bride's virginity. But Enkidu blocked his path. In the ensuing days, Gilgamesh found it impossible to stop thinking about Enkidu. They went on expeditions hunting together. Every night, Enkidu made Gilgamesh a shelter in which to sleep. All around the shelter, Enkidu sprinkled flour to protect Gilgamesh from evil. The two men spent days hunting, ending up in a wondrous forest guarded by a giant called Humbaba. On his return to Uruk, in a steaming bath surrounded by shields to hide his naked body, with perfumes and herbs in the water, Gilgamesh's mind drifted to Enkidu. A noise caused him to jump and the bathwater slopped over the sides. Standing before his bath was a beautiful woman, Ishtar, the goddess of sex and war. She suggested that they have sex and get married, but Gilgamesh refused, reminding her that all her sex-partners have the unfortunate habit of ending up dead. He turned his mind back to Enkidu.

We are told he loves Enkidu like a wife. When Enkidu died, Gilgamesh lamented for six days and seven nights, a mirror of the time he spent having sex with Shamhat. We are told that Gilgamesh covered Enkidu's corpse like a bride – in a striking similarity to David and Jonathan.[77] Searching for his lost lover, he crossed the Stream of Death to meet him once again. In a tearful final farewell, Gilgamesh spoke with Enkidu's ghost.

This story has been widely acknowledged by academics to have homoerotic language and to play with homoerotic themes. It is also possible that the love affair between Gilgamesh and Enkidu served as an early model for the story of David and Jonathan. The Epic of Gilgamesh was written at least 1,000 years before the Jewish account of David and Jonathan,[78] but we know Mesopotamian literature had a heavy influence on Jewish storytelling. It may very well be that storytellers had for generations unconsciously woven the two tales together, and this was the reason for David and Jonathan's romantic liaison in the Bible.

ANCIENT EGYPTIAN HOMOPHOBIA

From the 330s BCE (after Alexander's conquest), some Jewish people found themselves back in Egypt, in the city of Alexandria. As the Jewish people settled there and had children and grandchildren, their descendants no longer spoke Hebrew, preferring the Greek language spoken commonly in Egypt. They also came into contact with Greek philosophies like Stoicism. It was probably in Alexandria that the first five books of the Old Testament (known as the Pentateuch) were translated into Greek for the first time, during the reign of Ptolemy II Philadelphus (284–246 BCE). In these early translations, Greek prejudices against same-sex love mingled with the Bible's binary male and female categories, honing the text into a fresh attack on queer people. Though the meaning of Leviticus in Hebrew may be a subject for continued scholarly inquiry, the Greek translation of Lev. 18.22 is unambiguous: 'and with a man you should not have a woman's sex. It is a stain.'[79]

Egypt was much more like Judah or Middle Assyria than ancient Greece or Babylon, in that it had early codified hatred of queer sex. The Egyptian *Book of the Dead* (one of the few sacred texts we have inherited) explicitly states as a marker of holiness in a passage from the 15th century BCE, 'I have not had sex with a boy'.[80] Nonetheless, there are sporadic clues that same-sex partners lived together in ancient Egypt.

In 1967, a team of archaeologists unearthed a tomb in the northern area of Saqqara. The tomb is composed of two chambers in one – a structure usually used for married couples. However, in this case the tomb is dedicated to two deceased men.[81] It dates from the 3rd millennium BCE and belongs to Niankhkhnum and Khnumhotep. Niankhkhnum means 'his life belongs to Khnum' and Khnumhotep means 'Khnum is satisfied'.[82] In the tomb's artwork, the two men are depicted holding hands, embracing and possibly – though it is hard to make out – kissing. Early Egyptologists assumed that they were brothers, and resisted the idea that their relationship could have been romantic.[83] But they were at a loss to explain, in the words of one archaeologist, why it was that 'we do not find such an example of tenderness so pronounced [anywhere else] between two male individuals'.[84] The idea that the two men could have been lovers was seen as unnecessarily imaginative.[85] But even if you agree that the contents of the tomb would point to their romantic affection for one another, the evidence for other such tombs and complexes is exceedingly rare.

The most common depiction of same-sex sexual activity in ancient Egypt was rape used as a means of displaying masculine dominance.[86] In an inscription on one coffin, the deceased informs us that '[an unknown] Atum has no power over me, for I fuck him between his buttocks'.[87] Egyptian mythology contains a telling story involving the gods Horus and Seth. Horus, the son of Osiris and Isis, is often depicted as a falcon-headed young man. Seth on the other hand is the god of chaos and he is Osiris' brother. Seth murdered Osiris and so Horus goes to battle with his uncle. Whoever wins will reign over all the gods. However, Seth does not fight fair.

Late at night, while Horus is asleep, Seth sneaks into his bedchamber, holds him down and rapes him. This is intended as a sign of Seth's dominance over Horus. But on his mother Isis' advice, Horus takes Seth's semen, some of which has leaked onto his hand, and mixes it into Seth's food.[88] Such a gesture renders Seth emasculated, having consumed semen, he cannot be man enough to rule over the gods. Horus is triumphant. The tale underscores fears around masculinity and gender roles in Egyptian society and would provide the part of the backdrop to the translations of Leviticus centuries later in Alexandria. It is telling that in all of ancient Egypt's vast history, this land of extraordinary wealth inequality (a place of pyramids and pharaohs), the tomb of Niankhkhnum and Khnumhotep is one of the only credible examples of a same-sex couple.

A NEW MILLENNIUM APPROACHES

For many years, academics thought that a text they were reading had been written by an ancient Greek called Phocylides from the 6th century BCE. After subsequent analysis, it turned out that it was likely written much later (between the 1st century BCE and 1st century CE) in Alexandria by a Hellenistic Jew.[89] The author was renamed 'Pseudo-Phocylides'. Pseudo-Phocylides warns his reader that 'many men go mad at desire for sex with a man' and offers some advice: 'Do not have illicit sex, do not stir up desire for a man, do not plot tricks, do not stain your hand with blood.'[90]

His other obsession, besides policing the private lives of his Jewish followers, is primarily economic: 'Work hard, so that you may survive on your own. For every man who does not work lives through perfidious hands.'[91]

Alexandria was a place of immense wealth inequality and high indebtedness. This situation only worsened as the Roman Empire emerged (1st century BCE). One of the great influences on later Christian thinking was a Jewish thinker living in Alexandria around the time Jesus was born. His name was Philo. Steeped in Stoic philosophy, he was implacably opposed to same-sex desire, believing it to be against natural law.[92] We know very little about his life, as he tended not to write too much, but we do know that he served as an ambassador on the Jewish embassy from Alexandria to the court of Gaius Caligula in Rome (38–41 CE).[93] Philo tells us that he was horrified by what he saw there – a debauched and sexually promiscuous court that knew everything of excess and nothing of moderation.[94] With an astonishing eye for detail, Philo describes some of the more outrageous parties, where the boys and even some of the men had shaved off all their hair and wandered around wearing chitons cut off just after the groin.[95] He frowns at the men he sees pursuing other men and closely associates the opulence and wealth of the Roman court with queer desire. As with Theopompus' account of the court of Philip II of Macedon, we may have cause to doubt the full truth of Philo's claims.

Philo's particular problem with homosexuality is that it disturbs the traditional household, which in turn he sees as a bulwark against poverty. Philo expends a great deal of energy proselytizing about the importance of sound household economics,[96] and is especially concerned with how self-discipline is the means to spiritual and personal prosperity: 'They say the most profitable of virtues is self-control, which is protected by sound economy, frugality, and making do with little, against the more harmful [instincts] of depravity and excess.'

Philo writes that homosexuality is 'the disease of effeminization'[97] and expresses paranoia about what may happen to gendered roles should this sacred (and artificial) boundary be transgressed. He considers same-sex sex to be one of the most terrible of sins, though admits that bestiality just pips it to the post as the very worst.[98] He recommends that the punishment in Leviticus, of death by stoning, cannot be carried out quickly enough. You should not wait even an hour before executing them, he writes.[99]

To deal with the instability, wealth inequality, poverty and debt, inflexible ideas about the world were constructed. Homosexuality, which violated the neat categorization of men from women, became the flashpoint for political rage. Philo may have been shocked by the queer culture and lavish lifestyles of the court of Gaius Caligula, but he was not the only ruler accused of sexual deviancy in the Roman world, whose vast armies and imperial structures of power were increasingly encroaching on the Hellenistic and Jewish spheres.

KING HEROD AND HIS BOYS

King Herod, famous for his alleged baby-killing antics in the Bible, was anxious to maintain his power in Jerusalem. To do so, he needed to cement his relationship with Roman authorities, the new superpower which by that time controlled the entire

Mediterranean and Levant. He summoned his council, determined to send an envoy to Mark Antony, then governor in Egypt – and lover of Cleopatra. They suggested sending Herod's young brother-in-law, Aristoboulos III. But Herod refused, apparently because he had heard that Mark Antony had a penchant for sexually abusing young men and he wanted to protect Aristoboulos from humiliation.[100]

It is nearly impossible to discern slander from fact in ancient histories, but according to one source, Herod was apparently no stranger to queer sex. He was said to keep a harem of eunuchs at his court (a fact we will return to in a later chapter). 'Eunuchs', in the ancient world, is a catch-all term which closely overlaps with 'queer people': they often cross-dress, are sometimes intersex and often practise bottoming, and are sometimes forcibly castrated. The eunuchs poured his wine, served him food and – allegedly – 'took care of matters of the state', according to one near-contemporary Jewish writer Josephus.[101]

However, Herod was less amused when he found out that his son Alexander had also been having sex with his eunuchs. Furious, paranoid and convinced that Alexander was plotting against him, Herod had all the eunuchs rounded up and tortured until they confessed to their crimes.[102] Josephus' account echoes the hysterical tales related by Philo about the court of Caligula: it is possible that both are exaggerations that contain a kernel of truth. The court of a queer-leaning king may have offered something of a shelter to eunuchs and others who practised same-sex desire. But what is important is not whether Herod was gay, it is the fact that writers discussed his queerness as a means of slandering him and making him seem a weak and ineffectual ruler.

The texts which make up the Old Testament and the writings of Hellenistic Jews would later converge with Stoic teaching to form Christianity. They did so in the heart of the Mediterranean under the glare of the Roman Empire. The Romans would progress across the ancient Mediterranean and the Near East largely unchecked, subduing Greece, Jerusalem, Egypt and many more states to their will. With a combination of their immense military discipline and political will, the Romans came to establish dominion over all before them.

Popular history tells us that, unlike the homophobic Egyptians, Jews and various Greek philosophers and politicians, the Romans were immensely fond of and open about gay sex. Rome has earned this reputation in large part thanks to Roman writers discussing the sex lives of their emperors as well as the collection of queer artworks and treasures which we have inherited from sites like Pompeii. But, as we will see, all is not what it seems.

SEVEN

Toxic Masculinity in Ancient Rome

> And from my father I learned ... to stop my love of young men.
>
> MARCUS AURELIUS, Meditations 1.16.2

While King Herod was in bed with his eunuchs and Philo was remonstrating about the excesses of luxury, a new power had taken dominion over the European continent. By the end of the 1st century BCE around the birth of Jesus, Rome had subdued modern-day Portugal and Spain, Italy, Greece, France, Germany west of the Rhine, southern Britain, Israel, Egypt, Tunisia and the rest of northern Africa, Syria (with Palmyra joining the Roman Empire in the 1st century CE under the emperor Tiberius) and Turkey, and had made imperial forays into many other regions. Over the course of two centuries or more, Rome had successfully riveted together disparate parts of the world with a combination of highly efficient administration, governance, economic integration and – most importantly – terror.

Such success was accompanied by no little unease. The Roman historian Pliny the Elder, who died in the eruption of Mount Vesuvius (79 CE), worried about the excess of a certain metal that the empire was bringing to ordinary people. 'Our women despise baths that aren't made of silver,' he complained, 'for serving food at the table, the metal must also be employed!'[1] Even working-class Roman women had taken to wearing silver on their shoe-buckles, a report we may have some cause to doubt.

Moralists like Pliny worried incessantly about what all this wealth and luxury would mean for the morals of citizens. The Roman statesman Cicero (106–43 BCE), whose unwise choice of political enemy led to his hands being cut off and nailed to a podium in the centre of Rome, even grumbled about a friend who had decorated his house too nicely.[2] While some Roman people enjoyed gambling, savage spectator sports, drink and sex, others looked on in horror at what they saw as the decline of a great society. Rome was divided.

Roman ideas of queer sex were fraught with complexity.[3] We have frescoes from Roman bath houses showing two men in flagrante delicto; we have a silver cup depicting a twink riding a bearded young man while a small boy, probably a slave, looks on furtively; we have cheap, copycat vases that depict sex with hermaphrodites; we have tales of Roman emperors so consumed by power that they spend their days having sex with everyone in sight; and we have a rumour that boy-prostitutes were celebrated at an ancient festival on 25 April in honour of the god Robigus.[4] And yet, we also have Romans writing at exactly the same time of the horror of queerness and the fear of passive sex; we hear that there were Roman laws against gay sex; we hear there were violent raids against the rituals of Dionysus and particular concerns raised about queer sex;[5] and we hear of Roman soldiers punished for having sex with each other. At the heart of ancient Rome is a queer contradiction – some sources paint a picture of a divided, homophobic Rome, while others suggest a lurid interest in documenting the most over-the-top stories about gay sex possible. But even amid all the tales of sex-crazed gods like Jupiter and his boy Ganymede, heroes like Nisus and Euryalus, Emperor Hadrian and his lover Antinous – amid all the sex and sensual excess rumoured to take place in the courts and the brothels – it is exceptionally rare to hear of a happy, cohabiting queer couple.[6] Once noticed, this silence is deafening.

In many ways, queerness in ancient Rome was fraught with the same moral and ethical questions that cocaine is today. Actors and performers were closely associated with queer sex, which was regarded as morally inferior and dangerous by the political and legal elite. Having sex with a male slave in order to humiliate him into submission in a private household would not draw too much attention from polite society.[7] But throughout much of the Roman Empire's history, if a politician went anywhere near it, or a lawyer, or a member of a public office was in any way associated with queerness, their career would be over. Like cocaine, queerness in Rome was indistinguishable from wealth and luxury, and it was stalked by a guilt, an anxiety about decay, about status, about health and – above all – about a loss of self-control. Rome's path to this complex relationship with sexuality can only be understood via its 200-year path to dominance in the Mediterranean.

A BLOODY HUNDRED YEARS

The Roman Republic was said to have begun in 509 BCE,[8] after King Tarquin the Proud was overthrown. His son had raped a noblewoman known for her virtue called Lucretia, who took her own life in shame. In the ensuing years, which we know about only through a mix of legend and history, a new system of government was worked out. The Romans never had a formal constitution, but their government was complex and it changed to answer new needs as the city first conquered Italy and then the rest of the Mediterranean.[9]

For most of the republic (from 509 BCE until the first Roman emperor, Augustus, assumed power in 31 BCE), popular assemblies made up of male Roman citizens could approve laws and elect officials called magistrates. These magistrates had power over everything from managing the courts of justice to ensuring the roads were well maintained. There also existed a body of ex-magistrates called the Senate. The Senate could give advice to the elected magistrates, which was customarily followed, but – for the most part – they never made law themselves. The Senate in turn always relied on suggestions from the class of priests who were drawn from noble families. The system combined advice given by experienced ex-magistrates and noble families with democratically elected officials and assemblies – it was organized according to a veneration for the wisdom and experience of elders and religious leaders which is foreign to us today. How this system functioned remains somewhat of a mystery to scholars, since no formal code of rules survives and accounts tend to be quite inconsistent in their treatment of the system.[10] Like an old-boys' club, you only got Roman politics if you'd been born into it – if you needed a series of rules to follow, you were already out.[11]

A tricky balancing act was always at play in Roman politics. The common people known as the Plebeians (from the Latin word plebs for the masses or the majority) and the aristocratic, land-owning Patricians were often in conflict. A particular magistracy was created in the year 496 BCE whose sole function was to protect the interests of the Plebeians. This magistrate was called the Tribune of the Plebs and he had the power to veto any acts of magistrates. For most of Roman history, the Tribune of the Plebs obediently went along with what the Senate recommended but, every so often, they would rebel. This cost one tribune his life.

On 10 December 134 BCE, an aristocrat named Tiberius Gracchus was elected as Tribune of the Plebs. Rome had recently defeated their bitter archenemy, Carthage, a city in north Africa. But despite Rome's growing empire and wealth, its people were increasingly restless. While the aristocrats enjoyed the fruits of power, these profits had yet to trickle down.

Tiberius Gracchus' main concern was with the redistribution of land, a prospect which unsurprisingly did not meet with the senators' approval. However, an ancient law – the Lex Hortensia (from 287 BCE) – had established that the Roman assembly of the people had the power to make laws. In practice, the Senate made sure that it exerted enough pressure, usually with bribes, on tribunes to keep themselves at the prominent position of the trough as far as money and land were concerned.[12] Tiberius Gracchus, however, intended to redistribute public land to individual, poorer Roman citizens, and he passed a law in the assembly to do so.[13] The senate was furious.

Another tribune, loyal to the Senate, Marcus Octavius, vehemently opposed the reforms. Using his powers as an orator before the assembly, Gracchus had Marcus Octavius removed by popular assent. He succeeded in establishing a commission to investigate lands and redistribute them to the people. The recalcitrant upper-class senators could do nothing to prevent this, but they refused to release the funds required to run the commission. The result was a stalemate. Luckily, some money was on hand. King Attalus III of Pergamum, a man who had shown little interest in governing and preferred the quiet life of a gardener, had left no heirs. He made the unusual decision upon his death of bequeathing his entire kingdom and treasury to the Roman people. Tiberius Gracchus proposed the use of Attalus' fund to run the commission, and he had every power to do so.

The leader of Roman religion – the pontifex maximus – Scipio Nasica, an aristocrat himself, interrupted the assembly with a mob of senators. They stoned Gracchus alive and dragged his bruised body to the River Tiber where it was dumped and his blood could suffuse with the muddy waters of the city he had tried to rescue. And with that murder, Scipio Nasica and his men ignited the powder keg of a 100-year Roman civil war. The tug-of-war that emerged between the Senate and the Plebeians was the first of many scuffles to break out over the redistribution of wealth.

As its empire expanded, Roman Italy was becoming a place of unprecedented disparities in wealth. Although he had complained about a friend who decorated his house too nicely, Cicero himself paid 3.5 million silver sesterces for his lavish house on the Palatine Hill.[14] At a similar time, farmers all over Italy were living at subsistence levels.[15] Well into the reign of the emperors, the writer Appian (2nd century CE) would look back on the end of the republic as a period when 'the powerful became very, very rich, the slave population multiplied in the countryside, the Italian people became few and weak, worn out by poverty, taxes, and military campaigns'.[16]

At the time, a poorer Roman citizen possessed 1/714 of the wealth of a median Roman citizen.[17] These were still individuals with money who could vote in assemblies. Much of rural Italy and the empire was made up of tenant farmers who paid in cash to lease their farms from richer landlords.[18] The richest Roman aristocrats had 10,476 times the wealth of the poorest. This was a gap that is estimated to have far exceeded even that of Victorian London. With debt crises spiralling[19] and wealth inequality sky-high, the Romans responded – as had the Spartans before them – with a rigorous narrative of discipline.

CATILINE IS NOT A MAN

Less than 100 years after Gracchus was murdered, a series of political crises were sparked by debt inflation.[20] In 91 BCE, in the town of Asculum (modern-day Ascoli Piceno), local Italians struck back against land grabs by the Roman authorities and assassinated a visiting magistrate. In the ensuing Social War, 300,000 men were killed. Just a few years later, a conspiracy shook the very heart of Rome during Cicero's consulship.

Throughout the 60s BCE, Lucius Sergius Catilina (known today as 'Catiline') had tried unsuccessfully for consulship, the highest magistracy in Rome. He was plagued by personal debt and championed by a group of nobles who were also in financial peril and supported his proposals for debt relief. Despite his financial difficulties, Catiline was intelligent and said to be able to endure hunger, cold and sleep-deprivation to phenomenal degrees. However, the Roman historian Sallust, writing only 20 years later, described Catiline as 'depraved'. Catiline's reputation had soured when, after being thwarted once again in his bid for consulship, he resorted to a coup.

Taking to the floor of the Senate in 63 BCE, Cicero denounced Catiline and his followers as 'shameless and unclean men'.[21] Cicero conflates his political opponents with men who cannot handle their money (they are 'gamblers') and with sexual profligacy ('adulterers'). In Latin, Cicero refers to these 'shameless' men as *impudici*, a word which has associations with homosexual behaviour.[22] Cicero goes on: 'these boys are so clever and so delicate not just in their fucking but in that they [allow themselves] to be fucked'.[23] Cicero belittles Catiline's masculinity, calling him a boy and accusing him of having sex with men. In the same breath, he associates a loss of financial control with a loss of sexual control. Cicero was not alone. Sallust, when describing the events for posterity, put it this way: 'Avarice is characterized by a zeal for money, which no wise man desires. As if imbued with evil venom [avarice] makes effeminate the male soul and the body.'[24]

Another near contemporary to Cicero and Sallust writing love poetry addressed queer desire in similarly hostile terms. Catullus (84–54 BCE) died young, but his list of works has – like Keats – survived long after him. He led a colourful and dangerous life. After publishing a poem in which he accused Julius Caesar of having gay sex with one of his soldiers, a man called Mamurra, Catullus was described as having 'the eternal mark of infamy placed upon him'. Catullus apologized profusely and Caesar invited him to a cordial dinner and all was forgiven.[25] In the 16th poem of his catalogue, Catullus responds outrageously to claims by his critics that he has been too soft in his depiction of love.[26] He addresses two of his critics directly:

> I'm going to fuck you in the arse and in the face,
> You *pathicus** Aurelius and you *cinaedus*† Furius,
> Both of you who claim that in my little verses
> [are signs] of weakness, [that they] barely show modesty.[27]

In another poem, Catullus possibly undermines his own claims to modesty when he rages:

> Who can possibly see this, and who can possibly stand it,
> Unless you are immodest, gluttonous, and a gambler . . .
> You sodomite Romulus, will you be able to see these things and
>   bear [them]?
> You are immodest, gluttonous, and a gambler.[28]

---

* A pathicus comes from the Greek word *pathikos*, which literally means 'one who suffers'. The Romans define the term for us (unusually) as 'a man who suffers womanly things' (Juvenal 2.99). It seems to mean a bottom, or a man who plays the passive partner in gay sex. However, the term may also have been extended to anyone who had sex with a man.

† This is the Latin term for *kinaidos*, and probably is a more all-purpose term for a homosexual man. Some have tried to argue a *cinaedus* is a top, a view I don't share, though I can understand its etymological basis (*kineo* is Greek for 'I move' and can mean 'I fuck').

Catullus,[29] much like his near contemporary Cicero, associates same-sex desire with a lack of self-restraint and modesty, and with a love of gambling and other frivolous uses of money. Anal sex, being a bottom, and being useless with money were all ridiculed as failures of masculinity. He also uses threats of gay sex, as Romans often did, to insult and intimidate his enemies.

In the law, in history and in poetry during the Roman Republic, queerness was used as a trope to attack and ridicule another man. Catullus and Cicero both associate gay sex with gambling. Catullus uses tropes from same-sex rape to attack his critics. The culture around same-sex desire was evidently hostile, but what did the law say?

EARLY LAWS AGAINST QUEER SEX

In 226 BCE, an ambitious man named Marcus Claudius Marcellus had been elected to the magistracy of curule aedile with responsibility for many areas of Roman life such as markets, roads, food supply, public games and even the proper maintenance of brothels. It was in that same year that Marcellus confronted a case that was rather closer to home. His own son, who was said to be very handsome and to comport himself with immense dignity and self-control (at least, so the sources tell us), was seduced by none other than one of Marcellus' colleague whose name was Capitolinus. Marcellus did not take this well. He denounced Capitolinus to the Senate, but Capitolinus denied anything improper had taken place. The Senate summoned Marcellus' son, who appeared before them with a red face and began to cry in anger and shame. The Senate fined Capitolinus on the spot.[30]

Capitolinus' full name was Scantinius Capitolinus, and the Senate's decision to fine him for his sexual pursuit of the young Marcellus came to be known as the Lex Scantinia or 'the Scantinian Law'. This law would lie quietly in the background and, to our knowledge, was seldom used widely until the reign of the emperor Domitian (81–96 CE). There are other accounts of soldiers who abused their positions of authority and preyed on younger recruits being fined under Lex Scantinia.[31] Some scholars even think that these early laws existed to prevent freeborn Roman men from having sex in order to settle their debts.[32] If true, this establishes the financial relationship with fears about queer desire very early in the Roman tradition. The trouble with the Lex Scantinia, as well as all these other stories and laws, is it is never precisely clear in the tradition what was banned and why. We see a similar thing in 4th-century Athens: though the law under which Timarchus was prosecuted by Aeschines is not clear to us, we can tell that the defendant was under attack for queer sex.

There is another account from 108 BCE in which queer sex is discussed in the courts. That year, Quintus Fabius Maximus told two of his slaves that if they succeeded in killing his son, he would reward them with their freedom. The slaves did as they were ordered and murdered the young man, but Quintus was caught and put on trial. As his defence, Quintus claimed that his son had sold himself for gay sex, suggesting that queerness was considered a serious stain on the character of any Roman.[33]

Quintus' defence did not rely on the fact that his son had gay sex, but that he sold himself – therefore implying that he took the passive role. In an early passage from a contemporary Roman comedy, the comic Plautus (died 184 BCE) tells us that Roman citizens could have sex with anyone they wanted, providing they are not also freeborn Romans.

> As long as you abstain from a bride, a widow, a virgin,
> A Roman youth, free boys, fuck whomever you want.[34]

While prone to exaggeration as a comic writer, Plautus appears to show us a dividing line. It was completely acceptable to have sex with anyone, providing they were not protected Roman citizens. In practice, this leaves only the rape of slaves. In a poem extolling the dangers of unnecessary expenditure, a later Augustan poet asks, 'would it not be better to question the boundary Nature sets in place for lust?' He continues, 'do you ask for a golden cup when you're about to die of thirst? . . . so when your cock gets hard if there's a slave-girl at home or a slave-boy at hand whom [you could] attack at that moment, don't you prefer that than being broken by desire?'[35] The poet's suggestion is that nature does give us urges and the best way to alleviate them is to sexually abuse your slaves.[36] The poet is not concerned about the slave's gender.

These sources understand sexual abuse of a slave or a prostitute as acceptable outlets for pent-up sex drive. The sources all see sex as something much more violent than we do in the modern world. The use of this violent sexuality against a Roman citizen (whether female or male) was prohibited. The Romans found the idea of a man who actually *wanted* to be subjected to sex positively alarming. The *pathicus*, a Latin word imported from Greek *pathikos* (meaning 'he who likes to suffer'), is imagined as this man; the *pathicus* wants to be sexually dominated. This horrifying thought undermined the entire basis of Roman patriarchy. It is for this reason that Quintus is able to excuse murdering his own son, it is also why the Romans appear happy to discuss sex between a Roman and his slave, but condemn roundly the very notion of consensual sex between two freeborn Roman men. As for lesbians, there are stories (which we will see shortly) of their existence, but they are never told in a flattering light. This paranoia about sexuality is borne out in its relentless discussion and ridicule in Roman texts.

VIRTUE RULES

In 31 BCE, at the Battle of Actium, Julius Caesar's adopted son Octavian defeated Mark Antony and Cleopatra. Until that point, Mark Antony and Octavian had shared power. This great naval battle changed the balance of power in Rome and paved the way for Octavian to bring all the different branches of government gradually under his influence. He would become the first Roman emperor. In 28 BCE, Octavian was given the title Augustus or 'revered one' by the senate. After 100 years of civil war in Rome, the doors of the temple of Janus (the two-faced god) were sealed, symbolizing the end of military conflict among Romans. The Romans, reunified, began to look to their empire as a source of renewed pride, and as they did so, they began to wonder what made them so special. What endowed them with such power?

As part of this period of renewed self-investigation and inquiry, Augustus commissioned the best writers and artists of the time to examine what it meant to be Roman. Recognizing the importance of literature and art in his propaganda, Augustus paid Virgil to write a 12-book epic poem called the *Aeneid* narrating the grand events of how the Trojans – defeated by the Greeks – fled their native Turkey, travelled the ancient Mediterranean and eventually settled in Italy where their descendants would become the Roman people. Virgil, a talented poet raised in a middle-class family, has Jupiter pronouncing on the fate of the Roman people very early on his epic:

On these lands, I impose no limit of time nor place,
I have given [them] an empire without limit.[37]

Writing at a similar time, the historian Livy describes the exceptionalism of the Roman people, 'Never has a state been greater or holier or rich in examples of good men ... nor for so much and for so long has it had the honour of poverty and parsimony.'[38]

For a Roman to emphasize the empire's 'poverty' (*paupertas* in Latin) or its 'parsimony' (*parsimonia*) may strike the modern reader as strange. But for the ancient thinker great power came from great self-control, modesty and living within your means. The Roman writers looking back at their history were devoted to the idea that restraint and virtue had obtained for them mastery over all the world. A little later, Pliny the Elder wrote, 'of all the world's people, the Romans stand out most in their virtue'.[39] The Romans even romanticized their historic defeat of Carthage 100 years earlier. 'So it was that the Roman people overcame all others in virtue'.[40] What the Romans meant by 'virtue' was a performance of self-discipline, parsimony and duty. A key part of this performance of masculinity was the ability to sow seed in the ground (both an agricultural and sexual metaphor)[41] and being good with accounts.[42] Above all, it echoes the Stoic idea of never succumbing to one's desires.

Besides the Lex Scantinia, other discriminatory measures existed before Augustus' time. A longstanding custom in Roman law gave a true man the right to speak up on behalf of a friend on trial, known as *postulare pro aliis*, 'to argue on behalf of others'. This right was not available to women, blind men (whose lack of sight emasculated them), men who were paid to fight with animals or men who 'had suffered that their body [be used] in womanish ways'.[43]

As Augustus tightened his grip on power, he brought in a series of further morality laws. Perhaps not by coincidence, this was happening while wealth inequality was rising in Rome.[44] Augustus' moral reforms included strict laws forbidding adultery, which he blamed for bringing about the civil war crisis of the preceding century. But these laws also formalized the already harsh social views on same-sex desire. The crime of *stuprum* (often translated 'outrage') became illegal under Augustus and with it came further criminal penalties on same-sex desire.[45]

At the same time, Roman poets were hard at work expounding the dangers of all forms of desire.[46] Early in the *Aeneid*, Virgil introduces Dido, the Queen of Carthage, who falls desperately in love with the hero of the epic Aeneas. Aeneas and Dido sneak off under the auspices of Venus, goddess of sex, to marry in a cave, where they spend all night in each other's embraces. Unfortunately for Dido, Aeneas leaves for Italy – on the orders of Jupiter – so he can found Rome. Dido, distraught, sets herself on fire. The message Augustus' propagandist wanted the world to know was the consuming power of desire destroyed all in its path.

Virgil's *Aeneid* also discusses same-sex love, which also ends tragically.[47]

> From everywhere, come the Trojans mixed with the Sicilians,
> The first among them [were] Nisus and Euryalus.
> Euryalus was famous for his comeliness and his blossoming[48]
>   youth,
> And Nisus for his pious love of the boy.[49]

The phrase Virgil uses for the 'love of the boy' was likely a stock phrase for a Platonic sort of gay love.[50] Virgil is at pains in the case of Nisus to describe it as *pius* or 'pious', which seems to mean that Nisus – much like Plato and Socrates – longed for Euryalus but never consummated his desire. Queer desire is used in Virgil's work to emphasize Nisus' extraordinary self-restraint and masculinity. Like Aeneas (and unlike Dido), he can resist the love and desire that would otherwise overwhelm him. Later in the epic, when Aeneas and his troops move into Italy and make war with the native Latin people, Nisus' self-restraint cracks.

At night, Nisus and Euryalus sneak into the enemy camp. They stab the sleeping soldiers and their swords withdraw red with gore and the wine of last night's feast. But quickly, they are discovered by Volcens, the leader of the Latin army. He surrounds them and they flee into a black wood, tangled with brambles and thick trees. 'Poor Euryalus, where did I leave you?' cries a desperate Nisus, having lost his love in the dark.[51] Then, amid the branches, Nisus sees Euryalus backed onto the ground while all his foes surround him. With Euryalus' terrified screams echoing through the woods, Nisus prays to the goddess of the moon for help, begging her to guide his spear. He hurls it through the brier, and it strikes the back of one of his foes, Sulmo. The native Italians turn on the spot, staring blindly into the dark, when a second spear strikes and smashes open a second skull.

> Evil Volcens raged yet could not see the shaft's spearman,
> Nor where he should shout back in his rage:
> 'Whatever,' he said, 'you shall pay for both men you've slain in
>   hot blood'
> Then he withdrew his sword and it slid into Euryalus.
> Then in terror, out of his mind, Nisus let out a scream,
> No longer could he hide in shadow, or could he bear such pain.
> 'It's me! It's me! I am the one who did it, draw your sword
>   against me!
> O Rutulians! The whole idea was mine! This man could not have
>   dared,
> Nor would ever have been able,
> I swear by all of heaven: his only crime was to love his friend
>   too much.'[52]

Words approximating 'friend' are used in many cultures hostile to same-sex desire to euphemize a lover. In Latin, the word *amicus* (often translated 'friend') can be used of a sexual companion in the feminine, and it's likely the masculine *amicus* carries a similar implication. In the modern world, we want to see the story of Nisus and Euryalus as a triumphant tale of love that kept two men together until the end. But for Virgil, the warning is much the same as Dido.

Love and a desire for booty killed these two promising men, though it is not the only one. Virgil's queer lovers also die because they set out for wealth and plunder.[53] The idea of excess, both sexual and financial, is at the heart of the tale and it leads to their deaths. Virgil's final salute to the two lovers, 'lucky pair!',[54] is heavy with irony.[55] A trope which had begun in ancient Greece, describing how gay lovers ultimately prove bad warriors because they fail to make tactical decisions and act to preserve their favourites, is deployed by Virgil to show how passion leads to pain.[56]

Sex and love were fraught with danger. To the Romans, sex itself seemed to bristle with a martial quality. Nearly all their words for sex parts and sex acts come from the field of war. *Vagina* means a sword sheath, and they use *gladius* ('sword') for a penis.[57] Yet as these stories of doomed lovers show, the Romans were fascinated by romantic love. Poetry commissioned by Augustus would have been performed at private parties, often to elite audiences, and one of the common poetic themes was love and its intoxicating power. The Augustan poet Propertius writing about having sex with his lover Cynthia describes how 'true love knows no limit':[58] it is like streams returning to their source, it is like fish parched and beached on dry sands. It takes place when men and women are drunk and have lost control of their limbs. To the Romans, a limitless love was terrifying. In legal speeches and in histories, the Romans emphasized self-restraint as a virtue; in poetry and tragedy, they showed desire's power.

Ovid, a contemporary of Virgil, claims that same-sex desire can never satisfy both partners and says, 'I hate [these] embraces'.[59] He perhaps thought this because, as already mentioned, sex between men in ancient Rome was largely not an act between consenting equals – but a citizen and a slave. The Romans, like the Greeks and Egyptians before them, mostly associated gay sex with rape and domination (either of enemies in war, or of slaves). Despite his feelings about queer sex, Ovid wrote a series of poems encouraging noblewomen to take up lovers in a poem called the *Art of Lovemaking*. In 8 CE, he was banished from Rome by Augustus and was forced to live on the Black Sea, far from his friends.[60] The *Art of Lovemaking* was deemed so offensive that Augustus even had it removed from the libraries of Rome. Ovid's misstep was to take his description of sex too far: to encourage people to have sex, rather than focus on the horrors of desire. Much scholarly debate has been had over what Ovid's crime was. What was it about this text, unlike others, that had led to such a fierce reaction? Often ancient historians search for consistency and logical security in the cultures they study. In a modern society, it is understood that an authoritarian ruler can make an example of somebody without punishing other offenders. Ovid's punishment speaks to the illegality of discussing sex and the arbitrariness with which these laws were enforced.

Where Ovid does talk about queer love, he usually does so negatively, with certain curious exceptions.[61] When Orpheus finally realizes in *Metamorphoses* that he will not be able to rescue his beloved Eurydice from the underworld, he changes topic. Instead, the grieving singer picks up his harp and recites:

> Often have I sung of Jupiter's power,
> I have sung with heavier plucking on my harp about the Giants,
> And the conquering thunderbolts hurled on the Phlegraean fields.
> But now is the time for a lighter lyre, let's sing of boys,
> delightful [boys], loved by the gods, and girls, struck by the illicit fires of love
> Who are so deserving of their punishment.[62]

The reader could be forgiven for thinking Orpheus is about to sing about boys with whom girls, unable to control their emotions after the Roman, masculine fashion, fall haplessly in love. But this is not the case, for he then goes on to tell the story of how Jupiter fell for the boy Ganymede.

First told in Homer's *Iliad*, Zeus captures the son of the Trojan king Tros and takes him up to Olympus as a cupbearer.[63] Initially, it seems the myth was about abduction rather than gay sex;[64] a terracotta statue from the 470s BCE survives from the archaeological site at ancient Olympia (a site dedicated to Zeus' honour). The statue shows a bearded Zeus carrying under his arm a child, presumed to be Ganymede. He is first described as Zeus' bedfellow by Euripides.[65] Somewhere between these two points, it had become common to describe Zeus and Ganymede as lovers. It became so popular to do so that the word 'Ganymede' eventually turned into 'Catamite'.

The study of queerness in ancient Rome is in many ways more puzzling than in any previous period. Despite the laws forbidding homosexuals from speaking in court and criminalizing same-sex acts between freeborn men, and despite vicious homophobic attacks in the courts, there is still considerable homoerotic poetry from the period. Some scholars have pointed out that almost all of these poems are about same-sex love for slaves, posing serious questions about consent and the authentic nature of the love affair.[66] Others still point to certain exceptions: Catullus' Juventius is likely a freeman.[67] I do not think there is such thing as a society that is uniformly homophobic in every nook and cranny. Nor is it likely there is any such thing as a queer utopia. There will always be pockets of societies which are more tolerant and pockets which are less, the question is which pocket wields the political power. In modern-day Florida, queer books are taken from library shelves while gay men party at night in Miami. We should not expect the Romans to be free of the same contradictions.

REAL MEN DOMINATE

While queer sex for pleasure was viewed as repugnantly decadent, the same-sex rape of slaves remained a valid means of maintaining control over one's household. It was so normalized that, writing in the 1st century CE, the Stoic philosopher Seneca expresses sympathy for the plight of a slave:

He cannot escape his boyhood, he is dragged back, he may already have a soldier's body, but he is an effeminate man,[68] whose hair has been shaved or plucked out, he stands vigil all night long, and divides the night between his master's drunkenness and his libido. In the bedroom, he is a man. In the dining room he is a boy.[69]

Seneca's letter also ridicules the *pater familias* who fails to take up his rightful position at the head of the household and instead allows himself to be topped by his slaves.[70] Sex had always been forbidden with freeborn men, but as the Roman emperors rose to power, the obligation to enforce dominance in the household by having sex with slave boys became even more engrained. This was how Romans showcased their masculinity.[71] Queer sex had been fashioned by the Romans into a tool of subjugation and terror, and excised entirely from same-sex love. At the same time, sex – and particularly queer sex – was becoming synonymous with wealth.

All over Pompeii, cocks adorn the walls. The penis in Roman thought was, in part, a symbol of fertility, but it was also a symbol of domination and power.[72] From Pompeii, we have found a vast quantity of phrases etched into the wall which similarly speak to a macho culture. Some describe heterosexual sex, some homosexual sex; none of the homosexual etchings are the sweet words of pining lovers – all describe aggressive, violent sex from the aggressor's perspective. 'Lick me and my cock,' says one.[73] 'Little fountain says a big hey to his little fish,' says another (little fish, in antiquity, were synonymous with sex slaves).[74] Other graffiti describe some men as having enormous cocks, too large to control.[75] In a set of poems called the *Priapic Songs*, which were originally attributed to Virgil (but almost certainly were not written by him), a man warns off a thief from his patch: 'look at [my] cock which stands fierce and at the ready'.[76]

While archaic Greece produced thousands of examples of queer porn pottery showing all kinds of erotic scenes, a silver Roman cup in the British Museum collection is notable for its rarity.[77] On one side, a young man with a beard lies naked on a bed. Most Romans were clean-shaven, at least until Hadrian's reign (117–138 CE);

his beard does little, in the Roman mind, to enhance his virility. The untamed hairs which curl all over his chin were symbols of a wild man, not a self-contained and virile Roman. Holding delicately onto a strap, a clean-shaven young man eases slowly down onto his bearded lover. On the other side, we see another bearded man wearing a laurel wreath, looking down in concentration as he buries his penis into his male partner from behind. In this scene, the bottom arches his back and grasps some fabric in his hands. This silver artefact is known as the 'Warren Cup' and would have been far beyond the purchase power of an ordinary Roman.

Likewise, in the private collection of George Ortiz is an extraordinary piece of glasswork. It is a perfume bottle discovered in the earth at Ostippo (Estepa) in Spain near Seville. On one side, a muscled man leans over and penetrates a young man, whose buttocks are somewhat feminine in appearance. The glassware would have been extraordinarily expensive, possibly even more expensive than the silver of the Warren Cup.

Archaeologists have also found numerous examples of mass-produced ceramics from Arrentium (Arretine) which show same-sex and heterosexual scenes. On one, kept in the Boston Museum of Fine Arts, a man has sex with an androgynous figure. All these figures seem to be copycat images of much more expensive glassworks.[78] Paintings in the bath houses at Pompeii also show elaborate sex scenes both queer and heterosexual. For wealthy middle-class Romans imitating the rich, perhaps pornographic pots and murals connected them with luxury. Given the invective and the laws around gay sex in ancient Rome, however, it is unlikely that any owners of these rare artefacts felt safe to engage publicly with queer sex.[79] They may also have been part of discreet, private collections or the risqué decorations of a brothel and regarded with suspicion by others. We do not know.

THE ROMAN EMPERORS

Augustus paved the way for one man to have control over all parts of Roman government. His adopted son Tiberius inherited his powers over the city and the Senate. Initially, he ruled from his palace in Rome but eventually moved to the island of Capri in the Bay of Naples. Our main source for his life was a biographer working at the court of the emperor Hadrian almost a century after Tiberius' death. Suetonius, the biographer, initially thought of becoming a barrister and was encouraged in this by his mentor Pliny. But he walked away from the legal profession after postponing a court case on account of having suffered a bad dream the previous night.[80] Pliny then helped him to buy a small estate where he enjoyed sitting amongst the vines and thinking.

Suetonius did not write history; he wrote biography intended to inform and educate the ruling classes of his day. He was working from first-hand court documents and hearsay accounts of the courts of emperors before Hadrian's day. His account of Tiberius' life is consequently not an absolute rendition of fact, nor could it be said to be a polemic; both vices and virtues are exaggerated commensurate with whichever morals Suetonius wished to promote to his readership.

According to Suetonius, Tiberius was at first a restrained emperor. In times of financial difficulty, he slashed the pay of actors and limited gladiators to a fixed number to keep costs down. He proposed to fix prices on household furniture. To encourage the whole Roman people to follow this frugality drive, Tiberius pioneered the practice of serving cold meats at lunch from yesterday's dinner. It was in this period of austerity that Tiberius issued a moral clampdown, banning all kissing between Roman citizens.[81] But this austerity was not to last.

Retiring to the island of Capri in the Bay of Naples, Tiberius was said to host anal sex parties in the latrines of his house. He selected groups of girls and *monstrosi* (literally 'monstrous men'), a common Latin term for queer men.[82] He had whole rooms decorated with sculptures and paintings depicting explicit sex acts, and was said to retain a copy of Elephantis' works in his library. Elephantis had been a Greek writer, whose works are now lost to us, who wrote on exotic sex positions and how to prevent pregnancy. Tiberius organized parties in the woods where men and women dressed up as nymphs and the sex-crazed god Pan and had sex in the open outdoors. These parties soon failed to sate his appetites, and Suetonius tells us that Tiberius turned to grooming and abusing male children. When this also failed to satisfy him, he ordered mothers to surrender their newborn babies to him.

Suetonius also tells us that Tiberius failed in his duty as an emperor to build magnificent public works, and that he was so stingy that he refused even to pay salaries for foreign campaigns.[83] Suetonius paints a man of extremes: too debauched in the bedroom and too stingy in court, failing in his duty to restrain his perverse desires and redistribute wealth.[84] This would become a trope in the biographies of the emperors. The emperor Domitian (81–96 CE) presided over a period of economic disaster,[85] and he is attacked in the historical record for his keeping of a 'boy' for his own sexual pleasure.[86]

During the Emperor Nero's reign (54–68 CE), the city of Rome burned to the ground, and the tales of his court are sensational. Suetonius tells us that Nero kept a slave called Sporus, who is said to have been very handsome. So handsome that he had his balls removed in order to make him appear more feminine.[87] That same day, the emperor Nero dressed Sporus in women's clothes, took him around the streets of Rome in a litter carried by guards, and then married him in a ceremony. Suetonius tells us that Nero had himself locked in a cage at parties. He had men and women tied to stakes all around him and when he was finally released from the cage, he had sex with them all. Another of Nero's 'husbands' was the freedman Doryphorus – whose name is Greek for 'spear-carrier' – who used his huge manhood to dominate the emperor. The now infamous story of Nero singing of the burning of Troy while his city went up in flames taps further into the narrative that, as a singer, Nero was no true man in their eyes and was incapable of having the restraint and dignity to rule.

This biographical tradition continued well after Suetonius' time. In later accounts, we are told that the emperor Elagabalus (218–222 CE) sent emissaries to the docks to look for sailors with enormous penises.[88] He also constructed a public bath that was connected to his own private baths where hung men could be scouted out.[89] It seems very unlikely that much of this is true. If it was, it would mean that almost every emperor was gay. It served ancient writers' agendas to tell stories of queer debauchery, since it played into their narrative that these men were poor managers of the Roman economy. These tales represent the culmination of a steady process by which gay sex became increasingly associated in Western history with abuses of power and hoarding of wealth.

It has been common in popular culture to assume that these tales are realistic portraits of gay life in Roman times, to assume that Romans were tolerant of gay sex. But nothing about Suetonius' account of the lives of the emperors could be said to condone the behaviour; it was quite the reverse.

THE GAY SUBCULTURE

Across Roman literature,[90] queerness is suffused with scandal and financial imprudence. But historians do think it possible that a gay subculture existed on the fringes of Roman societies. We know that male prostitution existed in Rome, because male prostitutes are known to have paid taxes,[91] but this was never an option for free-born Romans, and those who chose to make a life as a prostitute were vulnerable to abuse and rape. These prostitutes were frowned upon by polite society[92] – Pliny calls gays sexually perverted men who suffer from a 'wickedness of nature'.[93] Male prostitutes were also barred from certain legal positions and from political office, and there may well have been other controls on their work. Though he does so cuttingly, the poet Juvenal (late 1st century CE to mid-2nd century CE) talks of a 'great harmony among pathici (the plural of pathicus)',[94] which implies the existence of a community of queers who were heavily disapproved of by civilized Romans. The Romans actively conducted violent raids against such groups. In 186 BCE a cult of Dionysus, where gay sex was actively practised as a religious ritual, was shut down and thousands of its participants were arrested and killed.[95] Romans knew that queers existed, and they regarded them with fear and a deep hostility.

Most of the sources for this group of 'pathics' come from hysterical writers. Reconstructing their lives from these sources is like basing a history of queer communities in the 1980s on *Daily Mail* columns. Nonetheless, we can try. Males in this group were lambasted for wearing make-up, for depilation and for wearing bright clothing.[96] These men were known to approach other men and scratch their heads lightly with a single finger as a gesture of their interest in sex.[97] They were also known to hang around at the theatre[98] and congregate at bath houses where (according to Roman writers) they would look around with a wandering eye to find the biggest dicks in the place.[99] A man named Hostius Quadra is singled out by the philosopher Seneca as a man who liked to select the very largest.[100]

There was a subgroup of the subculture, of men called *drauci*. A *draucus* would pay a craftsman to insert a pin into his penis so that he could not get an erection, enabling him to play the role of a bottom completely.[101] Men who participated in this hook-up subculture at bath houses and theatres did so in complete silence in full knowledge that they could never be open about their activities.

The evidence for this subculture is tantalizing, but fragmented. Deeply homophobic Roman writers tell us these gobbets of gossip in hysterical outbursts, often directed at their political opponents and personal adversaries, replicating the same trope used by Suetonius against the emperors. Just as with ancient Greece, we would be fools to take it all at face value – but tantalizing clues about the subculture remain. It seems that almost nobody in the public eye could escape the accusation that they had, at some point, engaged in gay sex.

EMPEROR HADRIAN'S BOYFRIEND

Suetonius, who reflected solemnly on the unrestrained lives of former emperors, was a resident of the court of the emperor Hadrian.[102] Though Hadrian dealt with serious, organized rebellions in his time, he did a great deal to secure the frontiers of the empire. On his tour of Upper Germany (120s CE), he drove thick wooden palisades into the ground and built a huge wall to solidify the borders of the empire. He did the same in Britain, building turrets and military fortifications all along the Scottish border.

Not only was Hadrian a superb military commander, but he was a gifted polymath. As a young man, he was nicknamed Graeculus ('little Greek boy') by his family and tutors who were deeply impressed by his knowledge and love for the Hellenistic world. He often wintered on his tours in Athens, and on his second Provincial Tour (128–132 CE), he lived for a time in Alexandria where he posed paradoxes and impossible riddles to the scholars of that thriving intellectual city.

It was Hadrian's love of learning and his fierce appetite for all things Greek that brought about a renaissance in Roman appreciation of the Greek world. For the first time, it became fashionable in Rome for men to grow their beards. Roman and Greek writers penned thousands of poems in Greek which we call the *Greek Anthology*, Book 12.[103] Some of its poems celebrate queer love as a thing of beauty in a glorified Greek past. Others would suggest queer love was alive and well at the court of Hadrian.

> Yes, the wandering hairs may skirt your chin and
> Yes, the delicate blonde curls adorn your head.
> But I shall not run from my love – his beauty
> Is mine, with all the beard and hair he has.[104]

This passage hints at love affairs at Hadrian's court between two men who grew their hair out after the fashion of their emperor. In another, the poet explicitly rejects heterosexuality.

> A woman's love is not for me nor tugs
> My heart, but male torches heap me with coals,
> Greater by far this heat that's stronger, manlier.[105]

Another writes, 'I say to all: love is the whetstone of the soul'.[106] For some at the court of Hadrian, there was an opportunity to explore their sexualities in a way that was freer than at many other times in Roman history. It was here that Suetonius wrote his histories of scandalously queer emperors, and it was under Hadrian's empire that Plutarch produced his histories which tell us about ancient Greek love affairs. There was a passion in the period for a renewed understanding of same-sex desire at court, though it is unlikely that any tolerance that did exist extended to freedoms for ordinary citizens. But the Romans' preoccupations with rape and sex with slaves also persisted and mixed with these nobler ideas to yield some troubling results.

Other poems in the *Greek Anthology* still exhibit Roman anxieties around same-sex love. They describe gay love as a sickness,[107] they fantasize about loving boys with shaven hair out of shame to love a fully grown man.[108] More disturbingly still, others praise the only sex act between members of the same sex the Romans had ever sanctioned: sex with a younger slave boy.

> It gives me deep pleasure to think of a boy of twelve,
> Though one of thirteen is more desirable still.
> A fourteen-year-old is a still sweeter flower of love,
> And one just beginning fifteen even more delightful.
> The sixteenth and seventeenth years are those of the gods and
>   not for me, they are for Zeus.
> If a man has desire for one older still than this, he is no longer
>   playing with boys,
> But now seeks in a fashion where he answers back.[109]

The court of Hadrian may have encouraged some to express their true desires while protected by the emperor's successes, but most would still have worried about compromising their Roman masculinity. It was his court where, for the first time in the Greek corpus, the 'love of boys' is explicitly defined as a sexual interest in pubescent boys. This was a cultural phenomenon, a product of the homophobic climate in Rome that made paedophilia with slaves the only socially acceptable form of gay sex.

In October 130 CE, Hadrian's own teenage lover Antinous drowned in the River Nile while on tour. It was said that Hadrian wept like a woman upon hearing the news. He threw a lavish funeral and had Antinous deified. Shrines to his dead boyfriend sprung up all over the empire and particularly in the eastern provinces.

We can only speculate based on the scanty primary evidence, but it is probable that Hadrian's court provided an enclave within a homophobic society wherein some men felt free to conduct their love affairs and even to write anonymously about them. But, in general, it was only acceptable to admit openly to a love affair with a subordinate, usually a slave. This colours many of the texts and has left some historians with the impression that same-sex desire only took place within this dynamic.

MARCUS AURELIUS

Stoicism continued to curry favour in Roman intellectual circles as wealth inequality climbed in Rome.[110] Roman Stoics – like Gaius Musonius Rufus, who was active half a century before Hadrian – wrote extensively about the dangers of excessive sex and spending. Their writings do not survive in full, but fragments are still with us. In one text, entitled *About Sex*, Musonius Rufus makes no bones about his view on all forms of sexual desire, calling it 'certainly not the smallest part of excess'.[111] He writes in Greek, not Latin, reflecting the Stoic tradition. The term used for 'excess', *truphē*, is used of both excessive consumption of food, excessive consumption of money, and of sex. Musonius Rufus continues, laying out his thoughts on the purpose of sex: 'men who are not excessive and not evil must think about sex as a matter only for marriage, and even then only allowed for the production of children'.[112] Those men who have sex with other men, he continues, are 'pigs'.[113] This was the consensus view of Roman Stoicism by the 1st century CE.

One of the world's most famous Stoics, and still one of the best-selling writers from the ancient world, was the Roman emperor Marcus Aurelius (161–180 CE). His reign was far from peaceful, with economic disasters and plague striking Rome during his time in power.[114] He left behind a series of *Meditations*, supposedly notes scrawled for his own benefit, on the measured use of power. However, Marcus' writings do not always provide the sound wisdom one may expect. He writes near the beginning of Meditations: 'And from my father I learned . . . to stop my love of young men.'[115]

He tells us elsewhere – with characteristic sobriety – 'I did not lay hands on Benedicta or Theodotus, but that afterwards when I did give way to sexual passions, I was cured of them'.[116] It seems improbable that Marcus Aurelius was admitting to being genuinely interested in men at any stage. Much more likely is the case that he was aware, having read the works of biographers like Suetonius, of the trope which connected men of power with gay sex and he was anxious to divorce himself and his image from that connection entirely. There are some, though, who believe Marcus Aurelius did have a gay phase.

In 1815, the scholarly world was set alight by the discovery of a series of truly earth-shattering letters penned by the young Marcus himself. A prodigious scholar of classics, Angelo Mai was working at the Ambrosian Library in Milan when he came across an ancient manuscript. Well trained and keen-eyed, Mai noticed that the manuscript had been written on twice – the original copy had been written over by a later user. This is a common practice in the medieval period, paper was scarce and expensive so monks would often repurpose older texts. Such manuscripts are known as palimpsests.

Mai set about using chemicals to remove the top layer and expose the bottom, chemicals which unfortunately damaged the manuscript permanently. Nonetheless, for a brief time, he was able to copy out the underlying text. It was a series of letters from a well-known Roman orator called Marcus Cornelius Fronto.[117] Fronto, historians had long known, had been Marcus Aurelius' personal tutor in his late teenage years.

Fronto was an African from Cirta, Numidia (now Constantine, Algeria), and came from a wealthy family. He came to Rome to make his fortune and succeeded in becoming an orator of the highest calibre. It was in 139 CE that he came to be employed by Marcus' adopted father (the emperor Titus). The letters uncovered by Mai were, to put it mildly, nothing short of explosive. In them, Marcus Aurelius details his deep affection and love for Fronto. He describes wanting to be always with Fronto and to take intimate baths with him (Letter 14). Was this Stoic philosopher who denounced his interest in men actually gay? Indeed, was this relationship reciprocated? Fronto writes:

> Oh, lucky me, entrusted to the gods by your lips! Do you think that any pain would know how to penetrate my body or mind in the face of such joy? . . . What have I done to make you love me so? What has this Fronto person of yours done that's so good you should hold him so dear?[118]

Academics express strong doubt that the two men were ever lovers, particularly because they waste most of their ink neurotically comparing various ailments and illness, perhaps indicting a deep fear of all manner of diseases (remember that since Aristotle, queerness had been regarded as a sickness).[119,120] It seems that Marcus and Fronto are discussing homosexuality among other conditions they regard as sicknesses and trying to cure themselves of each in turn. In Stoic thought, it was common to practise spiritual exercises designed to reduce temptations and open one to painful experiences.[121] Part of bringing these desires under your control was to experience them and then denounce them. In this sense, the letters may form a very typical part of the Roman custom of talking very openly about same-sex desires and its dangers as a means to avoid the horror of their corrosive effect on masculinity. But as with many of these queer or maybe-queer men, we can't know what went on behind closed doors.

Where Roman writing mentions the more permissive attitudes of early classical Greece, queer love was heavily associated with ridiculing the rich and powerful. A satirist called Lucian gives us a dialogue of two women talking:

> Clonarium: We've heard news about you, Leaena. The say Megilla from Lesbos – the wealthy one – loves you as if you were a man, that you live together. I've no idea what you get up to with each other. What is it? Why are you blushing? Tell me the truth whatever it is.

Leaena: The truth, Clonarium? I'm ashamed that it's not normal.
Clonarium: By the goddess, what is the deed? What does the woman want? What do you do, when you're together? Are you looking? Don't you love me, or you wouldn't hide such secrets from me?
... Clonarium: So tell me about it, Leaena, how did you proceed? What was tried first? How were you persuaded?
Leaena: She and another rich lady from Corinth, Demonissa, were throwing a drinking party. They had taken me to play music for them. When I had finished playing and it was late and time to sleep, they were drunk. Megilla said, 'Come on, Leaena, it's already a good time to go to bed, then you can sleep between us in the middle.'
Clonarium: You slept together? What happened after that?
Leaena: First, they kissed me like men. They did not just touch their lips to mine, they hugged me, they rubbed my breasts. Demonissa bit me as she kissed me. I didn't really have any idea what that meant! After some time, Megilla who was all hot and sweaty removed her wig from her head. She revealed the skin on her head like that of a shaved athlete's. 'Laeana,' she said, 'have you ever seen such a good-looking man?' 'I don't see one,' I said. 'Don't degrade me,' she replied, 'I am Megillos and I've been married to Demonissa for a long, long time.'[122]

It is so rare to hear about lesbians in the ancient world that this text has to be included. But, like those works discussing love between two men in Rome, it is a satire – written by a man famous for his novel about an adventurer fed up with earth who flew to the moon. His story about rich lesbians would have been seen as no less fantastical. It would have made the audience howl with laughter, and it placed these now excessive and bizarre sexualities in a location of extravagant wealth.

EIGHT

The First Christians

> '... men who have sex with men, thieves, greedy men, drunkards, slanderers, and swindlers will not inherit the kingdom of God'
>
> 1 COR. 6.9–10

In 1968 at Giv'at ha-Mivtar in Jerusalem, a body was found. Both his wrists were tied to a wooden cross. His legs were wrapped around the vertical beam, pinned in place with a long, iron nail that had shattered the heel of one foot. A soldier must have stood on the other side to hold his legs steady while the nail was hammered all the way through the beam and into his other foot. The cross would then have been hoisted into the air. The victim, his crime unknown, likely died struggling to breathe while his blood drenched the crucifix.

Was this how Jesus of Nazareth met his end? One of the few facts we know about this remarkable man is that he was crucified under the orders of Pontius Pilate. The Gospels are unanimous on this point, as are independent Roman sources.[1] How he was crucified, however, remains a mystery. Roman soldiers displayed a callous contempt for their enemies by hanging victims in all sorts of humiliating positions; sometimes they had all their limbs nailed down, other times they were tied in place.[2] Crucifixion was usually preceded by flogging so brutal it left the victim barely able to stand, he was then forced to carry his crossbeam (wood was expensive and the vertical pole would have been recycled from execution to execution) to the site of execution. The historical Jesus would have spent the final hours of his life broken, bloody and screaming.

In 71 BCE in Spain, Spartacus' slave revolt was put down and 6,000 slaves were crucified on the Appian Way, a road into Rome. The same punishment was meted out to Jewish rebels. Publius Quinctilius Varus had 2,000 Jews crucified in revenge for a revolt following the death of Herod the Great. Crucifixion was preserved for severe crimes against the state, as well as for the most egregious acts of arson and banditry. What crime could he possibly have committed that was so terrible that he deserved this of all ends? What were his politics which led him to be punished so cruelly under Roman-occupied Judea?[3]

The story of Jesus is mired in myth and legend. We are told that he was born in Bethlehem to a young woman called Mary.[4] In some of the Gospels, Mary is possibly described as a virgin,[5] but St Paul's Greek says that Jesus 'was born from the seed of David in flesh'.[6] It seems at least plausible that she had her son out of wedlock.[7] A long-held Roman tradition euphemistically claimed that bastard children who rose to any position of prominence had divine fathers. Romulus, the founder of Rome, was one such example: born to Rhea Silvia, his father was always said to be the Roman god Mars. Was Jesus one such illegitimate child, whose father was said to be God? It's a thought that would have been considered heretical for nearly two millennia.

Though Jesus' true origins remain mysterious, this does not give us a carte blanche to declare his whole life a complete fabrication. Many atheists and sceptics claim the mysterious early years of Jesus' life are evidence that we cannot take the Bible as a source. To give one example, the Gospels provide two different accounts of Jesus' ancestry – a discrepancy seized upon by Christopher Hitchens among others.[8] Apparently anticipating these blasphemous chancers, the early Church historian Eusebius of Caesarea (260–339 CE) explains that the difference in these genealogies can be traced to an ancient Jewish custom. In some traditions, fathers are listed by 'nature' (who actually fathered a son), and in others they are listed by 'law' (whose money the son inherits).[9]

Jesus was born likely in Bethlehem, where his father had returned with Mary (his betrothed) for a census. We are told this was the year of Quirinius' governorship of Syria, which places his birth close to 6 CE.[10] However, if it is true that Herod the Great ordered the death of all the babies out of paranoia that the Messiah was among them, then Jesus must have been born by 4 BCE (the date of Herod the Great's death). After his birth in Bethlehem, it is thought Jesus was raised in Nazareth.[11] This relatively humble beginning, shrouded in historical unknowns, begs the question: what was it about this illegitimate child that would one day ensure his status as the most famous man on earth? Why would the religion later founded in his name be used as the cudgel-in-chief against queer people for thousands of years to come?

A BRIEF HISTORY OF ROMAN-OCCUPIED JUDEA

A family of priests, the Hasmoneans, gained control of Judea centuries before Jesus' birth. Their arrival was celebrated by the Jewish people. For too long, they had suffered under the oppression of foreign powers. They had been exiled to Alexandria, or they lived captive under the Babylonians. But under the Hasmoneans, the people in Judea once again lived under a Jewish king. This was a time, at least we are told, of relative prosperity. The Hasmoneans resettled many Jews to Galilee, where they would continue to live until Jesus' time. Archaeological evidence implies Galilee was a place of some wealth,[12] but in the whole region, from the years 800 BCE to 200 CE, there was a steady increase in inequality.[13] Though the Hasmonean period would be looked back on as more peaceful than what was to come, it was probably not how it felt at the time. In 160 BCE, a terrible famine tore through Palestine, a pattern which would repeat until well after Jesus' time.[14]

Pompey the Great, once a friend and then a rival of Julius Caesar's, was a politician who was derided for being too soft since he spent far too much time with his wife at the expense of the republic.[15] Pompey brought the Hasmonean kingdom under Roman control and reduced the borders of Roman Judea to encompass only Judah, Jerusalem, Idumea, Galilee and the Jewish Perea. He also returned the Greek city-states on the coast to their own rule, away from the Hasmoneans who had squeezed them as provinces. Scholars are still not clear on what Judea's status was to the Romans in this period.[16] Was it a client-state, where Roman rulers had little say in day-to-day affairs but taxes were paid into the republic's coffers, or was it a province with a Roman ruler?

Shortly after Pompey's death, Herod the Great ascended to the Jewish throne. Although we've already heard the colourful story of his court of eunuchs, and the grim tale of his paranoid mass-murder of newborns, these accounts are shrouded in myth and hearsay. What is certain about Herod the Great's reign is that he expanded Judea's trade following the territorial incursions of Pompey's Rome. He built an artificial harbour at Caesarea Maritima, which became the largest harbour in the Mediterranean. Trade flowed into Palestine through this port, while pack animals carried goods from Asia through the Near East and into the Roman Empire via complex overland trade networks. But very little of this trade trickled down to the people, it was heavily concentrated at the top of society.[17] Scholars tend to hold one of two points of view on Herod's reign. From 40 BCE to 6 BCE, conditions under Herod the Great for the poor either worsened, or were already in a diabolic state of economic oppression by the time of Herod's accession.[18] Either way, the outlook for the 90 per cent of Palestinians who lived as peasants[19] was intolerable. Taxes were exorbitant, and rents were so high that tenants were forced into debt to pay them, and all the while there was lavish spending and building at the court.

While the majority could barely afford subsistence living, Herod the Great inherited vast estates in Jericho, Ein Gedi and the Jordan Valley. After Augustus defeated Mark Antony and Cleopatra at the Battle of Actium, he gifted further lands to Herod, including Gaza, Joppa, Strato's Tower, Samaria, Gadara and Hippus. As well as his own lands and inheritance, when he married his wife Miriam, Herod inherited further lands from her dowry.

The Palestine into which Jesus was born and where he grew up[20] was not only deeply unequal, but a hotbed of violence and disorder. Upon the death of Herod the Great, a vast crowd stormed the temple in Jerusalem. Their stated purpose was to lynch whoever had cut down a golden eagle positioned at the entrance to the Jewish temple. But this was not, at least according to ancient sources, their primary goal. The first signs of rebellion came from popular anger at tax rates.[21] Amid economic crisis and debt, a new king – one of Herod the Great's sons[22] – Archelaus reached for power. While Archelaus and his kin were at each other's throats vying for power, a series of violent uprisings took place in Jerusalem. Sabinus, a Roman appointee, took possession of Herod the Great's palace there and stole 400 talents of gold from the temple's treasury. Separately, 2,000 veterans of Herod the Great's army rebelled in Idumea. There were widespread attacks on property-holders by looters and rioters.[23]

Understandably, in 6 CE, Rome declared it had had enough. Archelaus was forced out, and a Roman governor installed over Judea. For the next 60 years, Rome had power over the region and exercised direct responsibility for it. In return for the stability they offered, the Romans expected taxation and a census was commissioned to ascertain how much wealth they could expect to bring in from the whole area. It is possible this is the census[24] mentioned in the Gospels which took Jesus' family back to Bethlehem.

The Roman governors and prefects who oversaw Judea in this time showed little interest in its fair governance. Appointed by Emperor Tiberius, Pontius Pilate took responsibility for the region and also took money to build an aqueduct – but given this money was already available from the Jewish temple, it seems probable this cash went only to line Pilate's own pockets. Pilate also showed disinterest in cultural sensitivity, merrily minting coins with Roman and pagan symbols on them for circulation among the outraged Jewish community.[25]

THE END OF THE WORLD

So turbulent were the 100-or-so years from Pompey's seizure of Judea to the death of Jesus of Nazareth that the very world seemed on the brink of collapse. In the heart of the empire, Rome was witnessing frequent acts of bloody political violence, precipitous wealth inequality and very high debt even among the aristocracy, as explored in the previous chapter. Even in Rome, the poet Virgil longed for a saviour to come, who would see an end to the poverty and the bloodshed.

> Now is the final age of the Sybil's (an ancient prophetess) song,
> A line emerges great in all of time,
> A Virgin comes afresh, with Saturn's kingdoms,[26]
> A new heir dispatched from high heaven falls.
> Give favour to the newborn son, by whom
> Iron's age shall end, and golden times will reign.[27]

Later Christians looked to this poem as proof that even non-Christians saw the coming of Christ. The promised child would be born to a virgin, and he would bring an end to the age of iron. 'Iron's age' hints not just a period in metallurgy but at a bellicose age of swords. In Hellenistic Alexandria, debt and inequality were closely associated with a longing glance over the shoulder, a nostalgia for a peaceful past. Rome and Judea were no different. Historically, Virgil and his contemporaries did not see a coming of Christ, but they did hope desperately for an end to the political and economic turmoil through which they lived. The symbols of this new age were peace, prosperity, gold and a virgin-born saviour. Sex had become so wrapped up in excess, so enmeshed with inequality and debt, that the symbolic ruler of this new era must be born of a virgin.[28] But while some dreamt wistfully of this new age, others fomented rebellion.

Village communities in Palestine likely had limited interaction with imperial forces. Their sole contact was when tax collectors came to take monies owed to the Jewish authorities or to the Roman imperial treasury. The locals had their own means of government. Men would organize in a *knesset*, or assembly. Here they met, either outdoors or in a suitable building, to pray, to read Torah or to organize politically. In modern translations of the New Testament, *knesset* is translated as 'synagogue'. When Jesus visits synagogues, this is what is meant.[29] The synagogue's job encompassed all aspects of village life; here disputes would be resolved and repairs to local infrastructure organized.

Banditry was commonplace. The Jewish historian Josephus tells us of one case where bandits destroyed the offices which held records of debt, a clear sign that these criminal acts were a response to hard-baked social inequalities.[30] The bandits were invariably dissatisfied peasants (the vast majority of the population of Palestine) and whenever there was a major revolt, there is evidence that peasants elected themselves a 'king' or Messiah who coordinated attacks from village to village.[31] In the mid-1st century CE, near Jesus' time, both Judean and Samaritan (a rival ethnic group) peasants formed movements headed by prophets. Not only did these brigands loot and pillage, Josephus tells us that discontented villagers also burned debt records in Jerusalem and Antioch.

A debt document survives from the reign of the emperor Nero (54–68 CE). Nero's reign was long enough after Jesus' crucifixion that he had begun the process of torturing and killing Christian missionaries in the capital. The document from Judea reports an unsecured loan of 20 zuzim (roughly 20 denarii) at a 20 per cent interest rate and, most tellingly, this document also talks of an agricultural sabbath, when there would have been no crop yield. This primary source gives us firsthand evidence of loans at very high rates of interest being commonplace in the period. In the Gospels, similar stories of usury emerge. Mt. 18.24–5 tells the story of a man who owed 10,000 talents which he could not pay. To make the payment, the man was forced to sell himself, his wife and his children into slavery, along with all his worldly possessions. Ten thousand talents is a vast and likely exaggerated sum of money, but between the Neronian document and the testimony of the Gospels,[32] a picture emerges of widespread debt.

Debt was so commonplace that it had become a metaphor for sin in both the Hebrew Bible and the New Testament. In Aramaic, Jesus' native language (though not the language in which the Bible was written), *hôbâ* means 'sin' and 'debt'. In the Lord's Prayer we have inherited from Luke's Gospel, still recited all over the world, the phrase 'forgive us our sins, as we forgive those who trespass against us' has a spiritual meaning of forgiveness of wrongs. In fact, the Greek words used (such as *opheilō*) mirror the language of debt.[33] The Lord's Prayer does exhort its followers to forgive others' transgressions, but it primarily asks them to forgive debts. This is in keeping with Old Testament tradition, which could not have been rigorously adhered to, that the good Jew forgives the debts of other Jews.[34]

Peasants were entirely dependent on the agricultural economy to survive and to pay their rent. Despite this, Palestine was agriculturally rich. They grew a wide variety of agricultural products. Millet, wheat, rice, barley, onions, leeks, garlic, cabbage, squash, beetroot, olives, figs, grapes, dates, lentils and beans were all staple crops. However, evidence suggests that these farmers rarely got to eat any of the products of their labour. Peasants survived off a humble diet of bread, salt, olives, olive oil and onions; if they were lucky, they might have enjoyed a bunch of grapes. Wealth and produce flowed directly to urban centres to be enjoyed by the richest in society.

Herod the Great placed taxes on products of agriculture, as these were almost exclusively the source of income in ancient Palestine. Unfortunately, the effect of taxation was to decimate the finances of the freehold land-owning peasantry. Unable to afford tax, they borrowed money and secured it against their properties. When they were unable to pay, they had to sell their properties. This cycle further concentrated the properties in the hands of the wealthy.

In 20 BCE, when a low agricultural yield made it impossible to ask peasants for any more money, Herod reduced taxation that year by a third. For those who dared rebel against his regime, he fought back with violence and forced the subdued to pay up. Following a revolt, the towns of Galilee were forced to pay a fine of 100 talents, roughly 10 per cent of Herod's annual income.[35] Herod wielded taxation as a punishment, and only begrudgingly relented when it was likely the taxation levels would become so insurmountable as to lead to open rebellion. In addition to Herod's taxes, peasants would have been expected to pay tithes to local Pharisees and religious leaders. We cannot know how much these figures were, but they are unlikely to have been trifling sums.

After Herod the Great's death, Rome imposed another direct taxation on top of taxes paid to Pharisees and the temple and debts owed by tenant farmers. We know little for certain about what taxes were imposed, but scholars believe there could have been six or more:[36] a tax on land produce which was likely 12.5 per cent or more; a tax on assets; a tax on houses; a tax on the sale of agriculture; a customs tax; and a tax on salt. In addition to these burdens, work security was precarious. Following the construction of the temple, 18,000 men were overnight put out of work. Peasants relied on good weather to secure crop yields, which they needed to pay their debts and their tenancies.

FAMINE

Beginning in 25 BCE and lasting through to 24 BCE in Herod the Great's reign, a famine struck Palestine. In this part of the world, and in a time without meteorological reports or reservoirs, drought was an uncontrollable fact of nature. Palestine was watered by western winter cyclones and when these failed to materialize, crops withered and an entire economy trembled to a halt. Usually though, when it struck, the Palestinians had recourse to go south. They could ask Egypt for grain. In these times, there was some reciprocity between the two states: when the Nile failed to yield crops, Egypt turned to Palestine for help. Pack animals laden with grain baskets trod wearily over dusty and winding roads to and from Egypt.

In the first year of the crisis, grain prices rose steeply. Herod the Great could not afford to reach out to Egypt for mass help. Farmers found themselves no longer able to feed their animals. Sheep and goats and possibly cattle were taken in from the fields and slaughtered. Their meat was sold in the stead of grain, as an intermediary way of feeding a population.[37] Meat prices plummeted. Josephus reports that the meat-laden diet of the Jews in these years of famine led to serious health conditions.[38]

Herod had to act. With the paltry amount of money in his coffers, he bought a wheat ship from Egypt.[39] He employed bakers all over Judea to make bread for the weak and feeble, and for the rest he doled out grain. Estimates of the quantity of grain handed out vary, but they often land somewhere between 35 million and 41 million litres.[40]

Famine repeated often in the following decades. It is hard to date, but there is a story of Queen Helena of Adiabene (in Mesopotamia) visiting Jerusalem on a pilgrimage. She found the city suffering dreadfully under famine: many were dying before her eyes from malnutrition. As part of her pilgrimage, Helena personally paid for a shipment of dried figs and grain from Alexandria in Egypt.[41] The story is thought to date from around the time of the emperor Claudius or Nero, which makes it roughly contemporary with Jesus' crucifixion.

In Jesus' time, the population was not just desperately poor, indebted, underfed, unemployed and burdened by an oppressive dual taxation system from Rome and the Jewish authorities. They were chronically sick too. Archaeological evidence tells us that 25 per cent of the population were unwell.[42] Serious eye conditions that caused blindness and torturous, chronic pain were endemic in Egypt. They spread through trade routes up into Canaan and Galilee. Roman doctors were at a loss to treat them effectively. The doctor Celsus, who mentions Jesus in his works, prescribes bloodletting and the consumption of wine as cures for ophthalmic disease.[43] Amid such desperation, there emerged a hunger for the miraculous.

The Christian writer Origen of Alexandria (185–253 CE) reports a fragment written by a Roman doctor called Celsus: 'It seems the Christians gain their strength from summoning certain demons.'[44] What Celsus means by 'demons' are magical spirits, less powerful than divine entities but more powerful than mortals. Celsus is accusing Jesus and his followers of something like witchcraft. Yet it cannot be denied that Jesus did achieve something. Why else would a pagan like Celsus seek to explain the causes of his miracles? There must have been hundreds if not thousands of reports circulating of miraculous cures. In fact, this is perfectly true and they were not all carried out by Jesus.

One such miracle-worker was Apollonius of Tyana. After Jesus' death, Apollonius travelled around the Greek world and found himself on the island of Crete. Ancient sources tell us that one day Apollonius stopped a passing bier. On it lay a dead girl's blue corpse. Apollonius raised the girl from the dead and she walked on home, presumably much to the delight of her distressed family.[45] There is also the story where Apollonius grouped the people of Ephesus into the theatre hollowed out in the rock, many suffering from plague. He found an old man in their midst and ordered they throw stones at him. Upon killing this old beggar, the people were miraculously cured.[46] Apollonius was also said to have risen from the dead himself. Historians, exercising scepticism, have suggested that pagans wrote these stories to compete with those circulating about Christ and his followers.[47]

Another Jewish miracle-worker named Honi ha-Ma'aggel was known as the 'circle-drawer' in the 1st century BCE. This was owing to his ability to draw circles in the ground and stand in them to make rain fall. Scholars have attributed these miraculous interventions to times of severe drought.[48] Another 1st-century CE prophet called Hanina ben Dosa lived in a small Galilean village some 10 miles to the north of Nazareth. He prayed for the sick and declared beforehand those who would live and those who would die. Those involved in organizing rebellions against Roman power were often called 'sign prophets' and thought capable of miracles.[49] There was a close intersection between rebellious figures, miracle-workers and those seeking to combat the terrible stressors in the daily lives of ordinary people.

A near contemporary of Jesus, Theudas, led a rebellion against Roman power. He also claimed to be a prophet and once commanded a river to part. Unfortunately, right before the miracle took place, the Roman procurator Fabius caught up with him. He and his cavalry dragged Theudas from the riverside and sliced his head off. Though Josephus calls Theudas a *goēs* (a fake prophet), he was still part of some rebellion against Roman injustices.[50]

THE POLITICS OF JESUS OF NAZARETH

Understandably, scholars have sought to place Jesus of Nazareth amid these other miracle-workers.[51] Whether he considered himself one, we cannot know; but the plethora of stories about miracles in his time point to a people desperate for magical relief from their suffering. Almost all that we know about Jesus comes from New Testament sources written decades after his death. The first account of Jesus' life comes from the Gospel of Mark, usually taken to have been written down somewhere between 60 and 80 CE.[52] The written Gospels may have been circulating in oral form for decades before that, passed between assemblies of Christ-followers, their stories changed and adapted to emerging philosophical and political needs. It is this gradual process of adaptation that makes them so relevant to such a vast array of different problems.

The later Gospels of Matthew and Luke are thought by some scholars to have been developed from a lost Gospel known as 'Q'. The authors of the Gospels we have inherited from the Bible cannot possibly have been the original disciples, indeed the first time in history anyone claimed their authorship to have been the disciples was Bishop Irenaeus of Lyons writing in around 190 CE.[53] Each Gospel has a different agenda, each was written at a slightly different time in a language different from that which Jesus spoke. Each responds to a different set of political and philosophical concerns.

But none of this should stop us from speculating what the politics of Jesus himself were.

Two debtors owe money to a lender. The first man owes 500 denarii, the second owes 50. Jesus asks his followers: 'which man will love him (the lender) more?'[54] Jesus' simple story speaks to a deep connection in his thinking between the forgiveness of sins and the forgiveness of debts. His own 'love' or *agapē* for mortals accompanies their forgiveness. In this sense, the tax collectors with whom Jesus dines and drinks are sinners: they have involved themselves in the pained process of extorting money and bringing about suffering in the community. His command to his followers was: 'love your enemies'.[55] The Greek word that he uses *agapaō* asks his followers to show compassion and awareness to those who may be suffering around them.[56] Jesus' mission of love was about understanding the motivations and empathizing with the suffering of others – he encouraged his followers to give money and to expect nothing in return.[57]

It seems hard to imagine that Jesus was not preaching to an indebted and poor population. The hatred many people felt towards lenders and tax collectors drove division in society. This was a man who called the hungry 'blessed',[58] who rebuked the Pharisees for not handing out bread to the needy on the Sabbath.[59] Even his miracles, such as filling the Lake of Gennesaret with fish, turning water into wine and feeding 5,000 people, provide plenty where there is poverty.

Jesus would have been strongly influenced by the disease and poverty and injustice which surrounded him, but it was also possibly that he had heard and was influenced by Cynic philosophy.[60] Diogenes the Cynic, who wandered around Athens farting, masturbating and encouraging others to give up their wealth, seems some way from the hallowed image of Jesus of Nazareth we have inherited, but Jesus' teachings are certainly consistent with the essential commitment to reject wealth and material riches. So too is Jesus' unwavering commitment to the unmarried life.[61]

Antipas was one of the sons of Herod the Great. He ruled as tetrarch (one of four native rulers over Judea) over Galilee and Perea in Jesus' lifetime. Antipas must have caused quite a scandal among Jewish natives when he divorced his first wife and took his brother's wife Herodias. This violated Mosaic law – the law based on Moses' teachings which was sacrosanct in the region – in no uncertain terms.[62] Lev. 18.16 ('Thou shalt not uncover the nakedness of thy brother's wife') would appear to ban marrying your brother's wife is not permissible. Jesus, perhaps motivated by popular hatred of Herod Antipas, took up a rigid anti-divorce line. In the Sermon on the Mount, Jesus says that divorce is only acceptable on grounds of marital infidelity.[63] He seems to go further in the older Gospel of Mark: 'therefore, what God has joined together, let man not separate,' he advises.[64] Not only does Jesus explicitly oppose one of the defining elements of Antipas' reign, he contrasts all those who live in 'kingly courts' and are 'dressed in soft clothing and live in luxury' with John the Baptist's ascetic ministry.[65]

Jesus' mentor[66] John the Baptist opposed Antipas' remarriage.[67] In fury, Antipas arrested John and had him beheaded in a dungeon of his fortress Machaerus in Perea.[68] Jesus claims that Antipas targeted him, believing him to be John's spirit resurrected from the dead.[69] There can be no doubt with such testimony that Jesus was seen as far more than a harmless miracle-worker – the Jewish authorities, and very likely the Romans to whom they reported, saw him as a troublemaker. It seems likely that Jesus' card was marked from an early period, which could explain why he spoke in riddles and parables, and why the Pharisees are so often shown in the New Testament trying to trick him. Even if Jesus himself did not foment violence, the authorities knew all too well the connection between a Messiah and his mob. Not only did he oppose the Pharisees and Jewish leaders' powers to collect taxes and tithes, but he was also accused at his trial of opposing taxation to the Roman powers.[70]

Jesus' call to 'love thy neighbour' and 'love thy enemies' was a radical politics aimed at healing a fractured society. Almost everything that could conceivably go wrong in an ancient society hit ancient Judea. Poverty, wealth inequality, debt, high taxes, sickness, unemployment and famine dogged its people. But Jesus' response to these cruelties was to encourage flexible thinking about Mosaic law. The categories imposed in Jewish law, which were attempts to order a terrifyingly unpredictable world, were called into question by Jesus.

Some archaic Greek city-states responded to wealth inequality and debt with debt cancellation and the manipulation of currency. Jesus did not have anything like the political power of Solon or the rulers of Megara. He could not pass laws, though it seems impossible to believe he did not try to pressurize those who had the authority to do so. But his response to the inequalities of his day was a far more significant contribution to the history of thought than that of Solon or the Megarians. He showed that divisions in society could be healed by loving compassion for your neighbour. He emphasized that even in desperate poverty, love could bind societies together. This was how he intended to build his kingdom of heaven here on Earth. He often ignored much of Mosaic law in doing so. One wonders what he might have thought, in the face of such poverty, of trifling rules like those in Lev. 18.22 which may have banned queer desire. What might he have thought of clearly defined gender boundaries, of the hard border between male and female, of all our roles in a patriarchal, domestic society? Throughout the centuries, and most particularly in the years following Jesus' death, many people asked this question.

WAS JESUS PRO-GAY?

Shortly after Jesus dismisses divorce as a sin, he addresses his own unmarried status. The challenge of reading the New Testament historically is to keep, as far as possible, words in context. For this reason, I've kept one word in the original Greek, as it needs elaboration and some explanation.

> The disciples say to him: if this is how a relationship of man with his wife is supposed to be, it is better not to marry. He said to them: not everyone adheres to this guideline,[71] but it has been given to them. There are *eunouchoi* who were made so from the moment of their birth, and there are *eunouchoi* who

were turned so by men, and there are those *eunouchoi* who do it to themselves for the kingdom of heaven.[72]

There has been a flurry of excitement around this passage, particularly in online queer Christian communities. Maybe the Gospel of Matthew makes an exemption for those who don't feel they want a relationship with a woman? Before we arrive at too hasty a conclusion, we have to ask who the *eunouchoi* are.

The earliest uses of 'eunouchoi' in Greek come from the archaic poet Hipponax, where it is a term of insult for one who lives a lavish and unrestrained life.[73] In the 5th century BCE, the Greek historian Herodotus used it to mean castrated oriental slaves; they were symbols to Herodotus of the luxury of the Persian court – of how other civilizations were prepared to sacrifice their masculinity for their rulers.[74] In Greek descriptions of ancient Persia and Babylon, the *eunouchos* (singular of 'eunouchoi') is often portrayed as devoted to a goddess making them chaste and virginal.[75] But recent research has shown the eunouchos to be far more than a chaste virgin. Rather, *eunouchoi* were frequently sexually active, as indeed in the story we heard before about Herod the Great and his *eunouchoi*.[76] Despite their sexual profligacy, they were trusted with the most delicate aspects of court life because they could not have penetrative sex with women. It seems impossible to deny that *eunouchos* was often used as a term which described queer identities. It is possible that Jesus is referencing something like the ancient Babylonian tradition of eunuchs in temples who had queer sex and belonged properly to neither gender.[77]

It is far from certain that Jesus is condoning queer lifestyles. But in the spirit of honest readings of ancient texts, we have to make a further admission: had the writers of the Gospels and Jesus himself wanted to give the impression they were staunchly opposed to queer identities, this is a very difficult passage to explain. The position of the Catholic Church is unequivocally that Jesus has called his followers to a life of celibacy, but this is far from a secure interpretation of the Greek. In the study of ancient languages, the job of scholars is to set up the parameters of what could be an acceptable reading rather than to pronounce on matters of exactness. The *eunouchos* is someone who could be sexually active, but was also devoted either to a court or to the worship of a god. The Catholic Church's position on the matter is a plausible reading, but so is the queer reading.

Some have even argued, though it's not especially convincing, that Jesus may have been gay himself. Christopher Marlowe, a contemporary of William Shakespeare, was a playwright renowned for his tragic tale of the demise of Edward II who fell in love with Piers Gaveston and invoked the jealousy of the whole court. Well after he'd penned *Edward II*, Marlowe was caught in a brawl outside a tavern where he was attacked and killed. At the inquest into the playwright's death, the spy Richard Baines said Marlowe believed that 'St. John the Evangelist was bedfellow to Christ and learned always in his bosome, that he used him as the sinners of Sodoma'.[78] The idea that John the Baptist was having sex with Jesus is not a new one. In fact, it seems that a sect of early Christians, those living in the immediate aftermath of Christ's life, believed it too.

In the last century, a manuscript appeared that claimed to contain evidence of this sect and the Secret Gospel of Mark that they followed. In the library of an Orthodox monastery at Mar Saba in Jerusalem, a Biblical scholar by the name of Morton Smith pored over a letter that had been copied out on the back of a manuscript. The letter was from Bishop Clement of Alexandria (~150–215 CE). In it, Clement warns of the heresies of a group of Christians called the Carpocratians. Clement tells us that the Carpocratians had their own text of the Gospel of Mark and transcribes a section of it for us. In it, Jesus raises a young man from the dead and falls in love with him. They then lie together all night long 'naked'. Clement rages against the Carpocratians as examples of heretics who 'stray from the narrow road of the commandment into a boundless abyss of carnal sins of the flesh',[79] and writes that true Christians are to be prevented from hearing about this Secret Gospel of Mark. He urges followers to lie even under oath about its existence.

Much later, the Carpocratians appear again in a dictionary of heresies compiled by John of Damascus. He writes, 'Carpocratians: those who [follow] a certain Carpocrates in Asia. This man taught that every shame must be achieved and every practice of evil'.[80] Coincidentally, John died in the year 676 CE at the very same monastery where Clement of Alexandria's letter was found in Mar Saba. Had John seen the letter from Clement which lay in that library? Did he know more of the practices the Carpocratians were said to sanction?

Unfortunately, it is impossible to re-examine the letter from Clement. After Morton Smith published his findings, the Archimandrite of the Jerusalem Greek Patriarchate who had jurisdiction over Mar Saba barred access to the manuscript, locking it away securely in a patriarchal library.[81] Smith did take photographs which are published in his book, but it is very hard to examine the text itself. The Greek does not look unconvincing, so most of the arguments against Smith's text rely on the fact that it appeared so briefly and does not fit with the rest of Jesus' narratives. But no one could suppose that the disparate early Christian sects, who all disagreed with one another on the interpretation of Jesus' life, were consistent.

ST PAUL AND GAY SEX

Eusebius reports that Jesus had as many as 70 devoted disciples in his lifetime. After the crucifixion, they spread out all over the Mediterranean, reaching Greece, Rome and Alexandria, as well as continuing their activism in Jerusalem. We do not know what they would have called themselves, but probably not yet Christians.[82] They were likely simply Jesus-followers, who – much like Virgil – were convinced of the coming of another saviour and a violent end to the present world order. When this end-of-the-world failed to materialize, Christians eventually reset the date to the year 1000 CE,[83] and when this failed to materialize, Armageddon's date-setting fell somewhat out of fashion.[84]

Most of the early Jesus-followers were exceptionally poor. Though some, including those in the Greek city Corinth which was famed for its sexual licentiousness, came from the middle economic bands.[85] Such people found themselves just above subsistence, and likely relied on a close network of other Jesus-followers to survive, which explains their tendency to dine together and share resources. Moreover, a small number of them, especially encouraged by St Paul, were very wealthy.[86]

Then named Saul, the future St Paul grew up in the city of Tarsus in modern-day Turkey. This city was steeped in Hellenistic culture. He came into close contact with the best minds of his day and was exposed to ancient Greek philosophies from an early age. It was here, presumably, that Saul learned – possibly to his great embarrassment – that when pronounced in Greek his Hebrew name sounded rather too like the word *saulos* (meaning 'camp', 'excessive' or 'effeminate').[87] He changed his name to Paul, preferring a name that sounded like the Latin word for 'small' or 'few' (*paulus*), connoting his moderation and restraint. His education included learning Greek, the language in which he would later compose all his letters and books. He was also taught rhetoric, mathematics, geography and category theory from texts by Plato and Aristotle. The other component of Paul's education was his deep immersion in Jewish law. One imagines that to a young Paul there was a close intersection between the Jewish law which divided the world into holy and unholy categories, and Greek thinking which also sought to compartmentalize the world. He almost certainly read Philo and thought extensively about his Stoicism and his Judaism. Unlike Jesus, Paul was educated in a critical discipline. When he first heard of Jesus-followers he was, to put it mildly, sceptical.

The Book of Acts in the Bible claims intimate knowledge of Paul's life. It tells how Paul was personally involved in the capture and murder of St Stephen.[88] Stephen was attacked by Jews and stoned to death as a Jesus-follower. Elsewhere in Acts, Paul is said to have dragged away men and women and prosecuted them without trial.[89] Scholars are less convinced that any of this took really took place. In the Roman Empire, only Roman authorities had the power to put people to death and the idea that Paul had much personal say in trial and execution is thought implausible.[90] For the purposes of narrative, though, Paul's sinful past makes for a powerful precursor to his transformation into a preacher of Jesus' message of love.

On the road to Damascus, Paul experienced a blinding white light, which rendered him sightless for three days. In that moment, he heard Jesus' voice asking, 'Saul! Saul! Why are you persecuting me?'[91] The story of blindness and white light is a common feature of many conversions in religions all over the world, and following his calling Paul also found himself usefully possessed of magical powers. Displaying exemplary Christian charity, he struck a false Jewish prophet named Elymas blind in Paphos on the island of Cyprus.[92] He also showed off his power to heal the sick, healing a man crippled from birth[93] and a man with dysentery.[94]

Once Paul had made up his mind to spread the word of Jesus' return, he began to write letters to followers all over the empire. He also embarked on missions around the contours of that world. His letters, preserved in the Bible, show a gradual refinement of his theology.[95]

Helping the weak and vulnerable was a core part of Paul's message, and he believed it would strengthen every follower's case before God. He did, however, ask for contributions from all followers, even the less well-off. In 1 Corinthians, Paul asks followers to put aside on the first day of each week any extra money that has been earned for him to collect.[96] Scholars have interpreted this as an attempt to ensure the new Jesus-follower movement was not too heavily influenced by the will of super-rich donors.[97] Occasionally, this went too far. In 2 Corinthians, Paul describes how the followers in Macedon gave beyond their means, though they are said to be joyful in doing so, finding abundance in a place of scarcity.[98] The Roman authorities would have been deeply confused by such in-group generosity. Romans did not share the same ideas of society and charity, having inherited the model from ancient Greece of an atomized, family-centred society. The message Paul preached was one of community work, each man and woman bringing what skills they could to the group.⁹⁹ In Paul's mind, this would bring about a communal cohesiveness;¹⁰⁰ to use a modern metaphor, Paul sought to glue back together a fragmented society. But despite Paul's focus on community, he is infamous for his letters condemning queer love.

St Paul could not be described as a romantic.¹⁰¹ Like many men of letters of his day, he was steeped in Stoic and Platonic teaching,¹⁰² and was implacably opposed to nearly all sex. Since he believed the end of times and the kingdom of heaven were at hand, one might have thought that simple concerns about whom one shared a bed with were beyond his immediate frame of interest. But in 1 Thessalonians, he makes his position on all matters of sex clear: '[You must] hold yourselves from sexual immorality, every one of you [must] know [how to] control your own body in accordance with holiness and honour.'¹⁰³

The Greek word for 'control' does not use any of the ancient Greek terms for bodily control previously discussed. It speaks of gaining possession of the body, taking ownership over it, using the language of material possession to do so.¹⁰⁴ It's a word more commonly used for getting one's hands on gold, money or clothes. His philosophy becomes one of turning inwards to the self and the body, not outwards to material possessions.¹⁰⁵

His stance on sex and the dangers it poses to his community informed a view (perhaps anticipated in the teaching of Jesus) that even marriage was dangerous. It was better, Paul said, to be completely celibate.¹⁰⁶ There was an exception to this rule, which Paul laid out: 'If they do not exercise self-control, let them marry, for it is better to marry than to burn.'¹⁰⁷

Evangelicals get very excited about this line, because they imagine Paul is saying that those who cannot control their impulses should marry, or they will burn in hell. But scholars do not usually think Paul is talking about hell here; for one thing, Paul isn't talking about the afterlife, he is talking about the present. The language in the Greek seems much closer to Plato's thinking about desire as a form of fire that eats up the soul.¹⁰⁸ Nonetheless, Paul sees all forms of sexuality as burdens not blessings; he sees celibacy as safety – relief from torment. Like in Plato's work, sexual self-continence is praised.

In a departure from the Jesus we see in the Gospels, whose focus was more on love than self-control, St Paul sees self-continence as a prerequisite to purity. Unlike Jesus, Paul was not trying to appeal to a small group of divided peasants in Judea. He sought to appeal to non-Jews all across the empire, and sought to convert whole Greek and Roman communities to his new message. Rome already saw sexual inhibition as a virtue. That Paul's adherents were largely of a poor background and needed to practise financial self-restraint only underscores the need for a self-control politics to feature heavily in his theology. The survival and promulgation of the Jesus-follower group depended upon it.

God is angry, St Paul claimed. For too long, all across the empire, his people had devoted themselves to the worship of false gods and idols, even animals such as birds and snakes.[109] To Paul, this was a perversion of the natural order. In the natural order, God sat on high and men sat beneath him and animals beneath them. For men to worship animals was a violation of nature. In vengeance, God contrived a subtle punishment: 'Their women exchanged use [of sex] which conforms to nature with a use [of sex] which runs contrary to nature. Likewise, the men gave up their natural use of womankind and were burned in each other's embrace.'[110]

As a sign of his displeasure at the perversion of his perfect world, God invented gay sex, so Paul says. Such a view is owed in part to Mosaic law, and in part to the Greek philosophers that had long thought the world glimmered with a perfect, secret order, one which mankind had corrupted and was in constant need of rediscovery. Gay sex had become, thanks to the work of generations of Greek and Roman philosophers, a sign of disordered nature. For Paul, these earthly sins contaminated the kingdom of heaven.[111] He even went so far as to blame all forms of passion and disordered emotions for the murder of Jesus.[112]

Paul uses rare Greek vocabulary to condemn gay sex. In 1 Corinthians, he condemns *arsenokoitai* and *malakoi* as unable to enter the kingdom of heaven. Both terms have been translated as 'homosexuals' at different points, not – I think – incorrectly.

> Don't you know that the unrighteous will not inherit[113] the kingdom of God? Do not be misled, the sexually immoral, idolaters, adulterers, *malakoi* (soft men), *arsenokoitai* (men who have sex with men), thieves, greedy men, drunkards, slanderers, and swindlers will not inherit the kingdom of God.[114]

All the figures who do not enter the kingdom of God either profit too much from the material world which has brought about so much economic misery, or they have disordered emotions (they are drunkards), or they have – in Paul's view – disordered sexual lives.

In recent years, a focus has renewed on the use of the word 'homosexual' in the Bible to translate 'arsenokoitai'. Some have claimed this is an anachronism: they argue that 'homosexuality' is a modern category that did not exist in the ancient world. But, pragmatically, there would have been those who exclusively felt attracted to members of their own sex. So, of course homosexuality existed in the ancient world, even if the trappings of modern LGBTQ+ categories did not – and 1 Corinthians appears to oppose it. I understand, from personal experience, the very real desire on the part of those who have suffered at the hands of Christian communities to prove that these words do not really censure their loves and their lives – but there are other ways of arguing that the New Testament does not condemn queer sex.

'Arsenokoitai' likely does mean something like 'people who have sex with men', since it was in use for legal contracts in the 1st century BCE to ban wet nurses from having sex with men.[115] Here Paul deploys the term in the masculine, which almost certainly means 'men who have sex with men' making the translation 'homosexual' perfectly legitimate. In fact, it may have had a derogative connotation to it too. A similar term, *metrokoites*, had been in use for hundreds of years and meant 'mother-fucker'.[116] 'Arsenokoites' here means a 'man-fucker' and must mean a homosexual, especially as it is paired with 'malakoi', which seems a direct translation of the Latin term 'molles' (literally 'soft men' who enjoyed passive sex with other men).

DID PAUL REALLY SAY IT?

Scholars are seldom convinced that Paul has been misunderstood in his condemnation of homosexuality. But there is a growing group of scholars with a new explanation about why Paul writes it. It's a theory that depends on how ancient texts have been passed down to us, from manuscript to manuscript copied down by monks and scholars over thousands of years. The dialogues of Plato, for instance, appear very straightforward when printed in translation. They read like lines from a play. Take this excerpt from the beginning of Plato's *Gorgias* as an example, and pay close attention to who is speaking:

> Gorgias: So whenever there's an election of the types of people you were talking about, Socrates, it's always those trained in rhetoric who get motions passed.
> Socrates: This is what amazes me, Gorgias, so I ask again what is the power of rhetoric?[117]

Nothing could be simpler than identifying who is speaking to whom. But in the original manuscripts in the ancient world that was not so. The text was written in continuous writing. Had we translated the text as it really was transmitted, it would look something more like this:

> Sowhenevertheresanelectionofthetypesofpeopleyouweretalkingabout Socratesitsalwaysthosetrainedinrhetoricwhogetmotionspassed This is what amazes me Gorgias sold ask again what is the powerofrhetoric

Not only are all punctuation remarks removed, but so are the names of the speakers. For the most part it's fairly easy to tell who is talking to whom, but not always. Paul, schooled in reading manuscripts of this sort, likely also wrote in this style in his letters. There is an emerging school of thought that argues Paul was not writing one continuous letter to his followers full of advice. Rather, he was writing a back-and-forth conversation either with himself or with an interlocutor, and possibly even a dialogue – which was the most common way, established by Plato and Xenophon, for Greek writers to discuss their ideas.[118,119] We would not be able to tell from the manuscript whether it was intentionally a dialogue or not, since the speakers' characters are not usually identified. So, it could be argued that some of the more fiery attacks against queer people were voiced by other characters in the dialogue who were meant to be Paul's opponents (of course, it could also be that the less homophobic voices are in fact Paul's opponents, we don't know). But Paul arguing with homophobes, rather than being homophobic himself, would be more logically consistent with Jesus' position on (and lack of vitriol towards) queer identities.

A sudden volte-face does seem to occur in Paul's view of homosexuals in a single letter. Directly after his firebrand call for homosexuals not to enter the kingdom of God, Paul writes: 'and some of you were like this, but you were cleansed, but you were made holy, but you were made righteous in the name of the Lord Jesus Christ and in the spirit of our God'.[120] Paul seems to argue against his previous position that homosexuals will never enter the kingdom of God, refuting himself. Is he unclear about his position? Or could this be a dialogue between one anti-queer speaker, who argues homosexuals, drunkards, cheaters and thieves will not enter the kingdom of God, and another speaker – perhaps Paul – who says they will? It's another possible reading, which is far from conventional but perhaps all the more interesting for it.

Legend has it that Paul met his death, like Jesus, at the hands of the Roman authorities. We are told that he was executed on the orders of the emperor Nero himself. When the executioner cut off Paul's head, milk and not blood was said to flow from his severed neck. In another legend, Nero is surprised when strolling in his garden the morning after the execution, he comes across an apparition of Paul, back from the dead. The angry apostle, face to face with his murderer, promises Nero great punishment for his crimes. Stories like these were whispered among believers and spread to embolden Christian revolutionaries all across the Roman Empire.

Following Paul's death, Christianity began its steep climb to become one of the world's dominant religions for the next 2,000 years. Some scholars believe that its community-focused, charity-oriented organization helped Christians to convert the poor and the sick in times of plague. Those who recovered from sickness inevitably attributed their survival to Christianity and began to recruit more followers.[121] However Christianity succeeded in becoming the official religion of much of Europe, its unique blend of Mosaic law and ancient Graeco-Roman philosophy only intensified homophobia in the West – even though Jesus never said a word against same-sex desire.

NINE

The Birth of Modern Homophobia

> In the whole world I believe there are no two sins more abominable than those that prevail among the Florentines
>
> POPE GREGORY XI

> A prospect of resting near Dennie for life would be very agreeable. Agreeable? It would be heavenly.
>
> A LETTER FROM ROGER VOSE TO HIS LOVER JOSEPH DENNIE IN 1790

Following the establishment of the Christian Church, queerphobia did not see a straightforward rise. Instead, as ancient history would suggest, it correlated very closely with changing social and economic conditions.

For hundreds of years before Christianity, we hear rumours of the 'Mysteries'. They begin with Demeter the goddess of agriculture and the harvest, and with Dionysus the god of wine and fertility and growth. We can't reconstruct the Mysteries practised by the ancient Greeks, but we have ideas about their general character. There are snippets about women's ritual deaths and rumours about *sparagmos*: the ritual tearing apart of live animals. These close-knit communities of secret members preserved a sense of community until, unsurprisingly, the Romans sought to eradicate them. In 186 BCE, members of the cult of Dionysus were arrested and its participants executed for many offences, including gay sex.[1]

The hyper-patriarchal culture of ancient Rome could not tolerate whatever it was that the Mysteries entailed.

The very early Jesus-followers may have seemed like members of a new set of Mysteries to the Roman authorities. The image of the early Church we are familiar with today is one of small, interdependent communities redistributing wealth and food and clothing to the sick and the needy – but very early on, the Church combined with Mystic-like practices to form sects. These sects would, centuries later, come to be known as the Gnostics and regarded as heretical. The Gnostics had very different views from those of the later Church. Some were reportedly known for welcoming women and having women leaders; the Carpocratians were no exception, they were said to have had a woman leader at one stage called Marcellina.[2]

Each group of Gnostics had their own versions of the Gospels. This has led to widely circulating and differing accounts of Jesus' life. Some Gnostics were less tolerant of women, as is shown in the Gospel of Thomas (which was excluded from the New Testament), which ends with Jesus explaining that Mary Magdalene can only enter the kingdom of heaven once he has transformed her into a man.[3]

Other Gnostics had non-marital sex – in fact, many made the choice not to marry, but to conduct sexually liberated relationships instead. There is not much direct evidence of same-sex relationships, but the existence of the Secret Gospel of Mark may suggest that some Gnostic groups celebrated queer love. It is always hard to know for certain because other early members of the Church made up scandalous stories about the Gnostics. One such writer, Epiphanius (310–403 CE), describes a Gnostic sect of which he had purportedly been a member. He tells us that during the Eucharist, men masturbated until they could pool their semen in their hands, then shared it around as a substitute for the body of Christ. Epiphanius tells us that the women of the community likewise collected their menstrual blood as a proxy for Communion wine.[4]

Despite the Gnostics' dizzying array of differing ideas and practices, it is possible to group them into two categories. The first category could be called the 'libertines'. They had a very egalitarian relationship between lay people and the clergy, often failing to distinguish between them; the libertines also enjoyed freer sex lives. On the other hand, the 'ascetics' held fast to Stoic-like teaching that self-control and abstinence from bodily pleasures were the means to spiritual salvation. Perhaps one of the most famous of the early ascetics was St Augustine.

LUST FOR LIFE

Today, the edifices that make up Souk Ahras in Algeria are coloured like autumn leaves. Mosques appear here and there. A little over one and a half millennia ago, in this municipality in Algeria, one of the most important figures in all of Christian history was born – a man who arguably did quite as much as Jesus or St Paul to shape the direction of attitudes to sex for the whole of the West.

Augustine was born in Thagaste in the year 354 CE. At the time of his birth, Thagaste was in trouble. Once a prosperous town, affluent off the proceeds of trade, its many building schemes had ground to a halt. There was no money for new public monuments and the old ones had been left to crumble; makeshift shanty towns popped up in and around the town. This was not a situation unique to Thagaste. The whole Roman Empire in the 4th century CE was continually at war. Taxation had doubled and possibly trebled. Meanwhile, the rich few – who had amassed stockpiles of wealth – continued to buy up more and more property. The emperor was even said to have written his edicts in gold on purple parchment.[5]

Against this deeply unequal, poverty-stricken backdrop, Augustine began his education. He was a very gifted student, accomplished in rhetoric, conversant with Plato's theories and deeply immersed in the words of Cicero and Virgil. As is traditional in the education of students of classics, Augustine was painstakingly taken through these works word by word, learning to pause, examine, analyse and criticize at microscopic levels of textual detail. It was this rigorous education that gave him extraordinary powers of memory and intellectual agility. His parents knew the importance of this education to their son's prospects; his father

Patricius was poor and yet saved to finance his son's education first in nearby Madaura and then Carthage. When he was 16, he had to wait to be sent on another educational expedition, because his father was low on funds. He describes this period of waiting and forced relaxation as one in which 'the brambles of sexual desires advanced over my head.'[6]

Despite his extraordinarily privileged education, Augustine had one great failing. He found ancient Greek boring. Throughout his whole life, Augustine never properly learned Greek, an astonishing fact given it is the original language of the New Testament, as well as the original language of the philosophies of Plato and Aristotle which greatly inspired him.[7]

Augustine had a complex but loving relationship with his mother Monica. She was a devout Christian and was said to love him very deeply, so much in fact that when Augustine decided his studies must take him to Rome, he was too ashamed to tell her that he was going. He stole away in the dead of night rather than face her tears.

Some time after he had left home, Augustine enjoyed a long love affair with a concubine, whose name is lost to history. He never married her but lived in sin (to use the modern Christian phrase), and they had a lot of sex. They even had a child together.[8] But it seems Augustine, in a fit of Christian propriety, abandoned her and possibly his child to live a life closer to God.[9]

The fact that Augustine had, unlike other fervent early Christians, experienced a life of sex and sin inspired him to write about the temptations of desire. Augustine writes in his *City of God* that the problem of lust is it defies free will. He reasons that he can move his hand and all his limbs at his will, but his penis moves according to its own will, according to lust.[10] In Augustine's view, only sex for procreation is an exercise of free will. Sex for any other purpose at all, whether to bond with others or simply for pleasure, was to succumb to desire.

Some Christian thinkers in Augustine's time maintained that in the Garden of Eden, Adam had maintained complete control over his penis. Spontaneous erections would never take place in paradise,[11] Adam could never become aroused unless it was entirely of his volition. This 'perfect' world was shattered when Adam and Eve ate the forbidden fruit, and carnal knowledge penetrated humanity. Thereafter, man lost power over the penis and it began to rule him.[12] With Augustine's writings, sexual self-restraint became even more embedded in Western theology at a time when the society and economy of the ancient Roman Empire were disintegrating.

A SAFE HAVEN IN BYZANTIUM

Given the political crises and crumbling wealth of the Roman Empire, we would expect to see, in the centuries following the fall of Rome, even more hatred of queer people. To the east of Rome lay the Greek-speaking city of Byzantium (modern-day Istanbul). In 410 CE, for the first time in 800 years, Rome was sacked and invaded by a people called the Visigoths. Then, less than 50 years later, it was sacked again, this time by the Vandals from eastern Europe. Rome lost its authority as the cultural and economic capital of the world and Byzantium took up the mantle.

In the 4th century CE, Byzantium oversaw a significant change in how it coined money, one which resulted in significant impoverishment. The city increased coin production and forced through a change from gold to silver coinage.[13] This was a means of debasing the currency which would have had an inflationary effect, decreasing wealth for the agrarian populations and increasing it for the city-dwelling merchants.[14]

In 342 CE, during this period of financial upheaval, the Byzantine emperors Constantius II and Constans I argued passionately that bottoming should be punishable by law. In 390 CE, Emperor Theodosios I took this a step further: all passive homosexuals who worked in brothels were to be burned alive at the stake. By 438 CE, the death penalty was extended to all bottoms regardless of where they had sex or whether they were paid for it.[15]

With the arrival of the Great Plague in 550 CE, which wiped out a third of the population, the economy took a sudden downturn, a crisis from which it took centuries to recover.[16] And whom did the emperor at the time – Justinian I – blame for all of these events?

> We know from the study of Holy Scripture that God visited His anger upon the previous inhabitants of the City of Sodom to punish these sorts of people, and consumed it with fire. This is how he teaches us that we should hate this behaviour, it is contrary to the laws of nature.[17]

Justinian I's invocation of the story of Sodom is one of the first times in history that it was used to justify the persecution of homosexuality. Homosexuality was already punishable with burning and Justinian weaponized the fear and hatred of queer people even further to explain the calamities Byzantium suffered.

But one of the complications in the history of homosexuality is the Byzantine Church, because despite the extreme homophobia of the state, there is evidence that within religious communities, same-sex desire flourished. At times, of course, the Church was a difficult place to be queer. Shenoute of Atripe, a 5th-century CE superior of the White Monastery in Egypt, chastized his monks for sexual impropriety and reprimanded 'those who sleep with men'.[18] But that said, it also seems that monasteries and nunneries could be a convenient refuge for some queer people who did not wish to marry.

Within the Church, we get tantalizing hints of queer lives lived well. And not just on the fringes, but weaved through the religious imagery that surrounded them. Explicitly homoerotic stories were exchanged about the moment when Thomas the Disciple felt Jesus' wounds – sliding his fingers in and out of them and massaging them.[19] Symeon the New Theologian wrote fervently of his dream that Jesus Christ would come to him and penetrate him in his sleep.[20] But monks fantasizing over Jesus' holy wounds and theologians imagining bottoming for the son of God were not the only expressions of queer life within the cloister confines.

For two men who were deeply close, usually within the Church, it was possible to form a spiritual union. They would step in front of a small table on which the Gospel was laid out and place their hands upon it, one man's hand on top of the other. A priest would then pray that the two men be granted oneness of mind, peace and love for one another. They would then embrace and thenceforth could call themselves 'brothers'. The ceremony is known as *adelphopoiesis* or 'brother-making'. This ceremony did not act as a full marriage: it did not confer inheritance rights, it did not exclude a man from marrying somebody else, but it did formalize a loving relationship.[21]

There can be little doubt that many queer men would have taken this opportunity to formalize their bond. But it would be wrong to suggest *adelphopoiesis* was exclusively for men who were romantically involved with one another. There must have been many straight men who formed great friendships and wished for whatever reason to cement their relationship.[22] The Church – unintentionally – provided a shadowy, mercurial cover for queer men to enjoy some form of sanctioned recognition.

Often, historians of the period have looked for consistency in Byzantium's approach to queer people, arguing that it was a relatively tolerant time for gay men at least.[23] Other scholars have refuted this (because of all the burnings). The truth is more nuanced. Byzantium's secular world subjected people to all sorts of sexual controls, but the Church – perhaps turning a blind eye – offered more cover for monks and nuns to carry out a discreetly queer life.

The period also shows some evidence of lesbians. The dictionary writer Hesychius preserves the little-used word *dietaristriai* (literally: 'rubbing women'), which he defines as 'women who turn to their female companions in sex, in the manner that men do'. The precision of this vocabulary, as in classical Greece, contradicts the claim that the first time queer lives were explicitly labelled was when the term 'homosexuality' was invented in the 1800s.

TRANS MONKS

Marinos was raised by his father after his mother died.[24] He had been born female, but his later actions in life tell us how he wished to be identified. One day when Marinos was still young, his father decided to join a monastery. Rather than marrying and starting his own family, Marinos asked to have his hair shorn so he could accompany his father and live as a monk.

By now, the ritual of asceticism was a widespread practice in Christianity. Ascetics were thought to be close to God – able to refrain from eating and sex, they starved their bodies to attain spiritual enlightenment. Legends tell us that Marinos ate only one meal every other day. This starvation would not only have brought him closer to God, but by depriving his body of crucial nutrients, Marinos' body fat would have been critically low, allowing him to pass more easily as a man.

Passing by an inn near the monastery one day, Marinos caught the eye of an innkeeper's daughter. He was later accused of raping her and of fathering the child she bore as a result. Marinos – unable to explain that he was physically incapable of having impregnated the innkeeper's daughter – could not protest and the monastery expelled him for three years. He died not long after his return, finally at peace in the place he had come to call home.

In the ceremonial washing of his corpse, the monks stripped Marinos' garb and sponged down his naked body. To their shock, they found not a penis, but a vagina. Marinos had fooled them for years, living out the life he wanted for himself in the gender he chose. He was far from alone; another monk called Anastasius begged on his deathbed that he be dressed in his monk's clothing so it would not be discovered that he had female genitalia. The text which recounts this explicitly describes his breasts as 'dried up from much fasting'.[25]

Byzantium was not the only place where the Church offered some slight refuge. Under the Carolingian Empire, which ruled much of western Europe in the 9th century, same-sex love letters were written within Church walls.[26] But outside these relatively closed religious communities, homosexuals were again blamed for the plague and for starvation.[27] In England and Scotland, the monk Aelred of Rievaulx is often cited as another example of queer tolerance.[28] The sources relate how at the court of David II of Scotland, Aelred had 'occasionally deflowered his chastity' with men.[29] Aelred was even said to have had two boyfriends, Hugh and Simon – Simon he described as a 'remarkably handsome' young lad.[30] But we must be guarded in imagining monasteries and nunneries as havens of queer abandon. There were many in the Church who were deeply intolerant of same-sex desire. The testimony of St Thomas Aquinas, a Dominican monk, who described 'the sodomitic vice' as unnatural, chimes with that of many other Church figures.[31] As we saw in Rome, no society is entirely tolerant or entirely homophobic.

THE FLORENTINE SIN

Following the Black Death in Europe of 1348–9, the Italian city-state of Florence did not collapse as Byzantium almost had after the Great Plague. Instead, the working classes gained significant bargaining power, as there were fewer people to do all the work. The result was a decrease in wealth inequality in the space of a few years.[32]

Only 30 years after the Black Death, Pope Gregory XI commented that 'in the whole world I believe there are no two sins more abominable than those that prevail among the Florentines', by which he meant fiscal excesses and homosexuality – the Germans started to use the word *florenzen* to mean 'to sodomize', and a *Florenzer* was slang for a homosexual man.[33] There were laws in 14th-century Florence that, in letter at least, criminalized same-sex desire, but for a period after the Black Death they were not enforced. Florence was briefly a relative haven for queer people. This, however, changed in the 15th century.[34]

The first move towards recriminalizing same-sex desire started in 1403. The legislative council established the Office of Honesty (*Ufficiali dell'Onestà*) with the express purpose of countering the rise in homosexuality that had occurred in the last half-century. To do this, the Florentines wielded an unusual tool – the Office of Honesty set up state-run and state-funded brothels so men could have subsidized sex with women. At the same time as they encouraged straight and bisexual men to have more heterosexual sex, the councils approved a proposal for the 'elimination and extirpation of sodomy'.[35]

The year before the Office of Honesty was inaugurated, Florence found itself deep in debt. From 1402 until the 1420s, the charges alone on the city-state's debt fluctuated from 167,000 to 280,000 florins. By 1424, combined debt repayments and military expenditure took Florence's debt to 628,000 florins. In 1427, it was 817,000.[36] From 1402 to 1420, an average year yielded just 200,000 florins, nowhere near enough to cope with city-state debt levels that were rising to four times that level. Worse still was to come, between 1424 and 1432, tax yields declined to 150,000 florins.[37] In 1432, the Office of the Night (Ufficiali di Notte) was established by the government. It was tasked with hunting down 'sodomites'.[38]

A law that had been written in 1325 was revived in light of these new economic conditions. According to this law, tops were to be castrated, bottoms were to be fined.[39] The court records are full of examples of queer men who were captured and persecuted. In 1480, a young man named Lorenzo di Francesco Ubertini was forced in court to confess to how a 64-year-old by the name of Antonio di Niccolò de' Nobili had ejaculated in his mouth.[40] This was labelled as a charge of sodomy 'ex ante parte' ('from the other part' in Latin, probably meaning 'from the other hole'). In a move with which we can sympathize, queer sex with minors constituted a still graver offence.

REFORMATION

When Henry VIII kicked off the English Reformation, self-control and prudence became embedded more firmly than ever in the fabric of both secular and religious life. For the Protestants, a man was encouraged to practise self-discipline relentlessly, to become a new kind of ascetic and fulfil his obligation from God[41] by making wealth for himself and his family.[42] In many ways, Protestantism represented a fresh incursion of economic thinking into the religious space.

The picture for the poor in late Tudor England was bleak. Starvation was routine in some parts of the country. People began to moralize the consumption of food; excesses of diet were seen as deep ethical failings, not just examples of greed.[43] Under Elizabeth I, the jurist Sir Edward Coke (pronounced cook) wrote down a summary of the country's laws and their justifications which survives to this day. He tells us that men found guilty of the crime of buggery would be hanged and women would be drowned. He describes buggery as 'so detestable' that good Christians cannot name it.[44] But Coke goes considerably further than denouncing queer sex, he even offers a spurious cause for these desires: '[Sodomites] came to this abomination by four means, viz. by pride, excess of diet, idleness, and contempt of the poor.'[45]

With the possible exception of pride, each of these causes is rooted in socioeconomic inequalities. Idleness, greed and contempt of the poor are all symptoms of excessive consumption. Even in Elizabethan England, Sir Edward Coke tells us quite plainly that queer love was considered an economic crime, an overstepping of the proper boundaries of self-restraint.

On 5 September 1640, a priest by the name of John Atherton was hanged at Gallows Green in Dublin. His tithe proctor John Childe was hanged at Bandon Bridge in March the following year. Both men were found guilty of sodomy, and Childe was also found guilty of 'avarice' and the 'extortion of fees'. An anonymous pamphlet written on the grim occasion of Atherton's execution warns:

Shun avarice, shun extortion, shun vain pride,
Shun hate, dissimulation, let your Guide,
Be godlinesse. Shun lust, shun buggery,
Shun incest, rape, and shun adultery.[46]

The connection between economic and sexual crimes is as alarming as it is predictable. This was not just the case in England. In France in 1605, a novel was published called *The Isle of the Hermaphrodites* which painted queer bodies and queer desires as motivated by gluttony and excessive consumption of food.[47]

With rising persecution and priests now encouraged to marry and have families, queer lives in the early modern period were made exceptionally difficult. But we did not go away. With monasteries and Church courts, queer people in Byzantium and throughout the Middle Ages were offered some very small shield. Without them, in Protestant countries, queer people had to find other ways to explore their identities in secret.

Speculatively, it is possible that the emerging theatrical scene in London was one such place where queer men could hide.[48] The sonnets of William Shakespeare attest plainly to his open exploration of homosexual desire. Sonnet 126 offers a case taken up by scholars of Shakespeare falling rapturously in love with a man. Most of his sonnets are written in a way that does not overtly advertise his sexual interest in other men, implying a need for coy discretion.

As in the ancient world, it's possible that certain royal courts may have provided some protection for queer people. When he was just 13 years old, King James VI of Scotland (1567–1625) and I of England (1603–25) met his cousin, the French nobleman Esmé Stuart. The future king was said to have appreciated Esmé's 'eminent ornaments of body and mind' and 'embraced him in a most amorous manner'.[49] On his ascent to the English throne, James continued his dalliances. On 30 December 1607, John Chamberlain wrote from court to his friend Dudley Carlton that a man named 'Sir Robert Carre a younge Scot and new favourite is lately sworn gentleman of the [king's] bedchamber'.[50] The romance between George Villiers and King James is also well documented in surviving letters.[51] In many of these, James refers to George – then approaching the age of 30 – as his 'sweet and dear child' and describes his tears at their parting. Other courtiers may have been scandalized by James' infatuation with men, but they were powerless to do anything about it. Those who had wealth and power, or the protection of an institution like the theatre, could afford to indulge their desires. But even while James was enjoying his prolonged love affair with Villiers, he oversaw a translation of the Bible into English which condemned sodomy to the Protestant population at large, and ordinary men and women continued to face the risk of prosecution.

REVOLUTION

In the late 17th century, Holland was a trading powerhouse of Europe and one of the world's first modern 'capitalist' economies. But a series of naval wars with England, coupled with a French invasion in 1672, caused major disruptions to the economy. In the 1690s, a sharp reduction in land rents took place, a serious blow for an economy built – in large part – on investments in real estate.[52] By 1713, 200 million guilders had been invested in the public debt by a small group of private individuals in the Netherlands. Interest payments at the time absorbed 70 per cent of the national budget, which caused wealth to concentrate in the hands of a few, very rich families.[53] Foreign writers became enormously interested in the decline of this once-great economy. The Prussian economist Jakob Friedrich von Bielfeld (1717–70) blamed – among many other factors – decadence, moral decay and a lack of religion among its people.[54]

Homosexuals were repeatedly subjected to criminal prosecutions in late-17th-century Holland.[55] Most notorious was the mass imprisonment and execution of gay men in Utrecht, which began in 1730 and spread across the Netherlands. Josua Wils, a local man from Utrecht, was employed to guard the Dom Tower but he was imprisoned for pelting passers-by with rocks and ringing the tower's bell at irregular times of the day.[56] In his defence, Wils claimed that Egmond Chapel, part of the Dom Tower, was a favourite spot for gay men to meet and have sex.

A few days later, some magistrates visited Egmond Chapel where – owing to 'good lighting' – they claimed to have found unimpeachable evidence that buggery had taken place there. One man, Gilles van Baden, was accused by both Wils and his sons. On 19 January, van Baden confessed to having had anal sex in the chapel with a soldier called Hendrik Corver. Corver was also arrested and, under interrogation, named others, including one Zacharias Wilsma who in turn named as many as 22 men – not just commoners but members of the Dutch elite. On 31 March 1730, a judge sentenced Corver, van Baden and a manservant named Adrianus van Wijck to death by strangulation in a dungeon.

A moral panic caught fire throughout the Netherlands, and dozens more men were captured by the authorities, tortured and executed.

In neighbouring France, under the ancien régime, queer people were burned to death at the stake. The French Academy's dictionary refused to print an entry for 'Sodomite', but another lexicographer in 1680 – César-Pierre Richelet – tells us that 'the sin of sodomy . . . [is] the sin of the flesh against nature . . . [which] every man with a drop of good sense should abhor',[57] giving us a flavour of contemporary feelings. The ancien régime was remarkable for its contempt of the poor and its hugely wealthy aristocracy – and stories of the royal court and some of its terrible misbehaviour eventually reached the ears of the public.

On a warm summer's evening in July 1722 in the gardens of the Palace of Versailles, a large group of noblemen apparently met to have sex. According to a letter from a scandalized Duchesse d'Orleans, one noble announced to the assembled garden, 'Here I am in my wedding outfit, who wants to marry me?', and three men volunteered their services enthusiastically.[58] Many of these men ended up in the Bastille. Tales such as this have the whiff of Suetonius' exaggerated claims about the Roman imperial court about them. They may say more about a society's homophobia and the connection in contemporary thought between homosexuality and aristocratic excess than they do about the true sexuality of people at court. But this moral panic among the upper classes precipitated a thorough crackdown on those lower down in society.

In 1723, the police ran a sustained campaign in Paris to apprehend and imprison gay men.[59] They posed as queers soliciting sex in the Jardins des Tuileries and the Luxembourg Gardens and on the Quai de la Ferraille. They found men giving certain gestures to one another, pulling out their penises and feeling the breeches of the other man to see whether he had an erection. Some of these men disappeared to local taverns or even into the bushes to have sex. The agents themselves declined sex and instead had the unfortunate men arrested.

Following the French Revolution a project was undertaken to redistribute money and land from the Church and the nobility;[60]

not long after, France decriminalized queer sex in 1791. It remains unclear just how much this change was attributable to economic redistribution and how much to a generally revolutionary attitude towards established norms – and it is equally unclear whether such a legal change was reflected in social attitudes. But decriminalizing queer sex would have still saved the lives of many people who would otherwise have been executed under the ancien régime.

On the other side of the Atlantic, Boston was engaged in a prolonged social wealth experiment. The lands that European Puritans had colonized were occupied by Native Americans, whose varied tribes had a broadly open and tolerant position on sexuality and gender. By contrast, the Puritans were extremely opposed to queer identities. What happened in Boston, shortly after the American War of Independence, would have shocked them.

Eighteenth-century Boston was hardly a utopia, but it has often been held up by historians as a rare example of economic equality.[61] Despite its proximity to the modern era, it is hard to measure its wealth distribution, but the Bostonians tell us themselves that a 'levelling principle' was at work in the economy and most men had enough property to vote.[62]

At 5 Pinckney Street lived the leader of the Bucks of America, an all-black American regiment. His name was George Middleton and he had served in the American Revolution. At the same address lived a French West-Indian hairdresser named Louis Glapion. They lived together until 1792 when Glapion married. It seems Middleton then found another man, for when he died, he left all his possessions to a certain Tristom Babcock.[63]

In a letter from 1790, Joseph Dennie, a Harvard-educated man who edited the Philadelphia *Port Folio* (which contained many essays on same-sex love), writes to a certain Roger Vose:

> Depend upon it, Vose, so well acquainted am I with your disposition and my own that united we should enjoy as much felicity as this sublunary state can furnish. Would to God this scheme

were practicable; and that for years to come one might be our table and one our bed. This top (sic) can never be exhausted.[64]

We also have the letter which Vose wrote to Dennie:

> Castle building apart; let us consider the subject of profession a little more attentively. In case we should both study physic or divinity, we could doubtless agree on a place, and be covered each night with the same blanket. But let us extend our views a little farther. Let us take the most effectual method to lay the foundation for a permanent friendship . . . A prospect of resting near Dennie for life would be very agreeable. Agreeable? It would be heavenly.

What is remarkable about Boston is the openness with which queer men and women wrote and cohabited, and the lack of criminal consequences. As well as Roger Vose and Joseph Dennie, Massachusetts later became home to gay writers like Walt Whitman and Herman Melville. There is also evidence in the 19th century of lesbian couples living together in 'Boston Marriages'. One such couple living together at the turn of the 20th century was Sarah Orne Jewett and Annie Adams Fields.[65] For a quarter of a century, Katharine Lee Bates and Katharine Coman lived together as well. When Coman went on a trip to England, she wrote to Bates:

> I am coming back to you, my dearest, whether I come back to Wellesley[66] or not. You are always in my heart and in my longings. I've been so homesick for you on this side of the ocean and yet so still and happy in the memory and consciousness of you.[67]

IMPERIAL BRITAIN

If Boston and France, in the immediate aftermath of revolution, were places of lower levels of inequality, imperial Britain offers a case study of quite extraordinary levels of inequality, subsistence living and social deprivation. The great migration into London and other cities during industrialization was met in 1780 with skyrocketing figures of arrests for queer men.⁶⁸ In 1810, a group of men were arrested at a gay tavern (a 'molly house') called the White Swan in Clerkenwell. They were put in the pillory and 50 women pelted them with 'mud, dead cats, rotten eggs, potatoes, and buckets filled with blood, offal, and dung'; the men were left nearly unconscious by the continuous assault.⁶⁹ On a two-month campaign in 1830, two policemen arrested 19 different men for homosexual offences in Hyde Park.⁷⁰ Oscar Wilde was famously prosecuted under indecency laws and sentenced to hard labour and incarceration in the latter part of that century. But in the 1830s, a far worse penalty was available to the Crown.

On 27 November 1835, James Pratt and John Smith saw each other for the very last time. They were both poor and married, but every so often, they met in a run-down boarding house in the Southwark area. All night on a small bed, they had sex and lay together. But on one of those nights, they were spotted by an attendant. James and John were arrested and incarcerated at Newgate Prison. On a cold day in November, John Smith stepped out into the yard and resolutely allowed the hangman to tie a noose around his neck. James Pratt was said to stumble and need assistance as he was taken to the gallows. The two men looked at each one last time, before the hangman pulled the lever.⁷¹

During the Second World War, gay men in the British army were court martialled for their affairs. That said, much like in the medieval Church, it was possible for queer men to experiment in the army ranks. One man writes of how otherwise heterosexual men on his ship 'used me sexually occasionally'.⁷² Another called Gerald Doherty recalls how he met up with a 'barrow boy' in the Fitzroy Tavern in Oxford Circus. They then walked down to Charing Cross station (metres from where the famous Heaven gay nightclub now pumps music), found an empty carriage and had sex.⁷³ No doubt these queer men felt more able to explore their identities with the police's attentions otherwise occupied.

Across the Channel, the story was very different. Many queer people were sent to concentration camps where they were forced to wear pink triangles to demarcate them from the rest, and they were often shunned even within the camps by other victims before the Nazi regime murdered them. At Buchenwald, a Danish doctor by the name of Dr Carl Peter Jensen (alias Dr Carl Værnet) was employed to experiment on gay men. In these experiments, men would have incisions made in their groin (without anaesthetic, as was routine in concentration camps) and a device for pumping hormones installed in their body. Værnet claimed this procedure was successful in his scientific publications, though given these studies relied on self-reporting, it is far more likely that the men reported a 'cure' only to stop the gruesome experimentation.[74]

In the aftermath of the Second World War, philosophers began to look back at the history of Western thought and wonder how it was that the extreme and violent ideology of Nazism had so successfully taken hold. Karl Popper theorized – in his book *The Open Society and Its Enemies* – that the belief that we are all in inevitable decline from perfection helped lay the groundwork for Nazi ideology, and for this he put the blame squarely at Plato's door. Like Plato, the Nazis argued against democracy and had a strict doctrine of purity and 'natural' law – and Plato proposes many different forms of eugenics in both his *Republic* and his *Laws*.[75]

After the war, in Britain, life did not immediately improve for queer people. In the 1960s, NHS hospitals administered aversion therapy to gay men and women.[76] Electrodes were attached to the wrist or the lower leg and shocks were delivered while the patient watched photographs of men and women in varying stages of undress. Patients were even given portable electric shock boxes to take home, so they could torture themselves. In other cases, apomorphine – a drug which induces vomiting – was injected. So-called 'outpatients' were subjected to these cruel and hopeless treatments for up to two years. Gay men were injected with oestrogen and chemically castrated, including, famously, Alan Turing. In the haunting words of one victim, 'mainly from a guilt-ridden Christian point of view it meant that at least I had tried to do something.'[77]

In 1965, Lord Arran succeeded in passing the partial decriminalization of homosexuality through the British House of Lords.

In 1967, homosexuality was decriminalized for consenting adults over the age of 21 in a private residence with only two people present. There is a traditional explanation for this change in policy – that too many members of the establishment were being placed under arrest for queer acts. But this had *always* been the case, from Bishop John Atherton to Oscar Wilde. I think the Attlee government's sweeping changes to the welfare state 20 years earlier – ending subsistence living – coupled with a general improvement in standards of living may have created the right conditions for the partial decriminalization of same-sex desire.

As Margaret Thatcher in Britain and Ronald Reagan in the US advanced neoliberal economics, a new age of self-reliance dawned. In an interview with *Woman's Own* magazine, Thatcher pugnaciously declared, 'there's no such thing as society. There are individual men and women, and there are families.' This commitment to social atomization included a rollback of welfare and a renewed attack on gay people. At the Conservative Party Conference, October 1987, she lambasted schools for teaching children – in a fantastically naive turn of words – that 'they have an inalienable right to be gay'. What followed was Section 28 of the Local Government Act, which banned teachers and other local government workers from discussing homosexuality in schools. Since the UK was not yet facing below-subsistence living on large scales, the case for recriminalizing queer sex would not have seemed prudent.[78] But the relationship between social atomization and homophobia observed throughout the ancient world doesn't seem to have gone away.

Since the early 2000s, queer rights have taken huge strides forward in many regions of the world. In recent academic literature, a correlation has been identified between GDP per capita (a measure of the wealth of the average person) and LGBTQ+ rights. One study even showed that for every $2,000 increase in the GDP per capita of a nation, a corresponding 8-point rise was seen on a scale of LGBTQ+ rights.[79] The global decline in LGBTQ+ persecution is also thanks to greater social connection and community brought about by the internet.[80] One of the challenges for the neoliberal agenda is the tension between traditional conservatism and individual freedom, a tension which continues to play out in right-wing attitudes to LGBTQ+ issues to this day. At the same time, America and other nations have become more comfortable and familiar with debt, which is more widely available than ever. A healthy relationship with debt is now considered a strong basis for increasing one's own wealth (providing the rate of appreciation on the debt is outpaced by the rate of appreciation on the purchased asset).[81] Self-restraint is no longer seen as the quickest and most reliable route to a good life.

It is no coincidence that in modern America and Europe, trans rights (the most vulnerable people in the queer community) have come under fresh fire in recent years. Since the 2008 financial crisis, and the recent conspiracy of price-inflation and stagnation in income,[82] the queer community has been subject to rising hostility. Hate crimes in the United Kingdom against trans people have risen by an astonishing 168 per cent in the last five years (with a 112 per cent rise in hate crimes against people based on their sexual orientation).[83] There is a degree of protection for some members of the LGBTQ+ community in liberal, metropolitan cities because of the sustained work that has been done both in the media and in the protest movement to make us visible to the wider public. But trans people have been eyed as a target by far-right political movements which favours ordered categories, social atomization and self-restraint over community and love.

HOW WE PROTECT QUEER LOVE AND IDENTITIES

Today there are sustained efforts by forces hostile to queer love and identities to eradicate us. They claim free speech gives them a right to spread lies: that we are medically abnormal, that we are deviant and excessive, that we don't understand healthy, ordered boundaries.

The next stage – if history is any teacher – will be a return to values of self-restraint, personal independence and hyper-masculinity. As in ancient Athens, we would expect to see queer people characterized as excessive aliens unable to contain themselves.

A recent computational model has shown increasing narratives against LGBTQ+ people designed to dehumanize them and present them as disordered.[84] The final stage, which in some senses is already widespread, would be to celebrate the ideal man and woman as heterosexual, sexually self-contained (only releasing this restraint as long as it takes to conceive children) and devoted to the duty of the family. Shame would be weaponized against those who fell short of this ideal.

If this does happen, then much of it will take place to mask the development of inequalities and unsustainable debt in society. We resist, as Jesus and other revolutionaries knew, by reaching out across communities. Nothing in history is inevitable, and we must safeguard our hard-won freedoms. In understanding the connection between these crises and the rise of political ideologies that target queer people, we have more of a chance of understanding where this hatred came from, noting it and stepping over it. We will face new crises, but next time we will know why some politicians and religious leaders and extremists want to point the finger at queer identities and queer love. When we know the origins of their hate, we can expose their moral philosophy for what it is – a very old lie.

Acknowledgements

With thanks to Armand D'Angour, Chris Cobb and Tara Venkatesan for reading the very first draft and their strong encouragement; to Alain de Botton who introduced me to Kat Aitken at Lexington Literary who became my steadfast agent and found the book a home; to Octavia Stocker, Sam Wells, Sarah Jones and Tomasz Hoskins who nurtured my writing; to Armand for always reading and helping to hone the argument; to the many academics and writers on the ancient world who contributed ideas and comments: Armand D'Angour, James Clackson, Caroline Lawrence, Jordan Dyck, Chris Scott, Joe Barber, Jim Bjork, Joe Watson, James Baker and Honor Cargill; to P – my therapist – who did so much to counter evangelism's work. Finally, a book can never come to fruition without the support and love of family and friends who have been my companions for life – thank you, Chris Bailey, Rachel Attwood, Karen Ciclitira, Olivia and Ruben Rowe-Menke, Mum, Stewart and George for all your love and help over the years.

Notes

CHAPTER ONE: THE MYTH OF GREEK SEX

1. For the details of the Wilde trial, see (Bristow, 2008, 2022).
2. (Bristow, 2022, pp. 176–77).
3. (Bristow, 2022, p. 165).
4. The evidence that is cited is nearly always from legal cases or comic speeches ridiculing lecherous old men. For a supposedly noble practice embedded in the fabric of ancient Greek culture, we hear very little about it from political writers and serious historians. The visual evidence may also be called into question: it has been assumed, for instance, that a man fondling the testicles of a boy is erotic, rather than a routine test of the boy's maturity (it is still common practice for doctors to test whether a boys' testicles have yet descended).
5. For the autobiography, see (Dover, Halliwell and Stray, 2023). For a highly critical account of Dover's life and its influence over his account of Greek sexuality, see (Davidson, 2008).
6. (Halperin, 1990, p. 56).
7. For the role of the Western mind in rendering other cultures exotic, see (Said, 1995).
8. (Parker, 1993, p. 309).
9. For example, see (Xenophon, *Anabasis* 7.4.7–8) and (Aristotle, *Nicomachaean Ethics* 1148b). Aristotle does not use the word *tropos* but clearly discusses the idea that some men are born queer.
10. Stoic literature in Greek, such as that of Gaius Musonius Rufus, is the exception.
11. For a history of this, see (Stray, Clarke and Katz, 2019).
12. E.g. (Boswell, 2009).
13. For same-sex rape in the transatlantic slave trade, see (Woodard, 2014).

14 For a history of Megara, see (Highbarger, 1927; Legon, 1981).
15 Plutarch, *Greek Questions* 18.
16 Theognis, *Elegies* 384–5.
17 Aristotle, *Politics* 1340b 35–40.
18 (Chairetakis, 2016, pp. 222–4).
19 Theognis cannot have written all his poems himself and they were certainly compiled later (Legon, 1981, pp. 106–7).
20 Theognis, *Elegies* 1335–6.
21 Sappho also refers to her same-sex female lover as καλὰ παῖς (Sappho, Fragment 132).
22 Theognis, *Elegies* 1269–70.
23 Theognis, *Elegies* 1305–10.
24 Theognis, *Elegies* 1249–50.
25 Though occasionally he laments how free they were in their attentions to other men, e.g. Theognis, *Elegies* 1311–13.
26 Theognis, *Elegies* 1251–2.
27 For details of these equal-age vases, see (Shapiro, 1981; Hupperts, 1988).
28 Theognis, *Elegies* 1295–7.
29 Theognis, *Elegies* 1359–60.
30 There is evidence of another *boy-lover* from Megara, called Diocles, who fled from Athens and died to protect his boyfriend. It had happened by the 430s BCE: See *Scholia on Aristophanes' Acharnians* 774c; Aristophanes, *Acharnians* 774. For a later, more explicitly homosexual account, see Theocritus, *Idyll* 12.27. That it seems to have been a common joke to swear using Diocles' name in Attic comedy (e.g. *Acharnians*, but also Eupolis Fragments 9 and 95) may imply he was homosexual.
31 Theognis, *Elegies* 184–5.
32 (Leroi, 2014).
33 Though the first recorded use of 'lesbian' for a same-sex female partnership did not take place until the Byzantine era, when Arethas of Caesarea uses it in his *scholia*, see (Betancourt, 2020, p. 123).
34 (Parker, 1993).
35 The word χλωροτέρα is often translated 'greener' or 'more yellow', neither of which makes any sense. The word was not regularly in use for colour at the time, but was commonly used of fearful people (Homer, *Iliad* 7.479; *Iliad* 8.77; *Odyssey* 24.33, among others) and pliable vegetation (Homer, *Odyssey* 9.320; *Odyssey* 16.47). It is much more likely that Sappho is poetically combining her fear at losing her lover to a pliable piece of grass. See (Tanner, 2024).
36 Sappho, Fragment 31.

37 Sappho, Fragment 16.
38 The phrase is not necessarily flattering in Homer, but a sign of her beauty as a harbinger of doom for the Trojans, see Homer, *Iliad* 3.158.
39 Sappho, Fragment 1.21–4; for wider discussion of Sappho's sexuality, see (Mueller, 2021, p. 40) for an overview.
40 Cicero, *Tusculan Disputations* 4.71.
41 Horace, *Odes* 1.32.11–12.
42 (Hupperts, 2005).
43 (Xenophon, *On the Spartan Constitution* 2.12). The Greek phrase I have translated as 'gay love' is '*tōn paidikōn erōtōn*'. Xenophon elsewhere makes it clear that there are those who have a *tropos* towards *eros* for *paides* (see Xenophon, *Anabasis* 7.4.7–8), see (Hindley, 1999, p. 75).
Xenophon's phrase 'man and boyfriend' is *anēr* (man) *kai* (and) *pais* (boyfriend). The cohabitation of same-sex couples seems a plausible reading of this relationship, and Xenophon makes it clear he views this living arrangement as analogous to marriage. We may be sceptical this is ritualized pederasty that will expire upon the teenager's attainment of a certain age. The blurred line, to the modern scholar, between homosexuality and pederasty speaks to the difficulty of studying ancient sexuality. However, it is necessary to explore this as a pre-cursor to later homophobic turns.
44 Black-figure Skyphos from circa 500 BCE, Akraiphia inventory number 19447, for discussion see (Hupperts, 2005, pp. 187–9).
45 (Lee, 2015, p. 75).
46 James Davidson has also discussed marriage-like ceremonies on the isle of Crete, see (Davidson, 2008).
47 At least according to Euripides: Euripides, *Children of Heracles* 724–6, 743–6.
48 Aristotle, Fragment 97.
49 (von Reden, 2007, p. 395).
50 Demosthenes, *Olynthiac* 3.25–6.
51 For an overview of the period, see (Ober, 1991, pp. 50–60).
52 (Ober, 1991, pp. 60–4).
53 Solon, Fragment 25.
54 Aristotle, *Athenian Constitution* 17.2.
55 Plutarch, *Solon* 1.2.
56 Plutarch, *Solon* 1.3; readers may be interested to note how English translations of this text read, '[he was not] proof against beauty in youth', even though no Greek correlate of 'youth' exists. The allure of age-unequal relationships seems irresistible to some translators.

57 The inference of precise ages of figures on vases is always something of a folly.
58 For an overview of age-equal same-sex vases in the period as well as an excellent discussion on the tendencies of some classicists to see age-unequal relationships where they do not exist, see (Hupperts, 1988).
59 See (Hubbard, 2003, p. 83) for a collection.
60 Plutarch, *Solon* 1.3.
61 Aristotle, *Politics* 1306b36–7a2.
62 For a history of Sparta's real economic inequality, see (Hodkinson, 2009).
63 Aristotle, *Politics* 1306b36–7a2.
64 Preserved in Alcaeus, Fragment 360.
65 Xenophon, *Spartan Constitution* 1.5.
66 Xenophon, *Spartan Constitution* 2.13.
67 (Hubbard, 2003, p. 26).
68 Though not uncontroversial, the dating of the text is given by (West, 2011).

CHAPTER TWO: HOW MONEY CORRUPTED LOVE

1 For a history of the sculptures, see (Azoulay, 2017).
2 For more detail on ancient Greek physical exercise and bodyweight training, see (Miller, 2004, pp. 63–4).
3 Many scholars of ancient Greece have sought to argue that homosexual acts played a role in a mentor-mentee relationship, the lack of potential advantage to either party here as explicitly related in Thucydides' story may encourage us to believe this relationship was more erotically and romantically motivated.
4 Thucydides tells us they were in love, see Thucydides, *History of the Peloponnesian War* 6.54; Aristotle, conversely, tells us that Harmodius was in love with Hipparchus, see Pseudo-Aristotle, *Athenian Constitution* 18.
5 For details of the procession, see (Mikalson, 1976).
6 Thucydides, *History of the Peloponnesian War* 6.56.2.
7 It is also possible that Persia entertained anti-queer laws, as the Videvdad states, 'the male who is sodomized and the male who sodomizes . . . is an evil spirit before death. The man who releases semen in another man is an evil spirit after death'. For the citation see (Joosten, 2020, p. 3).
8 (Bullough, 1973, p. 286).
9 Xenophon, *Hiero* 1.29–30.
10 For Xenophon's own possible dalliances with same-sex desire, see (Hindley, 1999).

11 Thucydides, *History of the Peloponnesian War* 2.43; (Wohl, 2002) has attempted to argue that same-sex desire and erotic language is implicit in this speech, which is unlikely to be true on philological grounds. But the speech does emphasize the importance in Greek thought of a connection between love and democracy, even if same-sex desire was not what Thucydides intended us to read into Pericles' words.
12 Alexandria – where the librarians worked – had by this time developed a relatively hostile approach to same-sex desire, as will be explored in later chapters.
13 Aeschylus, *Myrmidons* Fragment 135.
14 Aeschylus, *Myrmidons* Fragment 138.
15 Aeschylus, *Myrmidons* Fragment 139.
16 Aeschylus, *Myrmidons* Fragment 136.
17 See the Oxford *Archive of Performances of Greek and Roman Drama* database (Myrmidons | APGRD, no date).
18 (Sandhoff, 2019).
19 (Fisher, 2001, p. 33).
20 (Kron, 2014, p. 129).
21 (von Reden, 2007, p. 386).
22 (Adamidis, 2019).
23 Plutarch, *Precepts of Statecraft* 13.
24 For Cleon's speech in the Mytilene debate, see Thucydides, *History of the Peloponnesian War* 3.37; on Cleon and populism, see (Adamidis, 2019).
25 Thucydides, *History of the Peloponnesian War* 3.37.3.
26 Aristophanes, *Knights* 877.
27 *Scholia in Aristophanem in Equites* 877c Lh.
28 Whether Gryttus was actually homosexual or not is less important than the fact that the Athenians were – this early in their history – executing men for the crime of gay sex.
29 See (D'Angour, 2020).
30 (Leitao, 1995, p. 131).
31 *Scholia in Aristophanem in Equites* 877c Lh.
32 Aulus Gellius, *Attic Nights* 15.20.
33 Aelian, *Varia Historia* 13.4. συγκλιθέντα seems to imply a sexual reading of the banquet scene, it has been used elsewhere to refer to sex with a woman, e.g. Herodotus, *Histories* 2.181. Certainly, after a little too much pure wine, Euripides kisses Agathon.
34 Aelian, *Varia Historia* 13.4.
35 Aristophanes, *Women at the Thesmophoria* 57.
36 E.g. Aristophanes, *Knights* 364–5.
37 Aristophanes, *Knights* 428; Aristophanes, *Knights* 167.

38 Aristophanes, *Clouds* 973–4.
39 Aristophanes, *Birds* 139–42.
40 Aristophanes, *Frogs* 83–4 makes explicit the reason for Agathon's departure. Aristophanes has Dionysus say that Agathon is a 'ἀγαθὸς ποιητὴς καὶ ποθεινὸς τοῖς φίλοις', 'good poet and missed by his friends'. The phrase could be a double-entendre, as it's possible to interpret the dative not as an agent but as the indirect object, in which case it would translate 'a good poet and he's horny for his friends'.
41 There are even rumours Archelaus I partook himself, though they remain unsubstantiated (Diodorus Siculus 14.37.5). There is considerable evidence, however, that later Macedonian kings – Philip II and Alexander the Great – had gay sex. Throughout the book I'm more interested in what such accounts say about homophobia than the verifiable sexual predilections of the participants.
42 Suda Lexicon X 595.

CHAPTER THREE: QUEER AS MACEDON

1 Xenophon, *Hellenica* 1.6.24.
2 If Aristophanes, *Frogs* 702 is to be believed.
3 For populism in Athens, see (Adamidis, 2019).
4 For reading on Dionysus see (Seaford, 2006).
5 The role of drink is quite clear. The role of drugs is controversial. (Wasson, Hofmann and Ruck, 2008) have suggested that ergot grew as a fungus on crops and had LSD-like properties, but this theory has met with mixed reviews (Bell, 1980). There is tentative archaeological evidence to suggest that a mushroom-like substance was exchanged in a Pharsalus bas-relief between Demeter and Persephone (both associated with Mystery cults), see (Samorini, 2021). The *Homeric Hymn to Demeter* seems to reference explicit ecstatic states brought about by wine mixed with a certain type of honey; I have written that this may be an intoxicating form of 'mad honey' in a forthcoming piece, see (Tanner, 2025).
6 Euripides, *Bacchae* 1150–2.
7 Euripides, *Bacchae* 773–4.
8 For the history of the play, see (Allan and Swift, 2024).
9 For a brief biography of Philip II, see (Müller, 2010).
10 For archaeological details of the palace, see (Kottaridi, 2011).
11 Large sections of the surviving palace were built by Philip himself.
12 For more detail and for the full Pausanias and Philip story, see (Ogden, 2009).
13 On Theopompus' rhetoric and its relationship to historical truth, see ('Theopompus' Historical Accuracy', 1997).

14 Theopompus, Fragment 187.
15 Theopompus, Fragment 49.
16 Theopompus, Fragment 57.
17 Polybius, Histories 8.9.12. Theopompus also deploys the phrase 'trópon' which some scholars think was used in other authors like Xenophon to refer to sexual orientation, see (Hindley, 1999).
18 For a survey of Olynthus' house sizes as evidence for equality, see (Kron, 2014, pp. 128–9). The mean size of each house in square metres was 227.6, the median size was 220.6, indicating very little variation.
19 Ancient Olynthus is estimated to have had a very low Gini coefficient (a measure of economic inequality) of 0.14. By the end of the 4th century BCE, Athens had an estimated Gini coefficient of 0.7, showing climbing inequality. See (Kron, 2014, p. 129).
20 Demosthenes, *Olynthiac* 3.25–6.
21 For the archaeological findings, see (Lagia, 2015, p. 138).
22 (von Reden, 2007, p. 401).
23 E.g. Lysias, *On the Murder of Eratosthenes*.
24 (Kennedy, 1963, p. 209).
25 Aeschines 2.88.
26 Aeschines 3.167.
27 Aeschines 3.174; (Worman, 2004, p. 17) has interpreted this to undermine Demosthenes' 'child-making capacity', but his making himself into a *pais* (a homosexual partner) seems possible too.
28 It is on this basis that ancient historians have reason to be sceptical about the stories of Philip II and his lovers. But if that is so, Theopompus' attacks are evidence of the broad homophobia which had gripped Greece by that period.
29 For the lack of clarity, see (Fisher, 2001, p. 40). Fisher suggests the problem was that Timarchus had had sex with multiple partners, a claim for which there is no evidence. In light of the other attacks on gay men, it's probable that the law cited was a vague one against *kinaidia* of the sort that the Aristophanes scholiasts attest to Cleon bringing before the assembly (see the previous chapter).
30 Aeschines, *Against Timarchus* 159. It appears that Aeschines draws a distinction here between a chaste erastes-eromenos relationship bleached of any fear of homosexual desire and one which is perverted by predatory homosexuals.
31 Lysias, *Against Simon* 4.
32 Plutarch, *Pelopidas* 18. 4–5.
33 The Plutarch story suggests that Philip thought the men had been in love, but it's also possible they were simply in very close-knit mentor–mentee

34 See (Romm, 2021).
35 Although he is cautiously mute about the sexual reading of these relationships, Müller points out that Philip did want to establish a strong bond with his royal pages (Müller, 2010, p. 170).
36 Diodorus Siculus, *History Library* 16.93–4; for the involvement of homosexuality and sexual intrigue in the Royal *paides*, see (Sawada, 2010, p. 404).
37 (Sawada, 2010, p. 404).

CHAPTER FOUR: PLATO AND THE PHILOSOPHY OF THE CLOSET

1 In fact, there are conflicting accounts of where Plato may have died. But a scroll found in Herculaneum (one of the earliest surviving accounts) tells us it was in bed listening to a Thracian girl playing the flute.
2 For a history and reconstruction of the Academy, see (Baltes, 1993).
3 Cf. Romulus and Remus, Jesus Christ.
4 The Greek charges were: 'Σωκράτη φησὶν ἀδικεῖν τούς τε νέους διαφθείροντα καὶ θεοὺς οὓς ἡ πόλις', 'the city says that Socrates did commit offences both in corrupting young men and the gods' at Plato, *Apology* 24b.
5 Theodorus of Cyrene had been brought to trial for atheism in the late 5th century BCE.
6 If the phrase is used in the law court, to our knowledge it was a new coinage, since no collocation of νέος and διαφθείρω predates it. Lysias (writing after Socrates' trial) uses the collocation of γυνή and διαφθείρω for seducing women (Lysias, *On the Murder of Eratosthenes* 16.8). Theopompus apparently uses it of raping young men at Theopompus, Fragment 121.10: 'παῖδας καὶ νεανίσκους διέφθειραν'. It has an ambiguous meaning at Isocrates 15.56. Later writers mean rape, e.g. Plutarch, *Alexander* 22.2.
7 Xenophon, *Memorabilia* 1.2.2.
8 She has often been called his wife, but there is no evidence they married.
9 Plato, *Phaedo* 117d–e.
10 Aulus Gellius, *Attic Nights* 15.20. According to *The Lives of Euripides* 2, Euripides allowed his wife to run away with a slave.
11 For a life of Pythagoras, see (McKirahan, 2010, pp. 79–82).

12 A tablet in the Columbia University Plimpton collection from the 2nd millennium BCE attests to this (Plimpton 322).
13 The story is related to us by Proclus; see (Lloyd, 2014, p. 34).
14 Diogenes Laertius, *Lives of Eminent Philosophers* 8.4.
15 Herodotus, *Histories* 4.95.
16 Iamblichus, *Life of Pythagoras* 18.
17 Iamblichus, *Life of Pythagoras* 31.210–211. (Allen, 2006) – a work which has not been reviewed in scholarly literature – has claimed that Pythagoras opposed homosexuality, but I could not find any evidence that this is right.
18 Aristotle, *Metaphysics* 985b.
19 (Lloyd, 2014, p. 33).
20 Philolaus, Fragment 4.
21 For the miracles, see (McKirahan, 2010, pp. 79–80).
22 For details of the Grove of Hecademus, see (Baltes, 1993, pp. 6–7).
23 See (Baltes, 1993, p. 7); for Plato's own account of the importance of restricting sleep, see Plato, *Laws* 808b.
24 Plato, *Phaedrus* 275a.
25 For a beautiful account of the battle, see (D'Angour, 2020).
26 Plato, *Symposium* 215d.
27 Plato, *Symposium* 217a–b.
28 Plato, *Symposium* 216d and 217b.
29 For the perhaps lurid suggestion that Taureas was a place to observe naked men, see (Dover, 2016, p. 54). As is typical of Dover, he assumes that cognates of ἐρᾶν are always sexual in meaning, which is certainly not the case. It is never precisely clear when ἐρᾶν and its cognates refer to sexual desire or mere admiration, and it is quite plausible that in every one of Dover's examples those cognates refer to the admiration of a mentor for a mentee and vice-versa. It is clear there was a preoccupation in the sources that was alive to the corruption of this sacred relationship with homosexuality, which we explored in the previous chapter. For examples of this paranoia – among others – see: Aeschines, *Against Timarchus* 133–40; Lysias, *Against Simon* 4–6; Aristophanes, *Peace* 762; Aristophanes, *Birds* 139–42. The fear that this sacred, chaste relationship be corrupted by homosexuality makes a better case for homophobia than tolerance of same-sex desire.
30 Plato, *Charmides* 153a.
31 One of the cognates of ἐρᾶν for which many readers, including (Dover, 2016), have assumed a sexual connotation.
32 Often translated 'boys', they are referred to again at Plato, *Charmides* 155b where contextually they seem to be attendants rather than younger boys.

33 Plato, *Charmides* 154b–c.
34 Plato, *Charmides* 155d.
35 Plato, *Charmides* 171d–e.
36 Plato, *Lysis* 204d–e.
37 (Halperin, 1986).
38 (Roochnik, 2023).
39 For a history, see (Stray, Clarke and Katz, 2019). For my own solution to this problem, see (Tanner, 2024) and (Tanner, 2023).
40 The authenticity is not uncontroversial (Bowra, 1938).
41 I am indebted to Professor Angie Hobbs who very kindly pointed me to this.
42 Dion, oddly, is not in the vocative, but the nominative.
43 Diogenes Laertius, *Lives of Eminent Philosophers* 3.30.
44 Plato, *Phaedrus* 253e–354a.
45 Plato, *Gorgias* 494e.
46 Plato, *Phaedrus* 250e–1a. I am indebted to Samuel Woodward, a DPhil candidate in Classics at Oxford, for pointing this out to me.
47 For the background to the Symposium, see (Dover and Plato, 1980).
48 Plato, *Symposium* 220a.
49 Plato, *Symposium* 177d.
50 Plato, *Symposium* 210a–11c.
51 Plato, *Symposium* 211b.
52 Xenophon, *Symposium* 4.24–6.
53 For a review of the deleterious effects of debt in the ancient world generally, see (Graeber, 2011).
54 For discussion and sources on debt problems in the period, see (Millett, 1991).
55 See (Millett, 1991, p. 181).
56 Xenophon, *Ways and Means* 4.6.
57 Plato, *Republic* 555c.
58 Demosthenes 61.2.
59 Demosthenes 49.50.
60 Demosthenes 53.9.
61 (Millett, 1991, p. 77).
62 Xenophon, *Oeconomicus* 7.14–15.
63 Xenophon, *Oeconomicus* 9.11.
64 'Love of boys' in the Greek can reasonably be understood to refer to homosexuality generally; for the *pais* growing into an adult and still remaining a *pais* see Plato, *Symposium* 181d. Aristotle, *Nicomachaean Ethics* 1157a9–11 also references same-sex desire persisting into adulthood.
65 Xenophon, *Oeconomicus* 12.14.

66 https://www.theguardian.com/lifeandstyle/2017/may/15/australian-millionaire-millennials-avocado-toast-house (Accessed 3 July 2024).

67 Plato, *Letters* 7.332e–3a. The authenticity of the Seventh Letter has been contested by (Burnyeat and Frede, 2015) among others. However, their argument that the letter cannot have existed because there was no letter-preserving tradition before Epicurus leaves something to be desired. Additionally, the questions about style are always laden with subjectivity, see (Lewis, 2017). We should treat the letter cautiously, with a mind to its possible inauthenticity, but not dismiss it entirely. We must be mindful always of the big picture, where many different fragments of information cohere to form an argument. In any case, this part of the Seventh Letter is consistent with the rest of Plato's philosophy of self-restraint, as I argue below.

68 Plato, *Laws* 636c.

CHAPTER FIVE: ALEXANDER THE STRAIGHT?

1 For the description of Alexander, see Plutarch, *Alexander* 4.2.4.
2 We are also told that the Delphic Oracle referred to him in these terms, see Plutarch, *Alexander* 14.4.
3 For the lessons and details, see (Hamilton and Plutarchus, 1969, p. 19).
4 (Baltes, 1993, p. 9). It is likely that Plato despised rhetorical training as it could mislead the audience from his view of the truth.
5 It was common practice in the ancient world for famous writers to compile their own version of the text; the text we have inherited was not written by Homer but was compiled by scholars in ancient Alexandria centuries after Alexander the Great.
6 Plutarch, *Alexander* 8.2.
7 Pseudo-Aristotle, *Physiognomics* 808a.
8 Aristotle, *Nicomachaean Ethics* 1148b.
9 Aristotle, *Nicomachean Ethics* 1148b.
   I have translated 'nurture' where it is traditional to translate 'habit' to ease the reader more into understanding Aristotle's position.
10 Xenophon, *Anabasis* 7.4.8.
11 On Aristotle's relationship with alcohol, see Plutarch, *Alexander* 4.4.
12 Plutarch, *Alexander* 21.4.
13 Plutarch, *Alexander* 21.4.
14 Plutarch, *Alexander* 22.1.
15 Plutarch, *Alexander* 22.3.
16 Plutarch, *Alexander* 14.4.
17 For the ancient source, see Plutarch, *Alexander* 67.4.

18 For the story and Alexander's relationship with Hephaestion, see (Ogden, 2011, p. 155); see also Aelian, *Varia Historia* 12.7.
19 Curtius 10.5.32.
20 For his age, see (Ogden, 2011, p. 155).
21 For Hephaestion's death and the tomb, see (Ogden, 2011, p. 156).
22 For Hector, see (Ogden, 2011, p. 171).
23 For monetization following Alexander, see (Graeber, 2011, pp. 226–30). For minting in the Hellenistic period, see (Reden, 2022, pp. 66–9). For the monetization of the Macedonian economy, see (Bagnall and Bingen, 2007, p. 215). There had already been a practice of using money for dowries in Egypt for centuries, but the Macedonians formalized the use of money.
24 (Bagnall and Bingen, 2007, p. 223).
25 Diogenes Laertius, *Lives of Eminent Philosophers* 6.43.
26 Plutarch, *Alexander* 14.2.
27 For Diogenes' joy of farting, see (Krueger, 1997, p. 226) and Diogenes Laertius, *Lives of Eminent Philosophers* 6.20–81.
28 Dio Chrysostom 6.17.
29 Diogenes Laertius, *Lives of Eminent Philosophers* 6.65.
30 Diogenes Laertius, *Lives of Eminent Philosophers* 6.67.
31 Why Diogenes would have been in correspondence with Alexander is unclear and the letter is very probably a fake. Nonetheless its contents reveal what the tradition *after* Alexander and Diogenes knew of their respective beliefs and habits.
32 Diogenes of Sinope, Letter 24.1, cited in (Ogden, 2011, p. 159).
33 It is always a tricky thing to know what plant is exactly referred to by an ancient text. Often scholars make loosely educated guesses. It is possible this plant was not henbane, but a now-extinct plant. For the LSJ and Greek botany, see (Raven, 2000).
34 Xenophon, *Oeconomicus* 1.13.
35 Julius Pollux, *Onomasticon* 2.7.1.
36 (Scarborough, 2010, p. 158).
37 (Bresson, 2015, p. 411).
38 This was likely for practical reasons: it was harder to track profits honestly.
39 For the story and an overview of Zeno's philosophy, see (Sellars, 2006).
40 For Crates, see (Branham and Goulet-Cazé, 1997, p. 10).
41 (Skinner, 2013, p. 205).
42 For a history of the painted Stoa and reconstruction, see (Meritt, 1970).
43 See Pausanias, *A Description of Greece* 1.15.1.

44 It is unlikely that raping Cassandra was the chief concern here but violating Athena's protection. Women were captured in battle frequently in the Trojan War.
45 Diogenes Laertius, *Lives of Eminent Philosophers* 7.27.
46 Diogenes Laertius, *Lives of Eminent Philosophers* 7.16.
47 Some have argued that Jesus Christ himself was a follower of Cynicism. See initially (Downing, 1992) and then for the counterargument (Goulet-Cazé, 2019).
48 Womanhood was spoken about by men in antiquity as an inferior form of masculinity, rather than as an equivalent category.
49 Zeno, *Letter to King Antigonus* (Cited in Diogenes Laertius, *Lives of Eminent Philosophers* 7.8)
50 (Evenepoel, 2014).
51 Athenaeus, *Deipnosophistae* 13.15.10–14. In most translations it is still rendered as 'the most infamous of passions', but the Greek could not be clearer. Translated literally, it means 'Zeno . . . who never used a wife, always boys, as Antigonus . . .' As I have argued previously, unless a writer explicitly introduces term *arren*, 'man', the term 'boys' is age-blind. Indeed it is this writer who says he pursued men as old as 28.
52 Stoicorum Varia Fragmenta 1.204.
53 See (Price, 2002, p. 187). Modern philosophers have sometimes expressed this sentiment amusingly, Michel Foucault once remarked, 'I wasn't always smart, I was actually very stupid in school . . . there was a boy who was very attractive who was even stupider than I was. And in order to ingratiate myself with this boy who was very beautiful, I began to do his homework for him—and that's how I became smart, I had to do all this work to just keep ahead of him a little bit, in order to help him. In a sense, all the rest of my life I've been trying to do intellectual things that would attract beautiful boys.' (Miller, 2000, p. 56).
54 Stoicorum Varia Fragmenta 3.180.19.
55 *King Lear* Act 1 Scene 4; *Antony and Cleopatra* Act 2 Scene 1.
56 For the story, see (Sedley, 1976, pp. 121–2).
57 (Mansfeld, 2006, p. 464).
58 Epicurus in Diogenes Laertius, *Lives of Eminent Philosophers* 10.118.
59 *Vatican Collection of Epicurean Sayings* 18.
60 Usener Fragment 67, citation in (Jope, 2013, p. 423).
61 From the poet Baton, about whom we know very little.
62 Timon of Phlius, *Siloi* 3.
63 (Lagia, 2015).
64 (Ormand, 2009, p. 108).

65 (Olesen-Bagneux, 2014).
66 For discussion of the story, see (Ormand, 2009).
67 Herondas, *Miniambos* 6.
68 For a survey of female homoerotic stories in the ancient world, see (Boehringer, 2013).
69 The idea that women were freed sexually from their husbands and their households is a fantasy following the development of the household model of the economy (discussed above).
70 Theocritus, *Idyll* 23.7–10.
71 Theocritus, *Idyll* 23.36–8.
72 Indeed, he doesn't paint a positive picture of many forms of desire, he also shows the Cyclops hopelessly in love with the nymph Galatea, see (Konstan, 2021, p. 520).
73 Theognis had made this comparison centuries before, but he also wrote extensively about the *joys* of same-sex desire which are notably absent in this period.
74 Often blending Doric and Thessalian dialects.
75 Theocritus, *Idyll* 12.10, 11, 15–16.

CHAPTER SIX: LOVE IN THE TIME OF THE OLD TESTAMENT

1 (Beaulieu, 2018, p. 230); (Dalley, 1994).
2 (Pedersén, 2020).
3 (Peled, 2016, pp. 156–8).
4 Reconstructed in the 1980s by Saddam Hussein.
5 Though the Etemenanki ziggurat did not house the dead.
6 It is no coincidence that the God of the Old Testament also begins his creation by transforming chaos into order.
7 (Beaulieu, 2018, p. 232).
8 (Olyan, 1994, p. 192); as we saw in ancient Greece and Alexandria, the introduction of currency and debt often correlates with increased homophobia.
9 It is conventional to call them Israelites until the First Temple period, when some called them Judaeans. 'Jewish people' is sometimes adopted following the Babylonian capture of Jerusalem under Nebuchadnezzar.
10 For an attempt to reconstruct the history of the Old Testament narrative, see (Davies, 1979).
11 Much has been made by evangelical Christians of the 'clear' evidence for certain aspects of the Bible's story. This is often a form of confirmation bias and can be countered by asking *what else* the evidence could support. This is a feature of ancient history: little is certain and multiple interpretations of the same datum are possible.

12 For a fuller account, see (Bickerman and Tropper, 2007, pp. 962–71).
13 The Babylonian record gives us dates which can be mapped onto our modern dating system.
14 Or possibly 25 August 587 BCE.
15 The blinding of kings is a symbol of their inability to rule.
16 At least, according to Daniel 5.
17 E.g. (North, 1994).
18 (Douglas, 2000, p. 6).
19 Somewhat subjective criteria, but they can be relied upon in the absence of an original manuscript or a clear date from a scholiast tradition.
20 (Milgrom, 2007, p. 1319).
21 (Grabbe, 2002, p. 210).
22 Lev. 20.22.
23 E.g. (Nissinen, 1998, p. 38).
24 E.g. (Milgrom, 2007, p. 1361).
25 (*Bowers v. Hardwick*, 1986, p. 197).
26 (House of Lords, 1965, p. 628).
27 (House of Lords, 1965, p. 628).
28 Excellent work is underway led by the barrister Tim Otty KC to repeal these unjust laws.
29 (Joosten, 2020, p. 9).
30 (Milgrom, 2007, p. 1567).
31 (Olyan, 1994, p. 199).
32 (Walsh, 2001, p. 205).
33 (Bigger, 1979, p. 203; Thurston, 1990).
34 Hittite Law Codes 199–200a.
35 Some have claimed that Law Code A20 just bans same-sex rape, which cannot be true: the penalty for raping a woman is death (A19), and it seems impossible to believe that this would not be applied with added violence in the case of same-sex rape.
36 Middle Assyrian Law Code A8.
37 Thanks to Dr Joseph Barber for this.
38 For details on debt security in Middle Assyria, see (Abraham, 2001, p. 175).
39 (Creamer, 2024, p. 10).
40 We know that Judah did practise debt slavery around the time of the Leviticus law codes – Jer. 34.8–19; 1 Chron. 32; 2 Kings 25. See also (Hudson and Michael, 2018, p. 34). However, we also know that this wasn't practised among fellow Jews, see Deut. 23.20. Neh. 5.1–5 yearns for a prior time when there was more equality and less debt. Notably, Deut. 23.19 states, 'do not bring a fee for a prostitute or the recompense for a dog'; the 'dog' is often understood to be a euphemism

for a homosexual prostitute, see (Joosten, 2020, p. 1). If Joosten is correct, then anxieties about debt are found side by side with bans on homosexuals.
41 (Nagarajan, 2011, pp. 111–13).
42 (Hudson and Michael, 2018, p. 26).
43 Lev. 18.3.
44 For a biography of her life, see (Fardon, 1999).
45 (Fardon, 1999, p. 6).
46 (Douglas, 2005, p. 67).
47 Gen. 1–3.
48 Gen. 9.25.
49 (Cohen, 1974, p. 8).
50 *San* 70a.
51 (Goldenberg, 2005, p. 5).
52 (Pleins, 2004, p. 222). The slave-owning, white Presbyterian minister Robert Lewis Dabney wrote in his *A Defence of Virginia* (1867) a detailed theological argument from both the Old Testament and the New, citing the story of Ham and Noah, in passionate defence of what he saw as the right to keep Black people captive as slaves.
53 The story is related from Gen. 18–19.
54 The text says something like 'will I really have this joy?'.
55 Gen. 18.9–14.
56 Gen. 22.
57 The similarity to the entrance of the angels to see Abraham is noteworthy: both passages begin with a prepositional, both contain the same verb for 'sitting' (yōšeb). D'Angelo also noticed the striking similarity between the two passages (D'Angelo, 2013, p. 536).
58 The same verb is used for Lot as for Abraham, (wayištaḥū).
59 Mt. 10.15; at Mt. 10.11 it is made clear the comparison is about hospitality not sexuality.
60 Ezek. 16.49.
61 Judg. 19.25 and 20.
62 Judg. 20–21.
63 During the Renaissance, sodomy likely didn't mean anal sex, this was a later development. At that time, sodomy simply meant some form of illicit, unnatural sex. See (Goldberg (editor) *et al.*, 1993).
64 For an overview, see (Schroer and Staubli, 2000, p. 23).
65 Providing a historical date for any Biblical event is tricky without corroborating sources; it was possible in the case of the invasion of Jerusalem, since independent and precise records exist from Babylon.
66 1 Sam. 16.15–16.

67 1 Sam. 18.1–3.
68 (Stansell, 2011).
69 E.g. Gen. 34.2–3; see (Schroer and Staubli, 2000, p. 28).
70 The language mirrors the *Song of Songs* elsewhere, such as when David and Jonathan go together into a field (compare 1 Sam. 20.11 with Song 7.11).
71 (Lapsley, 2003, pp. 350–1).
72 2 Sam. 1.26.
73 (Ackerman, 2005, p. 181).
74 E.g. (Peleg, 2005, p. 179).
75 (Heidel, 1949).
76 (Foster, Frayne and Beckman, 2001, p. 19).
77 (Nissinen, 1998, p. 23).
78 For a comparison of the two texts, see (Ackerman, 2005).
79 Septuagint, *Lev.* 18.22.
80 See (Nissinen, 1998, p. 19).
81 Other tombs have been found where two men were buried together – such as the tomb of Nakht-Ankh and Khnum-Nakht – where DNA analysis has confirmed that they were half-brothers.
82 For the translation and other details, see (Matić, 2019, p. 184).
83 (Dowson, 2008, p. 35).
84 Cited in (Dowson, 2008, p. 35) in French, the translation is my own.
85 (Reeder, 2008, p. 146).
86 We will have occasion to comment later that same-sex rape is often permitted even in some of the most homophobic ancient cultures; enthusiastic historians have been quick to seize on these examples as evidence of tolerance which a more careful examination may be more sceptical about.
87 (Bullough, 1973, p. 286).
88 (Nissinen, 1998, p. 19).
89 (Wilson, 2012).
90 Pseudo-Phocylides 3–4.
91 Pseudo-Phocylides 153–4.
92 (De Marinis, 2019).
93 For an intellectual biography, see (Niehoff, 2018).
94 (Schwartz, 2009, p. 9).
95 Philo, *On the Contemplative Life* 50–2.
96 (Loader, 2011, pp. 125–27).
97 Philo, *On Special Laws* 3.37.
98 Philo, *On Special Laws* 3.43.
99 Philo, *On Special Laws* 3.38. The Jewish writer Josephus echoes this viewpoint, see Josephus, *Against Apion* 2.199–200.

100 For a fuller account, see (Zeichmann, 2020, p. 17). See also Josephus, *Antiquities of the Jews* 15.25–30.
101 Josephus, *Antiquities of the Jews* 16.230.
102 Josephus, *Antiquities of the Jews* 16.232.

CHAPTER SEVEN: TOXIC MASCULINITY IN ANCIENT ROME

1 Pliny, *Natural History* 33.54.
2 Cicero, *On Laws* 3.30–31.
3 In fact, especially as the imperial period dawns, the Romans are increasingly inconsistent on most aspects of moralism, see (Rudich, 1997, p. 1).
4 (Arkins, 1982, p. 104).
5 'Plura virorum inter sese quam feminarum esse stupra', 'there were more shameful things among the men with each other than the women' (Livy, *From the City's Foundation* 39.13.10–11), for scholars who've said this was anti-gay violence, see (Taylor, 1997, p. 329).
6 (Taylor, 1997, p. 320) says there are no sympathetic accounts, with the exception of Petronius' *Satyricon* and we may doubt this too. A reviewer raised the possible example of the Juventius poems in the Catullus series, but as (Arkins, 1982, p. 105) points out, this portrayal of queer love leads to Catullus' critics attacking him for softness and necessitating that he threaten them with rape to prove his masculinity. Additionally, the Juventius series is exceptionally tragic in nature: his love is never reciprocated and in fact is made to seem disgusting and torturous (Catullus 99).
7 This was a strategy also deployed in the transatlantic slave trade (Woodard, 2014).
8 The exact date is unknown, this is the date traditionally given.
9 For an introduction to Roman government in the republic, see (North, 2006).
10 (North, 2006, p. 256).
11 I'm grateful to Honor Cargill for this elegant analogy.
12 Land grabs by rich and powerful people from poorer people were a notable feature of the whole period, see Sallust, *Jugurthine War* 41.
13 For the full details, see (Von Ungern-Sternberg, 2004).
14 (Harris, 2007, p. 521).
15 (Frayn, 1979).
16 Appian, *Civil War* 1.1.7.
17 For the figures, see (Bastomsky, 1990).
18 (Kehoe, 2012, p. 116).
19 See (Collins and Walsh, 2015).

20 (Collins and Walsh, 2015, p. 125).
21 Cicero, *Against Catiline* 2.23.
22 See (Richlin, 1993).
23 Cicero, *Against Catiline* 2.23.
24 Sallust, *The War with Catiline* 11.3
25 Suetonius, *Julius Caesar* 73.
26 Indeed, the accusation seems to have been against the Juventius poems which Catullus disavows. As Arkins has argued the Juventius poems were probably never intended as serious expressions of love (Arkins, 1982, pp. 106–7).
27 Catullus 16.1–4.
28 Catullus 29.1–2 and 9–10.
29 A collection of Catullus' poems called the Juventius poems offer an interesting counterexample to the general narrative I am suggesting. The Juventius poems present an unrequited, obsessive love on the part of the poet (or the character he is impersonating) for a man called Juventius. I think it probable that it is an imitation of Hellenistic poetry like Theocritus (as he also imitates Sappho 31 with Catullus 51), and commentators have described them as unserious (Arkins, 1982, pp. 106–7). However, as I argue later in the chapter, we can be too seduced by the logical binary of a state being either homophobic or tolerant of homosexuality. Some states that have homophobic laws also have thriving gay subcultures. The existence of the Juventius poems, if we take them seriously, does not necessarily make Rome a tolerant society.
30 Related in Plutarch, *Life of Marcellus* 2.3–4.
31 For example the case of Marcus Laetorius Mergus, see Valerius Maximus, *Memorable Deeds and Sayings* 6.1.11.
32 (Fantham, 2011, p. 127).
33 Orosius 5.16.18.
34 Plautus, *The Weevil* 37–8.
35 Horace, *Satires* 1.2.116–18.
36 For a similar account of the need to relieve excess seed, see Lucretius, *On the Nature of Things* 4.1052–6.
37 Virgil, *Aeneid* 1.278–9.
38 Livy, *The Foundation of the City of Rome* 1.11
39 Pliny, *Natural History* 1.11.
40 Nepos, *Life of Hannibal* 1.
41 Servius, *Commentary on the Aeneid* 7.539.
42 Cicero, *On the State* 5.4.
43 For a full discussion of the law, see (Williams, 2010, p. 214).
44 (Bastomsky, 1990, p. 41).

45 (Treggiari, 1993, p. 263). For a fuller commentary on *stuprum* and the relationship between adultery and homophobia, see (Fantham, 2011, pp. 115–43).
46 For the relationship between sexual and financial excesses in the Roman Augustan poets broadly, see (Gibson, 2007). For a discussion of the topic specifically in one of Horace's poems, see (Dessen, 1968).
47 For an overview of Virgil's views on same-sex desire see (Oliensis, 1997).
48 Note the floral metaphor.
49 Virgil, *Aeneid* 5.293–6.
50 Cf. Ovid, *The Art of Lovemaking* 2.684.
51 Virgil, *Aeneid* 9.390.
52 Virgil, *Aeneid* 9.420–30.
53 Virgil, *Aeneid* 9.358–9.
54 In another ironic twist, 'felix' can also mean someone who has acquired wealth.
55 Virgil, *Aeneid* 6.466.
56 Xenophon singles out the Spartan general Thibron who was a poor leader because of his sexual desire for other men, see (Hindley, 1999, p. 77).
57 See (Adams, 1990).
58 Propertius, *Elegies* 2.15.30.
59 Ovid, *Ars Amatoria* 2.683.
60 Gibson has argued that Ovid's *Ars Amatoria* created a restrained form of desire which evaded the polarizing boundaries between a respectable woman and a whore created in Augustus' moral reforms, see (Gibson, 2007, pp. 113–14).
61 E.g. Ovid, *Tristia* 1.5 where he may be discussing an infatuation for a slave. Infatuation for slaves following their rape is commonplace in slave-owning societies and not indicative of tolerance towards homosexuality.
62 Ovid, *Metamorphoses* 10.149–54.
63 Homer, *Iliad* 5.265.
64 Homer possibly intended it as a divine correlate to the abductions which took place in the advent of the Trojan War.
65 Euripides, *Orestes* 1391.
66 (Williams, 2010).
67 (Verstraete, 2012). I am grateful to Dr Joe Watson for his guidance in trying to understand the strange queer-friendly parts of the Roman story.
68 A *glaber* in Latin.
69 Seneca, *Letters* 47.7–8.

70 The pater familias was originally defined, legally, as the head of a group of slaves, and rape was often one of the methods by which he asserted his power over his subordinates, see (Scheidel, 2012, p. 102).
71 For further discussion, see (Williams, 2010, p. 180; Cantarella, 2022, p. 98).
72 (Nissinen, 1998, pp. 48–9).
73 Diehl 504.
74 Diehl 540.
75 See Diehl 667. The Romans prided themselves on having shorter swords in combat than their enemies too.
76 *Carmina Priapea* 2.18.
77 (Zeichmann, 2020, p. 26). For a discussion of the Warren Cup, see (Pollini, 1999).
78 (Clarke, 1998, pp. 73, 275).
79 In his poetry, Catullus seems to allude to the fact that sexually explicit scenes were not about encouraging Romans to engage in sex acts, but were about satisfying one with imagery (Catullus 16.9).
80 (Wallace-Hadrill, 1983, p. 4).
81 Suetonius, *Tiberius* 34.
82 Suetonius, *Tiberius* 43. 'Monstrum' is often used of gay men. For the vocabulary of homosexuality, see (Richlin, 1993).
83 Suetonius, *Tiberius* 46.
84 (Charles and Anagnostou-Laoutides, 2010).
85 (Rogers, 1984).
86 See (Boswell, 2009, p. 67).
87 Suetonius, *Nero* 28.
88 Cassius Dio 80.2.
89 Historia Augusta, *Heliogabalus* 8.7.
90 (Taylor, 1997, p. 320) suggests Petronius' *Satyricon* may be an exception, but given it displays scenes of gay rape amid two men who cannot control their finances it still fits the pattern evinced here.
91 (Clarke, 1998, p. 84).
92 For the 'obnoxious threat' of the pathic, see (Taylor, 1997, p. 320).
93 Pliny the Elder, Natural History 10.83 and 10.172. See also, Caelius Aurelianus, On Acute and Chronic Illness 4.9.132, and (Fantham, 2011).
94 Juvenal 2.47.
95 Livy, *From the Foundation of the City* 39.13–18.
96 (Richlin, 1993, pp. 542–3).
97 (Taylor, 1997, p. 339), though (Williams, 2010, p. 244) suggests it was probably an attempt to secure neatly coiffed hair rather than

advertise for sex, which seems unlikely because many unmanly men were accused of doing it in contexts where sexual deviance is explicit, see (Edwards, 1993, p. 63).
98 Plautus, *The Carthaginian* 17–18.
99 Petronius 92. Martial 9.33. Juvenal 6.374–6.
100 Seneca, *Natural Questions* 1.16.3.
101 (Taylor, 1997, p. 368).
102 For the life of Hadrian, see (Birley, 2000).
103 For its authorship under Hadrian, see (Hine, 2001, pp. 9–10).
104 *Greek Anthology* 12.10.
105 *Greek Anthology* 12.17.1–3.
106 *Greek Anthology* 12.18.6.
107 *Greek Anthology* 12.81.
108 *Greek Anthology* 12.30.1–3.
109 *Greek Anthology* 12.4.1–8.
110 (Bastomsky, 1990, p. 41).
111 Musonius Rufus, Fragment 12.1 edidit Lutz.
112 Musonius Rufus, Fragments 12.4–6 edidit Lutz.
113 Musonius Rufus, Fragment 12.29 edidit Lutz.
114 (Gilliam, 1961).
115 Marcus Aurelius, *Meditations* 1.16.2.
116 Marcus Aurelius, *Meditations* 17.6.
117 For more details on the letters and their discovery, see (Richlin, 2007).
118 Fronto to Marcus, Letter 15, translation from (Richlin, 2007, p. 70).
119 (Richlin, 2007, p. 6).
120 (Richlin, 2007, p. 19).
121 (Sellars, 2023).
122 Lucian, *Dialogue of the Courtesans* 5.

CHAPTER EIGHT: THE FIRST CHRISTIANS

1 Tacitus, *Annals* 15.44. I characterize the Roman sources as 'independent', which requires some elaboration. The Roman sources we read have been passed down to us over thousands of years. For the majority of that time, the hands which copied and recopied those sources were those of Christian monks. A reasonable individual could have cause to question the true independence of these sources, though it's impossible to arrive at a firm conclusion either way.
2 Josephus, *War* 5.449–51.
3 The modern form of the Latin for Judah. Some historians prefer the term 'ancient Palestine', but this wasn't in use until the 2nd century CE by Romans and Greek historians.

4   For a history of the idea that Mary was a virgin, see (Lincoln, 2013).
5   Lk. 1.27 calls her a 'παρθένον', often translated 'virgin' in older Greek, but (Danker, Bauer and Arndt, 2000, art. παρθένος) says it means a young woman of marriageable age.
6   St Paul, *Letter to the Romans* 1:3. The Gospel of John also calls him Joseph's son at Jn. 1.45.
7   She is described as not yet married at the time of conception at Lk. 1.27.
8   (Hitchens, 2011, loc. 1619).
9   Hitchens is clumsy elsewhere. From the death of Herod the Great, a different Herod ruled in Galilee and Perea. His name was Herod Antipas. Yet Hitchens lambasts the Bible for inconsistency: how can it be, he says, that Herod was alive at the time of John the Baptist, yet also died in 4 BCE? (Hitchens, 2011, loc. 1627).
10 Reasoning by (Evans, 2006, p. 14).
11 (Evans, 2006, p. 14).
12 (Aviam, 2013). For a contrasting view, see (Fiensy, 2013, p. 165).
13 (Squitieri and Altaweel, 2022).
14 (Horsley, 2014, p. 49).
15 Plutarch, *Pompey* 8.5–7.
16 (Horsley, 2014, p. 77).
17 (Harland, 2002, p. 520).
18 (Horsley, 2014, p. 87).
19 (Harland, 2002, p. 515).
20 Assuming he did not flee into Egypt following Herod's alleged baby massacre, as some of the Gospels suggest. If the baby massacre did not take place, though, it seems unlikely that Jesus' family would have left.
21 Josephus, *Antiquities* 17.204–5.
22 Another of Herod's sons, Herod Antipas also ruled in Galilee and Perea as tetrarch.
23 For an overview of the political chaos, see (Horsley, 2014).
24 Census is ἀπογραφή in the Greek (Lk. 2.2), and had a looser sense of inventory of peoples for taxation purposes rather than a census we think of today, see (Danker, Bauer and Arndt, 2000, sec. ἀπογραφή).
25 For the details of the aqueduct and coin-minting, see (Horsley, 2014, p. 126).
26 Saturn reigned during the mythical golden age of Rome.
27 Virgil, *Eclogues* 4.4–9.
28 Likely thinking along similar lines, Augustus Caesar introduced strict laws on adultery and possibly homosexuality; see the previous chapter.
29 E.g. Mk. 1.22–29.

30 Josephus, *War* 2.427.
31 Josephus, *War* 2.184–203.
32 See Lk. 16.1–9 and 7.41–2 for similar debt stories.
33 Lk. 11.4. Interestingly, the Gospel of Matthew and the Didache contain a Lord's Prayer which does not use debt language, but rather focuses on forgiving class distinctions. I'm indebted to Dr Jordan Dyck for pointing this out.
34 Neh. 5.1–5.
35 Josephus, *War* 15.365.
36 (Horsley, 2014, p. 124).
37 Throughout ancient history, animal (and even human) sacrifice is associated with a failure of crops. Possibly, attempts to propitiate the divine overlapped with a need to kill a surplus of animals that could no longer be fed.
38 Josephus, *Antiquities* 15.9.1.
39 Josephus, *Antiquities* 15.299–316.
40 (Horsley, 2014, p. 108).
41 Josephus, *Antiquities* 20.51.
42 (Evans, 2008).
43 (Mansour et al., 2005, p. 740).
44 Origen, *Against Celsus* 1.6.
45 Philostratus, *Life of Apollonius* 4.45.
46 Philostratus, *Life of Apollonius* 4.10.
47 (Keener, 2012, pp. 89–90).
48 (Costa, 2012, p. 131).
49 For a full list, see (Gray, 1993).
50 Josephus, *Antiquities* 20.98.
51 (Mansour et al., 2005).
52 (Keith, 2020, p. 73).
53 Irenaeus, *Against Heresies* 3.1.1.
54 Lk. 7.42–3.
55 Lk. 6.27.
56 (Danker, Bauer and Arndt, 2000, sec. ἀγαπάω).
57 Lk. 6.35.
58 Lk. 6.21. This has a double meaning in the Greek, since spiritual hunger had long been a metaphor used in the Old Testament.
59 Lk. 6.2–5.
60 No archaeological or literary presence seems to point to the Cynics in the area (Evans, 2006, p. 13), but (Crossan, 1991, pp. 74–6) sees a resemblance between Cynic disavowal of law and embrace of poverty and Jesus' life and teachings. (Keener, 2009) is a biographer who's sceptical of Jesus' debts to Cynic philosophy.

61 Later Cynics, as we have covered in previous chapters, did marry, but Diogenes stayed single.
62 Roman authorities, by contrast, would have had little problem with it. Divorce was commonplace in Rome and could be performed by either party to the marriage without citing a reason. While Roman law generally forbade marriage between blood relations, in-laws may have had more leniency. For more reading on Roman marriage and divorce, see (Treggiari, 1993).
63 According to Mt. 5.32.
64 Mk. 10.9.
65 Lk. 7.25. The Greek word for 'soft' here is *malakos*, a term frequently used to condemn homosexual men, cf. 1 Cor. 6.9, where it seems to be used particularly of bottoms.
66 E.g. (Jennings, 2009).
67 Mt. 14.4.
68 (Keener, 2009, p. 296).
69 Mk. 6.16.
70 Lk. 23.1–4. Jesus also called upon his followers to cancel debts owed to them – Lk. 11.2–4; Mt. 6.9–14.
71 I have translated λόγος as 'guideline' here, since it cannot be law, since Jesus is providing an exception.
72 Mt. 19.10–12.
73 Hipponax Fragment 26, edidit West.
74 See (Asheri et al., 2011, p. 161).
75 ('Eunuchs in Ancient Religion', 1972, p. 10).
76 (Hester, 2005, p. 17).
77 See Chapter 6.
78 (Jennings, 2009, p. 81).
79 (Smith, 1982, p. 120).
80 John of Damascus, *On Heresies* 27.
81 According to (Welburn, 1994, p. 318), though the author's lack of citations on this and other matters may be a cause for concern in the critical reader. Others report more vaguely that the text was 'lost' or 'hidden' or 'destroyed', see (Frey, 2018, pp. 38–40), perhaps out of fear of angering the authorities over Mar Saba and never being allowed future access to manuscripts. There is a precarious politics to all manuscript work, especially if the texts are held by Orthodox authorities or the Vatican.
82 This has, at any rate, been the perspective of scholars writing on the period; that said, Luke-Acts does contain a reference to men being called Christians in Antioch, see Acts 11.26.
83 See, among others, (Cubitt, 2015).

84 However, in certain Church denominations (such as the Pentecostal Church) Armageddon date-setting is still very much in vogue.
85 (Longenecker, 2022, p. 185).
86 1 Cor. 1.26.
87 σαῦλος means 'waddling' or 'prancing' and is used of the 'loose, wanton gait of courtesans or Bacchantes' (according to the 19th-century LSJ dictionary of Greek). Hesychius the Lexicographer goes further, telling us of the existence of a colloquial verb 'σαυλοῦσθαι', meaning 'to be excessive, to break oneself, to destroy one's masculinity'.
88 Acts 8.
89 Acts 8.3.
90 (Roetzel, 2022, pp. 17–18).
91 Acts 22.7–8.
92 Acts 13.4–12.
93 Acts 14.8–18.7.
94 Acts 28.7–8.
95 (Roetzel, 2022, p. 11).
96 1 Cor. 16.2.
97 (Longenecker, 2022, p. 188).
98 2 Cor. 8.1–3.
99 Rom. 12.6–8.
100 Rom. 12.4.
101 (Dale, 2022, p. 638).
102 (Engberg-Pedersen, 2000).
103 1 Thess. 4.4–5.
104 (Danker, Bauer and Arndt, 2000, sec. κτάομαι).
105 This is often a feature of poetry and writing on the power of love, consider for example Rumi's *Masnavi-ye Ma'navi*, where the motif of looking outwards is replaced by a deliberate looking inwards to find the heart.
106 1 Cor. 7.8. Scholars like (Dale, 2022, p. 646) have suggested this is a more evolved position than we see in Thessalonians.
107 1 Cor. 7.9.
108 Just as Sappho and Plato described desire as forms of fire.
109 Rom. 1.23–4.
110 Rom. 1.26.
111 Gal. 5.19–20.
112 Gal. 5.24.
113 The language he is uses is a metaphor from inheriting property, reinforcing the connection to the economy in Pauline thought.
114 1 Corinthians 6:9–10.

115 (Hollenback, 2017).
116 Hipponax Fr. 12.2, edidit West.
117 Plato, *Gorgias* 456a.
118 (Thorsteinsson, 2003).
119 Thank you to Dr Jordan Dyck for raising this possibility. For the details of the argument, see (Dyck, 2017, pp. 228–62) where Dyck argues Paul might be writing *prosōpopoia*. For a brief history of different approaches to viewing Paul as a dialogue, see (Dyck, 2017, p. 235). For parts of Romans as a dialogue, see (Stowers, 1994, pp. 159–75). It is extremely controversial, but this whole conversation was provoked by (Campbell, 2009).
120 1 Cor. 6.11. (Peppiatt, 2017) has argued that 1 Corinthians could also be considered a conversation between Paul and an imaginary interlocutor.
121 (Stark, 1997, pp. 84–8).

CHAPTER NINE: THE BIRTH OF MODERN HOMOPHOBIA

1 Livy, *Ab Urbe Condita* 39.13–18.
2 (Filoramo, 1994, p. 177).
3 I have made a point throughout this work of refraining from labelling such ideas transgender. I don't think it respectful to the trans community to imply, in what has become a transphobic trope, that people only transition out of fear of their birth gender. For example, some have interpreted the Roman myth of Iphis and Ianthe as a trans story, but it is more likely that such an event was motivated out of a fear of being in a same-sex relationship than a desire to live as another gender.
4 For the details of the semen and menstruation rituals, see Epiphanius, *Panarion* 26.4–5.
5 Each of these details comes from (Brown, 2000, p. 13).
6 Augustine, *Confessions* 2.3.
7 (Brown, 2000, p. 24).
8 (Brown, 2008, pp. 387–88).
9 Augustine was heavily influence in his theological worldview by Cicero and other Stoics, he frequently cites Cicero's *Hortensius* in his work.
10 Augustine, *City of God* 14.24.
11 Augustine, *City of God* 14.16.
12 (Lansing, 1998, pp. 110–11).
13 (Banaji, 2007, pp. 87–8).
14 (Banaji, 2007, p. 215); for the growth of private industry and the urban economy, see (Laiou and Morrisson, 2007, pp. 23–42).
15 For all the dates, see (Cantarella, 2022, p. 229).

16 (Laiou and Morrisson, 2007, pp. 38–41).
17 Justinian I, Novellae 142.
18 (Betancourt, 2020, p. 125).
19 (Betancourt, 2020, p. 122).
20 (Rapp, 2016, p. 45).
21 (Smythe, 1999, pp. 146–7).
22 For a full survey, see (Rapp, 2016).
23 (Boswell, 2009).
24 For the life of Marinos, see (Betancourt, 2020, p. 92).
25 (Betancourt, 2020, p. 103). There have been many stories throughout history of those born as women who went to extreme lengths to present as men, including Joan of Arc, James Barry (I am grateful to Octavia for pointing this out to me) and Lavinia Edwards.
26 (Boswell, 2009, pp. 186–7). Boswell's blanket conclusion that same-sex desire was tolerated has been challenged repeatedly, see (Kuefler, 2018, p. 1260). The only way to reconcile both factions is to assume that queer identities could be explored clandestinely under cover of the Church, but the secular sphere offered no such protections.
27 *Concilium Parisiense*, Anno 829:69.
28 For example, by (Boswell, 2009).
29 (Mills, 2007, p. 11).
30 (Mills, 2007, p. 12).
31 Thomas Aquinas, *Summa Theologiae* 43:244–5.
32 (Alfani and Ammannati, 2017).
33 (Rocke, 1996, p. 3).
34 (Rocke, 1996, p. 4).
35 (Najemy, 2006, p. 246).
36 For the debt figures, see (Najemy, 2006, pp. 255–6).
37 For the tax figures, see (Najemy, 2006, p. 256).
38 (Rocke, 1996, p. 4). Rocke blames this rise on the need to find an excuse for arresting political dissidents. While this was doubtless true, it cannot be imagined that the only people persecuted were political opponents. Same-sex desire was being eradicated, and it was happening because of economic changes.
39 (Rocke, 1996, p. 89).
40 (Rocke, 1996, p. 92).
41 The Bible's parables became reinterpreted by new Protestants. The parable of the servant who was turned away because he could not increase the talent of gold that he was given was transformed from a metaphor for what the human being is supposed to do with Jesus' love into a literal commandment to make as much money as possible.

42 (Weber, 2001, pp. 108–9).
43 (Crow, 2018).
44 Coke 58 and 59.
45 Coke 59.
46 *The Shameful End of Bishop Atherton and his Proctor John Childe* 82–5.
47 The same was true in England. In 1729, a text entitled *Hell Upon Earth* recalls how a man named Tolson who lived in Charing Cross, 'whose constitution was so depraved and ruined that he could contain nothing within him', was executed for sodomy.
48 One manuscript of a play written by John Fletcher in 1611, *The Night Walker*, describes the penetration of an adult male by another male in a darkened room.
49 (Bergeron, 2002, p. 33).
50 (Bergeron, 2002, p. 70).
51 (Bergeron, 2002).
52 (De Vries and van der Woude, 1997, p. 674). While a useful source of data, I have concerns about de Vries and van der Woude's lack of footnotes and clear practices for citation.
53 (De Vries and van der Woude, 1997, p. 682).
54 (Reinert, 2009, p. 38).
55 For a review, see (Noordam, 1995).
56 For the history, see (Noordam, 1995, pp. 212–16).
57 (Merrick, 2007, p. 295).
58 (Merrick, 2007, p. 296).
59 (Merrick, 2007, p. 309).
60 (Horn, 2015, p. 618).
61 For example, see (Kron, 2014, p. 129).
62 (Warden, 1976, p. 585).
63 (*Improper Bostonians: lesbian and gay history from the Puritans to Playland*, 1998, p. 33).
64 The letters here cited can be found at (*Improper Bostonians: lesbian and gay history from the Puritans to Playland*, 1998, p. 34).
65 (*Improper Bostonians: lesbian and gay history from the Puritans to Playland*, 1998, p. 86).
66 i.e. Wellesley College.
67 Printed in (*Improper Bostonians: lesbian and gay history from the Puritans to Playland*, 1998, p. 88).
68 (Cocks, 2007, p. 110).
69 (Cocks, 2007, p. 111).
70 (Cocks, 2007, p. 117).
71 James Pratt and John Smith were the last men to be executed for the crime of gay sex in Britain. For their story, see (Cocks, 2007, p. 109).

72 (Cook, 2007, p. 148).
73 (Cook, 2007, p. 149).
74 For the camps, see (Grau, 1995, p. 281).
75 See (Kim, 2017). For the link between Plato, Aristotle and Nazism, see Karl Popper's *The Open Society and Its Enemies*. Popper does occasionally overreach in his argument, but the main thesis that Plato developed a Greek philosophy of purity and pre-destiny which has been a hallmark of fascist governments ever since is sound.
76 For details, see (Smith, Bartlett and King, 2004).
77 (Smith, Bartlett and King, 2004, p. 2).
78 Countries which have reintroduced criminal penalties in the modern world for same-sex desire are very often going through prolonged periods of economic difficulty with high levels of subsistence and below-subsistence living e.g. India, Uganda, Kenya, Romania (recriminalized 1996, then decriminalized 2001), Zimbabwe.
79 (Badgett, Waaldijk and Rodgers, 2019). There are occasional exceptions to this case, like the United Arab Emirates which maintains a death penalty for LGBTQ+ people and has a relatively high GDP per capita of around $49,000.
80 The internet has improved social connectivity offline in some studies, see (Ellison, Steinfield and Lampe, 2007; Wang and Wellman, 2010), but constant online contact may create a ghostly effect of pseudo-contact between people.
81 (Hyman, 2011).
82 For a history of this phenomenon, see (Piketty, 2014).
83 (*New data: Rise in hate crime against LGBTQ+ people continues,...,* no date)
84 (Mendelsohn, Tsvetkov and Jurafsky, 2020).

Bibliography

Abraham, K. (2001) 'The Middle Assyrian Period', in Jasnow, R. and Westbrook, R., *Security for Debt in Ancient Near Eastern Law (Culture and History of the Ancient Near East)*. Brill Academic Publishers (Culture and History of the Ancient Near East volume 9), pp. 161–222.

Ackerman, S. (2005) *When Heroes Love: The Ambiguity of Eros in the Stories of Gilgamesh and David (Gender, Theory, and Religion)*. Columbia University Press.

Adamidis, V. (2019) 'Manifestations of Populism in Late 5th Century Athens', in D.A. Frenkel and N. Varga (eds). Athens Institute for Education and Research, pp. 11–28. Available at: https://irep.ntu.ac.uk/id/eprint/36810/.

Adams, J.N. (1990) *The Latin Sexual Vocabulary*. Johns Hopkins University Press.

Alfani, G. and Ammannati, F. (2017) 'Long-term trends in economic inequality: the case of the Florentine state, c. 1300–1800', *The Economic History Review*, 70(4), pp. 1072–102. Available at: https://doi.org/10.1111/ehr.12471.

Allan, W. and Swift, L. (2024) *Euripides: Bacchae*. Cambridge University Press.

Allen, R.H. (2006) *The Classical Origins of Modern Homophobia*. McFarland.

Arkins, B. (1982) *Sexuality in Catullus*. Olms.

Asheri, D. et al. (eds) (2011) *A Commentary on Herodotus Books I - IV*. 1. publ. in paperback. Oxford University Press.

Aviam, M. (2013) 'People, Land, Economy, and Belief in First-Century Galilee and Its Origins: A Comprehensive Archaeological Synthesis', in D.A. Fiensy and R.K. Hawkins (eds) *The Galilean Economy in the Time of Jesus*. Society of Biblical Literature (Early Christianity and Its Literature 11), pp. 5–48.

Azoulay, V. (2017) *The Tyrant-Slayers of Ancient Athens: a Tale of Two Statues*. Translated by J. Lloyd. Oxford University Press.

Badgett, M.V.L., Waaldijk, K. and Rodgers, Y. van der M. (2019) 'The relationship between LGBT Inclusion and Economic Development: Macro-Level Evidence', *World Development*, 120, pp. 1–14. Available at: https://doi.org/10.1016/j.worlddev.2019.03.011.

Bagnall, R. and Bingen, J. (2007) *Hellenistic Egypt: Monarchy, Society, Economy, Culture*. Edinburgh University Press.

Baltes, M. (1993) 'Plato's School, the Academy', *Hermathena*, (155), pp. 5–26.

Banaji, J. (2007) *Agrarian Change in Late Antiquity: Gold, Labour, and Aristocratic Dominance*. Oxford University Press (Oxford Classical Monographs).

Bastomsky, S.J. (1990) 'Rich and Poor: The Great Divide in Ancient Rome and Victorian England', *Greece & Rome*, 37(1), pp. 37–43.

Beaulieu, P.-A. (2018) *A History of Babylon, 2200 BC-AD 75*. John Wiley & Sons Ltd.

Bell, J.M. (1980) 'The Road to Eleusis. Unveiling the Secret of the Mysteries by R. Gordon Wasson, Carl A. P. Ruck, and Albert Hofmann (review)', *Echos du Monde Classique: Classical News and Views*, 24(2), pp. 68–70.

Bergeron, D.M. (2002) *King James and Letters of Homoerotic Desire*. University of Iowa Press.

Betancourt, R. (2020) *Byzantine Intersectionality: Sexuality, Gender, and Race in the Middle Ages*. Princeton University Press.

Bickerman and Tropper, A. (2007) *Studies in Jewish and Christian History*. New edition. BRILL (Ancient Judaism and Early Christianity).

Bigger, S.F. (1979) 'The Family Laws of Leviticus 18 in Their Setting', *Journal of Biblical Literature*, 98(2), pp. 187–203. Available at: https://doi.org/10.2307/3265509.

Birley, A.R. (2000) 'Hadrian to the Antonines', in A.K. Bowman, P. Garnsey, and D. Rathbone (eds) *The Cambridge Ancient History*. 2nd edn. Cambridge University Press, pp. 132–94. Available at: https://doi.org/10.1017/CHOL9780521263351.004.

Boehringer, S. (2013) 'Female Homoeroticism', in T.K. Hubbard (ed.) *A Companion to Greek and Roman Sexualities*. 1st edn. Wiley, pp. 150–63. Available at: https://doi.org/10.1002/9781118610657.ch9.

Boswell, J. (2009) *Christianity, Social Tolerance, and Homosexuality: Gay People in Western Europe from the Beginning of the Christian Era to the Fourteenth Century*. University of Chicago Press.

Bowers v. Hardwick (1986) 478 U.S. 186.

Bowra, C.M. (1938) 'Plato's Epigram on Dion's Death', *The American Journal of Philology*, 59(4), pp. 394–404. Available at: https://doi.org/10.2307/291178.

Branham, R.B. and Goulet-Cazé, M.-O. (1997) *The Cynics: The Cynic Movement in Antiquity and Its Legacy (Hellenistic Culture and Society)*. 1st edn. University of California Press.

Bresson, A. (2015) *The Making of the Ancient Greek Economy: Institutions, Markets, and Growth in the City-States*. Princeton University Press.
Bristow, J. (2008) *Oscar Wilde and Modern Culture*. Ohio University Press.
Bristow, J. (2022) *Oscar Wilde on Trial: The Criminal Proceedings, from Arrest to Imprisonment*. Yale University Press.
Brown, P. (2000) *Augustine of Hippo: a Biography*. New ed. with an epilogue. Faber & Faber.
Brown, P. (2008) *The Body and Society: Men, Women, and Sexual Renunciation in Early Christianity*. Columbia University Press (Columbia classics in religion).
Bullough, V.L. (1973) 'Homosexuality as Submissive Behavior: Example from Mythology', *The Journal of Sex Research*, 9(4), pp. 283–8. Available at: https://doi.org/10.1080/00224497309550808.
Burnyeat, M. and Scott, M.F.E. by D. (eds) (2015) *The Pseudo-Platonic Seventh Letter*. Oxford University Press.
Campbell, D.A. (2009) *The Deliverance of God: An Apocalyptic Rereading of Justification in Paul*. Wm. B. Eerdmans Publishing.
Cantarella, E. (2022) *Bisexuality in the Ancient World*. Yale University Press.
Chairetakis, Y. (2016) 'Burial Customs of Megara during the 7th and 6th Centuries B.C.: The Case of the North-East Cemetery', in A. Robu and I. Bîrzescu (eds) *Mégarika: Nouvelles Recherches sur Mégare et les Cités de la Propontide et du Pont-Euxin Archéologie, épigraphie, histoire actes du colloque de Mangalia, 8-12 juillet 2012*. Paris: Éditions de Boccard (De l'archéologie à l'histoire, 66), pp. 219–38.
Charles, M. and Anagnostou-Laoutides, E. (2010) 'The Sexual Hypocrisy of Domitian: Suet., Dom. 8, 3', *L'antiquité classique*, 79. Available at: https://doi.org/10.3406/antiq.2010.3772.
Clarke, J.R. (1998) *Looking at Lovemaking: Constructions of Sexuality in Roman Art, 100 B.C.-A.D. 250*. University of California Press.
Cocks, H. (2007) 'Secrets, Crimes and Diseases, 1800–1914', in M. Cook et al. (eds) *A Gay History of Britain: Love and Sex between Men since the Middle Ages*. Greenwood World Pub, pp. 107–44.
Cohen, H.H. (1974) *The Drunkenness of Noah*. University of Alabama Press.
Collins, A. and Walsh, J. (2015) 'Debt Deflationary Crisis in the Late Roman Republic', *Ancient Society*, 45, pp. 125–70.
Cook, M. (2007) 'Queer Conflicts: Love, Sex and War, 1914–1967', in M. Cook et al. (eds) *A Gay History of Britain: Love and Sex between Men since the Middle Ages*. Greenwood World Pub, pp. 145–78.
Costa, T. (2012) 'The Exorcisms and Healings of Jesus within Classical Culture', in S.E. Porter and A.W. Pitts (eds) *Christian Origins and Greco-Roman Culture: Social and Literary Contexts for the New Testament*. Brill Academic Pub (Texts and Editions for New Testament Study 9; Early Christianity in Its Hellenistic Context 1), pp. 113–44.

Creamer, P.M. (2024) 'Inequalities in Wealth Distribution within Imperial Assyrian graves', *Antiquity*, pp. 1–16. Available at: https://doi.org/10.15184/aqy.2024.81.

Crossan, J.D. (1991) *The Historical Jesus: the Life of a Mediterranean Jewish Peasant*. T&T Clark.

Crow, A. (2018) *Ruling Appetites: The Politics of Diet in Early Modern English Literature*. Columbia University. Available at: https://doi.org/10.7916/D8709HTK.

Cubitt, C. (2015) 'APOCALYPTIC AND ESCHATOLOGICAL THOUGHT IN ENGLAND AROUND THE YEAR 1000', *Transactions of the Royal Historical Society*, 25, pp. 27–52. Available at: https://doi.org/10.1017/S0080440115000018.

Dale, M.B. (2022) 'Paul and Sexuality', in E. by M.V. Novenson and R.B. Matlock (eds) *The Oxford Handbook of Pauline Studies*. Oxford University Press, pp. 637–53.

Dalley, S. (1994) 'Nineveh, Babylon and the Hanging Gardens: Cuneiform and Classical Sources Reconciled', *Iraq*, 56, pp. 45–58. Available at: https://doi.org/10.2307/4200384.

D'Angelo, M.R. (2013) 'Sexuality in Jewish Writings from 200 BCE to 200 CE', in Hubbard, K., *A Companion to Greek and Roman Sexualities*. 1st edn. Wiley-Blackwell, pp. 534–48.

D'Angour, A. (2020) *Socrates in Love: The Making of a Philosopher*. Bloomsbury Publishing.

Danker, F.W., Bauer, W. and Arndt, W. (2000) *A Greek-English Lexicon of the New Testament and Other Early Christian Literature*. 3rd edn. Chicago: University of Chicago Press.

Davidson, J.N. (2008) *The Greeks and Greek love: a Radical Reappraisal of Homosexuality in Ancient Greece*. Pbk. ed. Phoenix.

Davies, G.I. (1979) *The Way of the Wilderness: a Geographical Study of the Wilderness Itineraries in the Old Testament*. Cambridge University Press (Monograph series / Society for Old Testament Study, 5).

De Marinis, A. (2019) *Philo on Male Homosexuality*. University of Oxford. Available at: https://ora.ox.ac.uk/objects/uuid:a5f1a652-a037-4be2-bf9e-945017f80669 (Accessed: 7 July 2024).

De Vries, J. and van der Woude, A.M. (1997) *The First Modern Economy: Success, Failure, and Perseverance of the Dutch Economy, 1500-1815*. Cambridge University Press.

Dessen, C. (1968) 'The Sexual and Financial Mean in Horace's Serm., I, 2', *The American Journal of Philology*, 89(2), pp. 200–8. Available at: https://doi.org/10.2307/293136.

Douglas, M. (2000) *Leviticus as Literature*. Oxford University Press.

Douglas, M. (2005) *Purity and Danger: an Analysis of Concept of Pollution and Taboo*. London ; New York: Routledge (Routledge classics).

Dover, K.J. (2016) *Greek Homosexuality*. Bloomsbury Academic.

Dover, K.J., Halliwell, S. and Stray, C. (2023) *Marginal Comment: A Memoir Revisited*. Bloomsbury Academic.

Dover, K.J. and Plato (1980) *Plato: Symposium*. Cambridge University Press (Cambridge Greek and Latin Classics). Available at: https://doi.org/10.1017/9780511813009.

Downing, F.G. (1992) *Cynics and Christian Origins*. Bloomsbury Publishing.

Dowson, T. (2008) 'Queering Sex and Gender in Ancient Egypt', in C. Graves-Brown (ed.) *Sex and Gender in Ancient Egypt: 'Don Your Wig for a Joyful Hour'*. ISD LLC, pp. 27–46.

Dyck, J.P. (2017) *Finding Lacan : St Paul and the Paradox of Jouissance*. Staffordshire University. Available at: https://eprints.staffs.ac.uk/3464/ (Accessed: 21 January 2025).

Edwards, C. (1993) *The Politics of Immorality in Ancient Rome*. Cambridge University Press.

Ellison, N.B., Steinfield, C. and Lampe, C. (2007) 'The Benefits of Facebook "Friends:" Social Capital and College Students' Use of Online Social Network Sites', *Journal of Computer-Mediated Communication*, 12(4), pp. 1143–68. Available at: https://doi.org/10.1111/j.1083-6101.2007.00367.x.

Engberg-Pedersen, T. (2000) *Paul and the Stoics*. Westminster John Knox Press.

'Eunuchs in Ancient Religion' (1972) in Nock, A. D., *Essays on Religion and the Ancient World*. Harvard University Press, pp. 7–15.

Evans, C. (2006) 'Context, Family, and Formation', in A.-J. Levine, D.C.A. Jr, and J.D. Crossan (eds) *The Historical Jesus in Context (Princeton Readings in Religions)*, pp. 11–24.

Evans, C.A. (2008) 'The Life and Teaching of Jesus and the Rise of Christianity', in J.M. Lieu and J.W. Rogerson (eds) *The Oxford Handbook of Biblical Studies*. Oxford University Press.

Evenepoel, W. (2014) 'The Stoic Seneca on Virtus, Gaudium and Voluptas', *L'antiquité classique*, 83, pp. 45–78. Available at: https://doi.org/10.3406/antiq.2014.3847.

Fantham, E. (2011) *Roman Readings: Roman Response to Greek Literature from Plautus to Statius and Quintilian*. De Gruyter, Inc.

Fardon, R. (1999) *Mary Douglas: An Intellectual Biography*. Taylor & Francis Group.

Fiensy, D.A. (2013) 'Assessing the Economy of Galilee In the Late Second Temple Period: Five Considerations', in D.A. Fiensy and R.K. Hawkins (eds) *The Galilean Economy in the Time of Jesus*. Society of Biblical Literature (Early Christianity and Its Literature 11), p. 165.

Filoramo, G. (1994) *A History of Gnosticism*. Reprinted. Translated by A. Alcock. Blackwell.

Fisher, N. (2001) *Aeschines against Timarchos*. Oxford University Press (Clarendon Ancient History Series).

Foster, B.R., Frayne, D. and Beckman, G.M. (eds) (2001) *The Epic of Gilgamesh: a New Translation, Analogues, Criticism*. 1st ed. New York: Norton.

Frayn, J.M. (1979) *Subsistence farming in Roman Italy*. Centaur Press.

Frey, J. (2018) 'Texts about Jesus: Non-canonical Gospels and Related Literature', in A.F. Gregory et al. (eds) *The Oxford handbook of Early Christian Apocrypha*. Oxford: Oxford University Press. pp. 13–47.

Gibson, R.K. (2007) *Excess and restraint: Propertius, Horace and Ovid's 'Ars Amatoria'*. London: University of London, Institute of Classical Studies (Bulletin supplement, 89).

Gilliam, J.F. (1961) 'The Plague under Marcus Aurelius', *The American Journal of Philology*, 82(3), pp. 225–51. Available at: https://doi.org/10.2307/292367.

Goldberg (editor), J. et al. (1993) *Queering the Renaissance*. Duke University Press.

Goldenberg, D.M. (2005) 'The Words of a Wise Man's Mouth are Gracious' (Qoh 10,12)', in M. Perani (ed.) *Festschrift for Günter Stemberger on the Occasion of his 65th Birthday*. De Gruyter, pp. 257–66. Available at: https://doi.org/10.1515/9783110901399.257.

Goulet-Cazé, M.-O. (2019) *Cynicism and Christianity in Antiquity*. Wm. B. Eerdmans Publishing.

Grabbe, L. (2002) 'The Priests in Leviticus—is the Medium the Message?', in R. Rendtorff and R. Kugler (eds) *The Book of Leviticus: Composition and Reception*. Boston, UNITED STATES: BRILL, pp. 207–25. Available at: http://ebookcentral.proquest.com/lib/ulondon/detail.action?docID=253684 (Accessed: 11 February 2025).

Graeber, D. (2011) *Debt: The First 5,000 Years*. Melville House.

Grau, G. (1995) *Hidden Holocaust? Gay and Lesbian Persecution in Germany 1933-45*. Cassell.

Gray, R. (1993) *Prophetic Figures in Late Second Temple Jewish Palestine: The Evidence from Josephus*. 1st edn. Oxford University Press, USA.

Halperin, D. (1990) *One Hundred Years of Homosexuality and other Essays on Greek Love*. Routledge.

Halperin, D.M. (1986) 'Plato and Erotic Reciprocity', *Classical Antiquity*, 5(1), pp. 60–80. Available at: https://doi.org/10.2307/25010839.

Hamilton, J.R. and Plutarchus (1969) *Plutarch: Alexander: A Commentary*. Oxford Clarendon Press.

Harland, P.A. (2002) 'The Economy of First-Century Palestine: State of the Scholarly Discussion', *Handbook of Early Christianity: Social Science Approaches*.

Harris, W.H. (2007) 'The Late Republic', in *The Cambridge Economic History of the Greco-Roman World*. Edited by W. Scheidel, I. Morris and R. Saller. Cambridge University Press.

Heidel, A. (1949) *Gilgamesh Epic and Old Testament Parallels*. University of Chicago Press.

Hester, J.D. (2005) 'Eunuchs and the Postgender Jesus: Matthew 19.12 and Transgressive Sexualities', *Journal for the Study of the New Testament*, 28(1), pp. 13–40. Available at: https://doi.org/10.1177/0142064X05057772.

Highbarger, E.L. (1927) *The History and Civilization of Ancient Megara*. The Johns Hopkins Press.

Hindley, C. (1999) 'Xenophon on Male Love', *The Classical Quarterly*, 49(1), pp. 74–99.

Hine, D. (2001) *Puerilities: Erotic Epigrams of the Greek anthology*. Princeton University Press.

Hitchens, C. (2011) *God Is Not Great*. eBook. Atlantic Books.

Hodkinson, S. (2009) *Property and Wealth in Classical Sparta*. Classical Press of Wales.

Hollenback, G.M. (2017) 'An Overlooked Backdrop to the Coining of αρσενοκοιτης', *Early Christianity*, 8(2), p. 269. Available at: https://doi.org/10.1628/186870317X14950055760665.

Horn, J. (2015) 'Lasting Economic Structures', in D. Andress (ed.) *The Oxford Handbook of the French Revolution*. Oxford University Press, p. 607.

Horsley, R.A. (2014) *Jesus and the Politics of Roman Palestine*. University of South Carolina Press.

House of Lords (1965) Sexual Offences Bill. 269. Hansard.

Hubbard, T.K. (ed.) (2003) *Homosexuality in Greece and Rome: a Sourcebook of Basic Documents*. University of California Press.

Hudson and Michael (2018) *...and Forgive Them Their Debts: Lending, Foreclosure and Redemption from Bronze Age Finance to the Jubilee Year*. Illustrated edn. Islet (Volume 1 of Tyranny of Debt).

Hupperts, C. (1988) 'Greek Love: Homosexuality or Paederasty? Greek Love in Black Figure Vase-Painting', in J. Christiansen and T. Melander (eds) *Proceedings of the 3rd Symposium on Ancient Greek and Related Pottery Copenhagen August 31–September 4 1987*. Ny Carlsberg Glyptotek and Thorvaldsens Museum, pp. 255–68.

Hupperts, C. (2005) 'Boeotian Swine', *Journal of Homosexuality*, 49(3–4), pp. 173–92. Available at: https://doi.org/10.1300/J082v49n03_06.

Hyman, L. (2011) *Debtor Nation: The History of America in Red Ink*. Princeton University Press.

Improper Bostonians: Lesbian and Gay History from the Puritans to Playland (1998). Boston: Beacon Press.

Jennings, T.W.J. (2009) *The Man Jesus Loved*. Seattle: Pilgrim Press.

Joosten, J. (2020) 'A New Interpretation of Leviticus 18:22 (Par. 20:13) and its Ethical Implications', *The Journal of Theological Studies*, 71(1), pp. 1–10. Available at: https://doi.org/10.1093/jts/flaa002.

Jope, J. (2013) 'Platonic and Roman Influences on Stoic and Epicurean Sexual Ethics', in Hubbard and K, T., *A Companion to Greek and Roman Sexualities*. 1st edn. Wiley-Blackwell, p. 417.

Keener, C.S. (2009) *The Historical Jesus of the Gospels*. Wm. B. Eerdmans Publishing Co.

Keener, C.S. (2012) 'Jesus and Parallel Jewish and Greco-Roman Figures', in S.E. Porter and A.W. Pitts (eds) *Christian Origins and Greco-Roman Culture: Social and Literary Contexts for the New Testament*. Brill Academic Pub (Texts and Editions for New Testament Study 9; Early Christianity in Its Hellenistic Context 1), pp. 85–112.

Kehoe, D. (2012) 'Contract Labor', in W. Scheidel (ed.) *The Cambridge Companion to the Roman Economy*. Cambridge University Press (Cambridge Companions to the Ancient World).

Keith, C. (2020) *The Gospel as Manuscript: An Early History of the Jesus Tradition as Material Artifact*. Oxford University Press, USA.

Kennedy, G.A. (1963) *The Art of Persuasion in Greece* (*A History of Rhetoric*, vol. 1). Princeton University Press.

Kim, A. (2017) 'An Antique Echo: Plato and the Nazis', in *Brill's Companion to the Classics, Fascist Italy and Nazi Germany*. Brill, pp. 205–37. Available at: https://doi.org/10.1163/9789004299061_010.

Konstan, D. (2021) 'Eros and the Pastoral', in Kyriakou, P., Sistakou, E., and Rengakos, A., *Brill's Companion to Theocritus*. BRILL (Brill's Companions to Classical Studies), pp. 517–33.

Kottaridi, A. (2011) 'The Palace of Aegae', in R.J.L. Fox (ed.) *Brill's Companion to Ancient Macedon*. Brill, pp.297–333.

Kron, G. (2014) 'Comparative Evidence and the Reconstruction of the Ancient Economy: Greco-Roman Housing and the Level and Distribution of Wealth and Income', in de Catallay (ed) *Quantifying the Greco-Roman Economy*, pp. 123–46. Available at: https://doi.org/10.4475/744.

Krueger, D. (1997) 'The Bawdy and Society', in Branham, R. B. and Goulet-Cazé, M.-O., *The Cynics: The Cynic Movement in Antiquity and Its Legacy* (Hellenistic Culture and Society). 1st edn. University of California Press.

Kuefler, M. (2018) 'Homoeroticism in Antiquity and the Middle Ages: Acts, Identities, Cultures, Christianity, Social Tolerance, and Homosexuality: Gay People in Western Europe from the Beginning of the Christian Era to the Fourteenth Century, by John Boswell', *The*

American Historical Review, 123(4), pp. 1246–66. Available at: https://doi.org/10.1093/ahr/rhy023.

Lagia, A. (2015) 'Diet and the Polis: An Isotopic Study of Diet in Athens and Laurion during the Classical, Hellenistic and Imperial Roman Periods', in Papathanasiou et al. (eds) *Archaeodiet in the Greek World: Dietary Reconstruction from Stable Isotope Analysis*, pp. 119–45.

Laiou, A.E. and Morrisson, C. (eds) (2007) *The Byzantine Economy*. Cambridge University Press.

Lansing, C. (1998) *Power and Purity: Cathar Heresy in Medieval Italy*. Oxford University Press.

Lapsley, J.E. (2003) 'Feeling Our Way: Love for God in Deuteronomy', *The Catholic Biblical Quarterly*, 65(3), pp. 350–69.

Lee, M.M. (2015) *Body, Dress, and Identity in Ancient Greece*. Cambridge University Press.

Legon, R.P. (1981) *Megara, the Political History of a Greek City-State to 336 B.C.* Cornell University Press.

Leitao, D.D. (1995) 'The Perils of Leukippos: Initiatory Transvestism and Male Gender Ideology in the Ekdusia at Phaistos', *Classical Antiquity*, 14(1), pp. 130–63. Available at: https://doi.org/10.2307/25000144.

Leroi, A.M. (2014) *The Lagoon: How Aristotle Invented Science*. Viking.

Lewis, V.B. (2017) 'The Authenticity of Plato's Seventh Letter', *The Classical Review*. Edited by M. Burnyeat, F. M., and D. Scott, 67(2), pp. 355–7.

Lincoln, A. (2013) *Born of a Virgin?: Reconceiving Jesus in the Bible, Tradition, and Theology*. Wm. B. Eerdmans Publishing.

Lloyd, G. (2014) 'Pythagoras', in Huffman, C. A., *A History of Pythagoreanism*. Cambridge University Press.

Loader, W.R.G. (2011) *Philo, Josephus, and the Testaments on Sexuality: Attitudes towards Sexuality in the Writings of Philo and Josephus and in the Testaments of the Twelve Patriarchs*. Grand Rapids, Mich: W.B. Eerdmans Pub. Co (Attitudes towards Sexuality in Judaism and Christianity in the Hellenistic Greco-Roman Era).

Longenecker, B.W. (2022) 'Paul and Economic Resources', in M.V. Novenson and R.B. Matlock (eds) *The Oxford Handbook of Pauline Studies*. Oxford University Press, pp. 180–97.

Mansfeld, J. (2006) 'Theology', in K. Algra et al. (eds) *The Cambridge History of Hellenistic Philosophy*. Cambridge University Press, pp. 452–78.

Mansour, A.M. et al. (2005) 'Jesus and the Eye: New Testament Miracles of Vision', *Acta Ophthalmologica Scandinavica*, 83(6), pp. 739–45. Available at: https://doi.org/10.1111/j.1600-0420.2005.00608.x.

Matić, U. (2019) 'Out of Touch', in Naujoks et al. (eds) *Von der Quelle zur Theorie*. Brill, pp.183–97. Available at: https://doi.org/10.30965/9783957437815_011.

McKirahan, R.D. (2010) *Philosophy before Socrates: an Introduction with Texts and Commentary*. 2nd ed. Indianapolis: Hackett Pub. Co.

Mendelsohn, J., Tsvetkov, Y. and Jurafsky, D. (2020) 'A Framework for the Computational Linguistic Analysis of Dehumanization', *Frontiers in Artificial Intelligence*, 3, p. 55. Available at: https://doi.org/10.3389/frai.2020.00055.

Meritt, L.S. (1970) 'The Stoa Poikile', *Hesperia*, 39(4), p. 233. Available at: https://www.jstor.org/stable/147646.

Merrick, J.W. (2007) *Order and Disorder under the Ancien Régime*. Cambridge Scholars Publishing.

Mikalson, J.D. (1976) 'Erechtheus and the Panathenaia', *The American Journal of Philology*, 97(2), p. 141. Available at: https://doi.org/10.2307/294404.

Milgrom, J. (2007) *Leviticus 17-22 (Anchor Bible Commentaries): A New Translation with Introduction and Commentary (Anchor Bible Commentary)*. Yale University Press.

Miller, J. (2000) *The Passion of Michel Foucault*. Harvard University Press.

Miller, S.G. (2004) *Ancient Greek Athletics*. Yale University Press.

Millett, P. (1991) *Lending and Borrowing in Ancient Athens*. Cambridge University Press.

Mills, R. (2007) 'Male–Male Love and Sex in the Middle Ages, 1000–1500', in M. Cook et al. (eds) *A Gay History of Britain: Love and Sex between Men since the Middle Ages*. Greenwood World Pub, pp. 1–44.

Mueller, M. (2021) 'Sappho and Sexuality', in P.J. Finglass and A. Kelly (eds) *The Cambridge Companion to Sappho*. Cambridge University Press.

Müller, S. (2010) 'Philip II', in Roisman, J. and Worthington I., (eds), *A Companion to Ancient Macedonia*. 1st edn. Wiley-Blackwell (Blackwell Companions to the Ancient World).

Myrmidons | APGRD (no date). Available at: http://www.apgrd.ox.ac.uk/ancient-performance/performance/556 (Accessed: 1 October 2024).

Nagarajan, K. (2011) 'The Code of Hammurabi: An Economic Interpretation', *International Journal of Business and Social Science*, 2.

Najemy, J.M. (2006) *A History of Florence 1200–1575*. 1st edn. Blackwell Pub.

New Data: Rise in Hate Crime against LGBTQ+ People Continues,... (no date) Stonewall. Available at: https://www.stonewall.org.uk/news/new-data-rise-hate-crime-against-lgbtq-people-continues-stonewall-slams-uk-gov (Accessed: 11 March 2025).

Niehoff, M.R. (2018) *Philo of Alexandria: an Intellectual Biography*. New Haven (Conn.): Yale University press (The Anchor Yale Bible reference library).

Nissinen, M. (1998) *Homoeroticism in the Biblical World. A Historical Perspective*. Augsburg Fortress.

Noordam, D.J. (1995) *Riskante relaties: vijf eeuwen homoseksualiteit in Nederland, 1233–1733*. Uitgeverij Verloren.

North, G. (1994) *Leviticus: An Economic Commentary*. Institute for Christian Economics.

North, J.A. (2006) 'The Constitution of the Roman Republic', in N.S. Rosenstein and R. Morstein-Marx (eds) *A Companion to the Roman Republic*. Malden, MA ; Oxford: Blackwell Pub (Blackwell Companions to the Ancient World), pp. 256–77.

Ober, J. (1991) *Mass and Elite in Democratic Athens: Rhetoric, Ideology, and the Power of the People*. Princeton University Press.

Ogden, D. (2011) *Alexander the Great: Myth, Genesis and Sexuality*. 1. publ. Exeter: Univ. of Exeter Press.

Olesen-Bagneux, O. (2014) 'The Memory Library: How the Library in Hellenistic Alexandria Worked', KNOWLEDGE ORGANIZATION, 41(1), pp. 3–13. Available at: https://doi.org/10.5771/0943-7444-2014-1-3.

Oliensis, E. (1997) 'Sons and Lovers: Sexuality and Gender in Virgil's Poetry', in C. Martindale (ed.) *The Cambridge Companion to Virgil*. Cambridge: Cambridge University Press (Cambridge Companions to Literature), pp. 294–311. Available at: https://doi.org/10.1017/CCOL0521495393.020.

Olyan, S.M. (1994) 'And with a Male You Shall Not Lie the Lying down of a Woman': On the Meaning and Significance of Leviticus 18:22 and 20:13', Journal of the History of Sexuality, 5(2), pp. 179–206.

Ormand, K. (2009) *Controlling Desires: Sexuality in Ancient Greece and Rome*. Praeger (Praeger Series on the Ancient World).

Parker, H.N. (1993) 'Sappho Schoolmistress', Transactions of the American Philological Association (1974), 123, p. 309. Available at: https://doi.org/10.2307/284334.

Pedersén, O. (2020) 'The Glazed Bricks that Ornamented Babylon – A Short Overview', in A. Fügert and H. Gries (eds) *Glazed Brick Decoration in the Ancient Near East*. Archaeopress (Proceedings of a Workshop at the 11th International Congress of the Archaeology of the Ancient Near East (Munich) in April 2018), pp. 96–122. Available at: https://doi.org/10.2307/jj.15136077.9.

Peled, I. (2016) *Masculinities and Third Gender: The Origins and Nature of an Institutionalized Gender Otherness in the Ancient Near East*. Ugarit-Verlag.

Peleg, Y. (2005) 'Love at First Sight? David, Jonathan, and the Biblical Politics of Gender', Journal for the Study of the Old Testament, 30(2), pp. 171–89. Available at: https://doi.org/10.1177/0309089205060606.

Peppiatt, L. (2017) *Women and Worship at Corinth: Paul's Rhetorical Arguments in 1 Corinthians*. James Clarke & Company Limited.

Piketty, T. (2014) *Capital in the Twenty-First Century*. Harvard University Press.

Pleins, J.D. (2004) 'When myths go wrong: deconstructing the drunkenness of Noah', *Culture and Religion*. Available at: https://doi.org/10.1080/1438300420000225448.

Pollini, J. (1999) 'The Warren Cup: Homoerotic Love and Symposial Rhetoric in Silver', *The Art Bulletin*, 81(1), p. 21. Available at: https://doi.org/10.2307/3051285.

Price, A.W. (2002) 'Plato, Zeno, and the Object of Love', in Nussbaum, M. C. and Sihvola, J., *The Sleep of Reason : Erotic Experience and Sexual Ethics in Ancient Greece and Rome*. 1st edn. University of Chicago Press.

Rapp, C. (2016) *Brother-making in Late Antiquity and Byzantium: Monks, Laymen, and Christian Ritual*. Oxford University Press.

Raven, J.E. (2000) *Plants and Plant Lore in Ancient Greece*. Leopard's Head.

von Reden, S. (2007) 'Classical Greece: Consumption', in Scheidel, W., Morris, I., and Saller, R., *The Cambridge Economic History of the Greco-Roman World*. Cambridge University Press.

Reden, S. von (2022) 'Hellenistic Economies', in Reden, S. von, *The Cambridge Companion to the Ancient Greek Economy*. Cambridge University Press (Cambridge Companions to the Ancient World).

Reeder, G. (2008) 'Queer Egyptologies of Niankhkhnum and Khnumhotep', in Graves-Brown, C., *Sex and Gender in Ancient Egypt: 'Don Your Wig for a Joyful Hour'*. ISD LLC, pp. 143–56.

Reinert, E.S. (2009) 'Emulating Success: Contemporary Views of the Dutch Economy before 1800', in Gelderblom, O., *The Political Economy of the Dutch Republic*. Farnham: Ashgate, pp. 19–40.

Richlin, A. (1993) 'Not Before Homosexuality: The Materiality of the Cinaedus and the Roman Law against Love between Men', *Journal of the History of Sexuality*, 3(4), pp. 523–73.

Richlin, A. (2007) *Marcus Aurelius in Love: the Letters of Marcus and Fronto*. University of Chicago Press.

Rocke, M. (1996) *Forbidden Friendships: Homosexuality and Male Culture in Renaissance Florence*. Oxford University Press (Studies in the History of Sexuality).

Roetzel, C.J. (2022) 'The Man and the Myth', in E. by M.V. Novenson and R.B. Matlock (eds) *The Oxford Handbook of Pauline Studies*. Oxford University Press, pp. 11–30.

Rogers, P.M. (1984) 'Domitian and the Finances of State', *Historia: Zeitschrift für Alte Geschichte*, 33(1), pp. 60–78.

Romm, J. (2021) *The Sacred Band: Three Hundred Theban Lovers Fighting to Save Greek Freedom*. Scribner.

Roochnik, D. (2023) 'Plato's Lysis and the Erotics of Philia', *Revista Archai*, 32. Available at: https://doi.org/10.14195/1984-249X_32_42.

Rudich, V. (1997) *Dissidence and Literature under Nero: the Price of Rhetoricization*. Routledge.

Said, E.W. (1995) *Orientalism*. Penguin Group.

Samorini, G. (2021) 'Psychoactive Plants in the Ancient World: Observations of an Ethnobotanist', in *The Routledge Companion to Ecstatic Experience in the Ancient World*. Routledge, pp. 73–89.

Sandhoff, B. (2019) 'Romancing the Sexes: Representations of Marital Love in Etruria', in K. Gardiner and S.V. Pfister (eds) *Past and Present: Perspectives on Gender and Love*. Brill, pp. 91–106.

Sawada, N. (2010) 'Social Customs and Institutions: Aspects of Macedonian Elite Society', in Roisman, J. and Worthington I., (eds) *A Companion to Ancient Macedonia* (Blackwell Companions to the Ancient World). 1st edn. Wiley-Blackwell (Blackwell Companions to the Ancient World).

Scarborough, J. (2010) *Pharmacy and Drug Lore in Antiquity: Greece, Rome, Byzantium*. Ashgate Pub (Variorum collected studies series, CS904).

Schroer, S. and Staubli, T. (2000) 'Saul, David and Jonathan — The Story of a Triangle? A Contribution to the Issue of Homosexuality in the First Testament', in A. Brenner (ed.) *Samuel and Kings*. 1st edn. Bloomsbury T&T Clark (Feminist Companion to the Bible), pp. 22–36.

Schwartz, D.R. (2009) 'Philo, His Family, and His Times', in Kamesar, A., *The Cambridge Companion to Philo*. 1st edn. Cambridge University Press (Cambridge Companions to Philosophy), pp. 9–31.

Seaford, R. (2006) *Dionysos*. Routledge.

Sedley, D. (1976) 'Epicurus and his Professional Rivals', in J. Bollack and A. Laks (eds) *Études sur l'Épicurisme Antique*. Publications de l'Université de Lille III (Cahiers de Philologie), pp. 119–59.

Sellars, J. (2006) *Stoicism* (Ancient Philosophies). 1st edn. University of California Press.

Sellars, J. (2023) 'Marcus Aurelius and the Tradition of Spiritual Exercises', in M. Garani, D. Konstan, and G. Reydams-Schils (eds) *The Oxford Handbook of Roman Philosophy*. OUP USA, pp. 74–86.

Shapiro, H.A. (1981) 'Courtship Scenes in Attic Vase-Painting', *American Journal of Archaeology*, 85(2), pp. 133–43. Available at: https://doi.org/10.2307/505033.

Skinner, M.B. (2013) *Sexuality in Greek and Roman Culture*. 2nd edn. Wiley-Blackwell.

Smith, G., Bartlett, A. and King, M. (2004) 'Treatments of Homosexuality in Britain since the 1950s—an Oral History: the Experience of Patients', *BMJ : British Medical Journal*, 328(7437), p. 427. Available at: https://doi.org/10.1136/bmj.37984.442419.EE.

Smith, M. (1982) *The Secret Gospel: The Discovery and Interpretation of the Secret Gospel According to Mark*. Dawn Horse Press.

Smythe, D.C. (1999) 'In Denial: Same-Sex Desire in Byzantium', in L. James (ed.) *Desire and Denial in Byzantium: Papers from the 31st Spring Symposium of Byzantine Studies, University of Sussex, Brighton, March 1997*. Ashgate/Variorum, pp. 139–48.

Squitieri, A. and Altaweel, M. (2022) 'Empires and the Acceleration of Wealth Inequality in the pre-Islamic Near East: an Archaeological Approach', *Archaeological and Anthropological Sciences*, 14(10), p. 190. Available at: https://doi.org/10.1007/s12520-022-01659-3.

Stansell, G. (2011) 'David and his friends: Social-Scientific Perspectives on the David-Jonathan Friendship', *Biblical Theology Bulletin*, 41(3), pp. 115–31.

Stark, R. (1997) *The Rise of Christianity: How the Obscure, Marginal Jesus Movement Became the Dominant Religious Force in the Western World in a Few Centuries*. HarperSanFrancisco.

Stowers, S.K. (1994) *A Rereading of Romans: Justice, Jews, and Gentiles*. Yale University Press.

Stray, C., Clarke, M. and Katz, J.T. (eds) (2019) *Liddell and Scott: The History, Methodology, and Languages of the World's Leading Lexicon of Ancient Greek*. Oxford University Press.

Tanner, H. (2023) *Ancient Greek Lexical Semantics: Word Meanings as a Function of Context*. National University of Ireland, Galway.

Tanner, H. (2024) *Beyond LSJ: How to Deepen Your Understanding of Ancient Greek – Antigone*. Available at: https://antigonejournal.com/2024/04/. (Accessed: 31 January 2025).

Tanner, H. (2025) 'Ancient Greek Lexical Meaning in Context', *Journal of Greek Linguistics* [Preprint], (25.2).

Taylor, R. (1997) 'Two Pathic Subcultures in Ancient Rome', *Journal of the History of Sexuality*, 7(3), pp. 319–71.

'Theopompus' Historical Accuracy' (1997) in Flower, M. A., *Theopompus of Chios: History and Rhetoric in the Fourth Century BC*. Clarendon Press (Clarendon paperbacks), pp. 184–210.

Thorsteinsson, R. (2003) *Paul's Interlocutor in Romans 2: Function and Identity in the Context of Ancient Epistolography, Coniectanea Biblica, New Testament Series*. Lund University.

Thurston, T. (1990) 'Leviticus 18:22 and the Prohibition of Homosexual Acts', in M. L. Stemmeler and J. M. Clark (eds) *Homophobia and the Judaeo-Christian Tradition*. Monument Press.

Treggiari, S. (1993) *Roman Marriage: Iusti Coniuges from the Time of Cicero to the Time of Ulpian*. Oxford University Press.

Verstraete, B. (2012) 'Reassessing Roman Pederasty in Relation to Roman Slavery: The Portrayal of Pueri Delicati in the Love-Poetry of Catullus, Tibullus, and Horace', *The Journal of International Social Research*, 5(20).

von Ungern-Sternberg, J. (2004) 'The Crisis of the Republic', in H.I. Flower (ed. & tran.) *The Cambridge Companion to the Roman Republic*. Cambridge University Press, pp. 78–100.

Wallace-Hadrill, A. (1983) *Suetonius: the Scholar and his Caesars*. Duckworth (Classical Life and Letters).

Walsh, J.T. (2001) 'Leviticus 18:22 and 20:13: Who Is Doing What to Whom?', *Journal of Biblical Literature*, 120(2), pp. 201–9. Available at: https://doi.org/10.2307/3268292.

Wang, H. and Wellman, B. (2010) 'Social Connectivity in America: Changes in Adult Friendship Network Size from 2002 to 2007', *American Behavioral Scientist*, 53(8), pp. 1148–69. Available at: https://doi.org/10.1177/0002764209356247.

Warden, G.B. (1976) 'Inequality and Instability in Eighteenth-Century Boston: A Reappraisal', *Journal of Interdisciplinary History*, 6(4). Available at: https://doi.org/10.2307/202533.

Wasson, R.G., Hofmann, A. and Ruck, C.A.P. (2008) *The Road to Eleusis: Unveiling the Secret of the Mysteries*. North Atlantic Books.

Weber, M. (2001) *The Protestant Ethic and the Spirit of Capitalism*. Routledge (Routledge Classics).

Welburn, A.J. (1994) *Gnosis, the Mysteries and Christianity: an Anthology of Essene, Gnostic and Christian Writings*. Floris Books.

West, M.L. (2011) *The Making of the Iliad: Disquisition and Analytical Commentary*. Oxford University Press.

Williams, C.A. (2010) *Roman Homosexuality: Second Edition*. 2nd edn. Oxford University Press.

Wilson, W.T. (2012) *The Sentences of Pseudo-Phocylides*. De Gruyter. Available at: https://doi.org/10.1515/9783110892765.

Wohl, V. (2002) *Love among the Ruins: The Erotics of Democracy in Classical Athens*. 1st edn. Princeton University Press.

Woodard, V. (2014) *The Delectable Negro: Human Consumption and Homoeroticism Within US Slave Culture*. NYU Press.

Worman, N.B. (2004) 'Insult and Oral Excess in the Disputes between Aeschines and Demosthenes', *American Journal of Philology*, 125(1), pp. 1–25. Available at: https://doi.org/10.1353/ajp.2004.0011.

Zeichmann, C.B. (2020) 'Same-Sex Intercourse Involving Jewish Men 100 BCE–100 CE'. Available at: https://doi.org/10.1163/18785417-01001001.

Index

abortions, 90
Abraham, 115–18
Achilles and Patroclus, 24–5, 32–4, 57, 75, 85
Acropolis, 18, 29, 32, 52
Actium, Battle of, 138, 160
Adam and Eve, 186–7
adelphopoiesis ('brother-making'), 189
Adey, More, 3
adultery, 55, 134, 140, 179, 193, 228n
Aegae, 50, 61
Aelred of Rievaulx, 190–1
Aeneas, 140–1
Aeschines, 55–8, 73, 137, 212n
Aeschines of Sphettos, 76
Aeschylus, 15, 32–6, 42, 98
  Myrmidons, 33–5
  Oresteia, 32
  Persians, 36
Affecter, The, 34
Agamemnon, 24, 33
Agathon and Pausanias, 43–5, 60, 75, 211n
Agave, 49
Ajax, 92
akousmata, 68–9
Alcaeus, 15–16
Alcibiades, 71
Alcman, 23
Alexander the Great, 61, 81–7, 89–90, 97, 101, 123, 211n, 217n
Alexander, king of Epirus, 61
Alexander (son of Herod), 127
Alexandria, 87, 97–101, 123, 125, 151, 159, 162, 166, 174, 210n, 216n, 219n

Dildo of Alexandria, 99–100
  Great Library, 98
Amazons, 92
American War of Independence, 197
amicus, 142
Anactoria, 15
Anastasius, 190
andreios, 40
Andromache, 25
animal sacrifice, 229n
Anniceris of Cyrene, 67
Antigonus, king of Macedon, 93
Antigonus of Carystus, 94
Antinous, 130, 152
Antioch, 230n
Aphrodite, 15, 74, 95
Apollo, 35, 51, 64, 68
Apollonios, 86
Apollonius of Tyana, 167
apomorphine, 200
Appian, 133
Appian Way, 158
Aramaic language, 164
Archelaus, king of Judea, 161
Archelaus I, king of Macedon, 43–4, 211n
Arginusae, Battle of, 47–8
Aristides, 53
Aristoboulos III, king of Judea, 127
Aristodemus of Sparta, 22
Ariston of Collytus, 64
Aristophanes
  Knights, 27, 38–9
  Wealth, 54–5
  The Women at the Thesmophoria, 43–4

Aristotle, 14, 17, 20, 22, 77–8,
    81–3, 85, 94–5, 155, 175, 186,
    206n, 215–16n, 235n
Armageddon, 174, 231n
Arran, Lord, 109, 200
Arrentium, 146
arsenokoitai, 178–9
Artemis, 18
Aruru, 121
Asculum, 134
Ashurbanipal, king of Assyria, 121
assinnus, 104, 114
Assyrians, 103–4
  law codes, 111–12, 123, 220n
atheism, 64, 95, 158, 213n
Athena, 18, 29, 70
Athens, ancient, 5, 16, 18–21, 25,
    27–32, 34–40, 42–5, 50, 52–9, 61,
    81, 98, 137, 151, 169, 202
  debt problem, 76–80
  democracy, 9–10, 29, 31, 37, 48, 64
  Diogenes and, 87–9
  graves and tombs, 53–5
  hostility to atheism, 64, 95
  Macedonian conquest, 58–9
  Mytilene debate, 37–8
  painted Stoa, 92, 94
  Panathenaia festival, 28–9
  Peloponnesian War, 37, 47–8, 64, 71
  Persian wars, 27, 29–30, 32, 34–5
  Plato and, 66–7, 70–1, 73, 75–8
  wealth and incomes, 35–7, 52–5
  Zeno and, 90–2
Atherton, Bishop John, 193, 201
Attalus III, king of Pergamum, 133
Attalus, 60–1
Attica, 36
Atum, 30, 124
Augustus, Emperor, 131, 138–40,
    142–3, 146, 160, 228n
aversion therapy, 200

Babcock, Tristom, 197
Babylonian Talmud, 115
Babylonians, 67, 103–6, 109, 111–12,
    114, 121, 159, 172
Bagoas, 85
Bandon Bridge, 193
Barry, James, 233n
Barsine, 83
Bates, Katherine Lee, 198

Belshazzar, Prince, 106
ben Dosa, Hanina, 167
Bible
  confirmation bias, 219n
  English translation, 194
  Lord's Prayer, 164, 229n
  New Testament, 107, 163–4, 168,
    170–1, 179, 184, 186
  Old Testament, 103, 105, 107, 110,
    115, 117–19, 121, 123, 127, 164,
    219n, 221n, 229n
  parables, 169–70, 233n
  Sermon on the Mount, 170
  textual scholarship, 107–8
  see also individual books
Bielfeld, Jakob Friedrich von, 195
Black Death, 191
Boeotia, 16–18, 21, 25
Book of Acts, 175
Book of Deuteronomy, 109
Book of Ezekiel, 117
Book of Genesis, 114, 116–17, 121
Book of Judges, 118
Book of Leviticus, ix, 107–14, 118–19,
    123, 125, 170–1
Book of Samuel, *see* David and Jonathan
Boston, 197–8
Briseis, 24
Buchenwald, 200
Buddhism, 68
buggery, 111, 193, 195
Burger, Warren, 109
Byzantium, 9, 187–91, 194
  Great Plague, 187, 191

Caesarea Maritima, 160
Caligula, Emperor, 125–7
Callicles, 74
Capitolinus, 136
Capri, 147
Carlton, Dudley, 194
Carolingian Empire, 190
Carpocratians, 173–4, 184
Carre, Sir Robert, 194
Carthage, 132, 139, 186
Cassandra, 92, 218n
castration, 111, 115, 127, 172, 192,
    200
Catholic Church, 172–3
Catiline, 134
Catullus, 135–6, 144, 223–4n, 226n

celibacy, 172
Celsus, 166–7
Chaeronea, battle of, 58–9, 81, 87
Chamberlain, John, 194
Chaos, 95
chastity, 58, 190
Choerilus of Samos, 45
Christianity, viii–xi, 6, 67, 75, 92, 98, 101, 118, 127, 162, 182
  and asceticism, 190
Chrysippus, king of Pisa, 43
Cicero, 16, 130, 133–6, 185
cinaedus, 135
Claudius, Emperor, 166
Cleanthes, 94
Clement of Alexandria, Bishop, 173–4
Cleon, 37–40, 42, 56, 75
Cleopatra, queen of Egypt, 127, 138, 160
Cleopatra (daughter of Philip of Macedon), 61
Coke, Sir Edward, 193
Coman, Katharine, 198
concentration camps, 199–200
Constans I, Emperor, 187
Constantius II, Emperor, 187
conversion therapy, ix
Corinthians, 71, 156, 174–6
Corver, Hendrik, 195
Crates, 91–2
crucifixion, 157–8
Curtius, 85
Cyclops, 219n
Cynicism, 89–90, 92, 169, 218n, 229–30n
Cynthia, 142

Dabney, Robert Lewis, 221n
David II, king of Scotland, 190
David and Jonathan, 1, 103, 118–23
de' Nobili, Antonio di Niccolò, 192
death penalty, 187, 235n
debt, 19, 87, 93, 169, 192, 195, 202–3, 219n
  in ancient Athens, 76–80
  in ancient Rome, 125–6, 134, 137
  in Judea/Palestine, 160–6, 170–1
  in Middle Assyrian law codes, 111–12
Delian League, 35
Demeter, 18, 183, 211n

democracy, 9–11, 16, 29, 31, 37, 48, 58, 64, 77, 97, 131, 200, 210n
Demosthenes, 53, 55–7, 61, 73, 76–7, 81–2
Dennie, Joseph, 183, 197–8
Dido, queen of Carthage, 140–2
Didyma, Temple of Apollo, 68
dietaristriai ('rubbing women'), 189
Diocles, 207n
Diodorus Siculus, 61
Diogeiton, 54
Diogenes of Sinope, 87–91, 169, 217n, 230n
Diogenes Laertius, 66
Dion, 73, 80
Dionysius I, king of Syracuse, 66–7, 73, 78, 80
Dionysius II, king of Syracuse, 80
Dionysus, 16, 18, 48–9, 75, 130, 149, 183
divorce, 170, 230n
Doherty, Gerald, 199
Domitian, Emperor, 136, 148
d'Orléans, Duchesse, 196
Doryphorus, 148
Douglas, Lord Alfred, 2
Douglas, Mary, 112–13
Dover, Sir Kenneth, 4, 6–7, 214n
drauci, 150
drugs, 48, 89–90, 95, 200, 211n
Dublin, Gallows Green, 193

e gradibus entium, 96
Ecbatana, 86
Edward II, King, 173
Edwards, Lavinia, 233n
Egypt, ancient, 11, 30, 86–7, 97–101, 105–6, 123–8
Egyptian Book of the Dead, 123
Elagabalus, Emperor, 148
Elephantis, 147
Elizabeth I, Queen, 193
Elymas, 176
English Reformation, 192
Enkidu, 121–3
Ephesus, 167
Epicurus of Samos, 94–7, 216n
Epiphanius, 184
Epistle to the Corinthians, 157, 176, 178–9
Epistle to the Thessalonians, 177

Eryximachus, 75
Etemenanki, 104
Etruscans, 34
eunouchoi, 171–3
eunuchs, 104, 127, 129, 160, 172
Euphorbus, 68
Euripides, 15, 42–5, 66, 98, 144
  Bacchae, 48–50, 54, 71
  Electra, 43
  Hippolytus, 43
  Medea, 42
  Orestes, 43
Eurymedon vase, 30
Eusebius of Caesarea, 158, 174
Euthydicus, 57

Fabius, procurator, 168
farting, 88, 169
Fields, Annie Adams, 198
Fletcher, John, *The Night Walker*, 234n
Florence, 191–2
Foucault, Michel, 218n
France, 196–7

Gaius Musonius Rufus, 153
Galatea, 41
Gedrosia, 85
gender fluidity, 40–1, 114
Gilgamesh, 121–3
Gill, Charles, 1
gladius, 142
Glapion, Louis, 197
Glaucias, 86
Gnostics, 184–5
Goliath, 119
Gospel of Luke, 164, 168
Gospel of Mark, 168, 170
  Secret Gospel, 173, 184
Gospel of Matthew, 117, 163, 168, 172, 229n
Gospel of Thomas, 184
Greek Anthology, 151–2
Gregory XI, Pope, 183, 191
Gryttus, 27, 39, 42, 56, 210n
gymnasia, 1, 4, 7, 12, 18, 27–8, 40, 43–4, 55, 57, 70, 72

Hadrian, Emperor, 130, 145, 147, 150–3
ha-Ma'aggel, Honi, 167
Harmodius and Aristogeiton, 27–9, 31, 34, 57
Hasmoneans, 159–60
Hebrew language, 110, 119–20, 123
Hector, 24–5, 85
Hecuba, 73
Helen of Troy, 15
Helena, queen of Adiabene, 166
henbane, 89–90, 217n
Henry VIII, King, 192
Hephaestion, 85–6, 89
Heracles, 17–18, 49
Herculaneum, 213n
Hermes, 92
Herod the Great, king of Judea, 126–7, 129, 158–61, 164–6, 169, 172, 228n
Herod Antipas, tetrarch, 169–70, 228n
Herodias, 170
Herodotus, 45, 172
Herondas, 98–9
Hesiod, 12, 15, 95
Hesychius the Lexicographer, 189, 231n
Hipparchia of Maroneia, 91
Hipparchus, 28–9
Hippias, 28–9, 32
Hippocrates, 41–2
Hipponax, 172
Hippothales, 72
Hitchens, Christopher, 158, 228n
Hittites, 111
Homer, 15, 24–5, 32–3, 77, 82, 144, 216n, 225n
homosexuality, decriminalization of, 109, 197, 200–1, 235n
Horace, 4, 16
Horus, 124
Hostius Quadra, 150
House of Lords, 109, 200
Humbaba, 122

Illyrians, 60
Inanna, 104
Iolaus, 17
Iphis and Ianthe, 232n
Irenaeus of Lyons, Bishop, 168
Ischomachus, 78–9
Ishtar, 104–5
Isis, 124
Isle of the Hermaphrodites, 193

James VI and I, King, 194

INDEX

Janus, temple of, 138
Jehoiakim, king of Judah, 105–6
Jensen, Dr Carl Peter, 200
Jerusalem, 105–6, 108, 117, 126–7,
    157, 160–1, 163, 166, 219n, 221n
  Mar Saba monastery, 173–4, 230n
Jesus Christ, 6, 71, 107, 129, 157–9,
    161–4, 166–74, 182, 184–5, 203,
    229n
  and homoerotic stories, 188
  parables, 169–70, 233n
  and St Paul, 175–8, 181
  Sermon on the Mount, 170
Jewett, Sarah Orne, 198
Joan of Arc, 233n
John of Damascus, 174
John the Baptist, 170, 173
Josephus, 127, 163, 166, 168
Judea/Palestine
  famine, 165–6
  miracle-workers, 167–8, 170
  Palestinian Hills, 105–6
  Roman-occupied, 159–68, 227n
Julius Caesar, 97–8, 135, 159
Julius Pollux, 90
Jupiter and Ganymede, 130, 144
Justinian I, Emperor, 188
Juvenal, 149

kakoi ('evil ones'), 19
kalûs, 104, 114
Kerdon, 99
Kerkylas of Andros, 6
kinaidia, 56, 82, 135n, 212n
knesset, 163

Laius, King, 43
Lampros, 41
Laurion silver mines, 53
leitourgiai, 36
lesbians, 6, 138, 155–6, 189, 198,
    207n
  see also queer women
lesbiazein (fellatio), 15
Lesbos, 14–16, 37
Leto, 41
Lex Hortensia, 132
Lex Scantinia, 136–7, 139
LGBTQ+ rights, 201–3
Livy, 139
Lot, 116–17

Lucian, 155
Lucretia, rape of, 131
Lycourgos, 21–3
Lysias, 58, 90, 213n

Macedon, 43–5, 50–6, 58, 60–1, 81–2,
    176, 217n
Machaerus fortress, 170
Mai, Angelo, 154
malakoi, 178–9, 230n
Mamurra, 135
Marcellina, 184
Marcus Aurelius, 129, 153–5
Marcus Claudius Marcellus, 136
Marcus Cornelius Fronto, 154–5
Marcus Octavius, 132
Marduk, 104
Marinos, 189–90
Mark Antony, 127, 138, 160
Marlowe, Christopher, 173
Mars, 158
Mary Magdalene, 184
masturbation, 4, 88–9, 169, 184
mathematics, 67, 69–70, 175
Mattatiah, king of Judah, 106
Medea, 49
medicine, ancient Greek, 40–2, 83, 83
megara, 11
Megara, 10–14, 18, 21, 25, 54, 171
Melville, Herman, 198
'memory palace' techniques, 98
menstrual blood, 184
Messenia, 21–2
metempsychosis (transmigration of
    souls), 68–9
Methone, 50
Metro and Koritto, 98–9
metrokoites, 179–80
miasma, 28
Michelangelo, 1
Middleton, George, 197
Mieza, 82
Migge, Antonio, 2
Miletus, 34
Miltiades, 53
Misgolas, 57
misogyny, xi, 66
'molles', 180
molly houses, 199
Monica, 186
monstrosi, 147

Mosaic law, 170–1, 178, 182
Moses, 105, 170
Mount Cithaeron, 16
Mount Helicon, 16
Mount Hymettus, 64
Mount Vesuvius, 97, 129
Mure, William, 6
Mystery cults, 183–4, 211n
Mytilene, 15, 37–8

Nabopolassar, king of Babylon, 104
Nakht-Ankh and Khnum-Nakht, 222n
Native Americans, 197
Nazi Germany, 17, 36, 200, 235n
Nebuchadnezzar II, King, 104–8, 117
Neocles, 95
Nero, Emperor, 148, 163, 166, 181–2
Netherlands, 195–6
NHS hospitals, 200
Niankhkhnum and Khnumhotep, 124–5
Nineveh, 121
Ninmah, 104
Nisus and Euryalus, 130, 140–2
Noah and Ham, 114–15, 118
Nysaius, 51

Odysseus, 77
Oedipus, 49
oikousi (economics), 38
Olympia, 144
Olynthus, 52–3, 55, 212n
Orestes and Pylades, 43
Origen of Alexandria, 167
Orpheus and Eurydice, 143
Ortiz, George, 146
Osiris, 124
Ostippo perfume bottle, 146
Ovid, 142–3, 225n

paidopoiia, 56
pais, 12–13, 81, 215n
Palace of Versailles, 196
Palmyra, 129
Panathenaia festival, 28–9
Paphos, 176
Papua New Guinea, 5
Parker, Charles, 2
Parker, William, 2
Parthenon, 36, 50, 52
'pathics', 149–50

pathicus, 135, 138
Patricius, 186
Pausanias, *Description of Greece*, 92
Pausanias of Orestis, 60–1
Peisistratus, 20
Peloponnesian War, 37, 47–8, 64, 71, 103
Pentheus, 48–9, 71
Pericles, 31, 36
Perictione, 64
Persians, 27, 29–30, 32, 34–5, 172, 209n
Petronius, 223n
Phaistos, 41
Phaon, 15
Pharisees, 165, 169–70
Pharsalians, 51
Philadelphia Port Folio, 197
Philip II of Macedon, 50–2, 55–9, 61–3, 66, 81–2, 87, 126, 211–13n
  royal pages, 51–2, 59–61, 213n
Philippians, 176
Philo, 125–7, 129, 175
Philoxenus, 66, 84
Phocylides, 125
Phrynichus, 34
Pisthetaerus and Euelpides, 44
Plato, 1–2, 14, 25, 63–7, 69–80, 88, 94, 98, 141
  Academy, 70–1, 78, 82
  Charmides, 63, 72, 214n
  his death, 63, 213n
  and fascism, 200, 235n
  Gorgias, 74, 76, 180
  Laws, 80, 200
  Letters, 216n
  Lysis, 72–3
  Phaedo, 65
  Republic, 200
  Symposium, 44, 75–6
  and St Augustine, 185–6
  and St Paul, 175, 177–8, 180–1, 231n
Platonism, 92, 96
Plautus, 137
Pleiades, 69
Pliny the Elder, 129–30, 139, 147
Plutarch, 10, 59, 82–4, 151
polygamy, 59
Pompeii, 128, 145–6
Pompey the Great, 159–60, 162

INDEX 257

Pontius Pilate, 157, 161
Popper, Karl, 200
pornographic pottery, 34–5, 39, 57,
　145–6
postulare pro aliis, 140
Potidaea, Battle of, 72
Pratt, James, 199
Propertius, 142
Protestantism, 192–4, 233n
Psamtik II, pharaoh, 106
Pseudo-Phocylides, 125
ptochoi ('beggars'), 77–8
Ptolemy II Philadelphus, pharaoh, 123
Ptolemy III Euergetes, pharaoh, 87, 97–8
Publius Quinctilius Varus, 158
Puritans, 197
Pythagoras, 67–70, 214n
Pythagoreanism, 67–70, 79–80, 88, 93

queer women, xi, 15
Quintus Fabius Maximus, 137–8
Quirinius, 159

rape, 9, 28, 30–1, 40, 43, 83, 92, 111,
　124, 152, 193, 213n, 220n, 222–
　3n, 225–6n
　accusation against Marinos, 190
　in ancient Rome, 131, 136, 143–4,
　149
　in the Bible, 115–18
　of Pausanias, 61
Reagan, Ronald, 38, 201
Rhea Silvia, 158
Richelet, César-Pierre, 196
Robigus, 130
Roman Empire, 10, 125, 127–31,
　138–56
　bearded men, 145–6
　in decline, 185, 187
　gay subcultures, 149–50
　lesbians, 155–6
　lives of the emperors, 146–9
　male prostitutes, 149
　pornographic artefacts, 145–6
Roman Republic, 131–8
　civil war, 133
　gambling, 130, 134–6
　Social War, 134
Romulus, 158
Ross, Robert, 3
Rumi, 231n

Sabinus, 161
Sacred Band of Thebes, 59
St Augustine, 185–7
St John the Evangelist, 173
St Paul, 158, 175–82, 185
　and *prosōpopoia*, 232n
St Stephen, 175
St Thomas Aquinas, 191
Sallust, 134–5
Salmoxis, 68
Samos, 67
Sappho, 6, 15–16, 23, 231n
Saqqara tomb, 123–4
Saul, King, 119–20
Scepticism, 96
scepticism, of religion, 95
scholia, 39
Scipio Nasica, 133
Scythians, 42
Second World War, 199–200
Section 28, 201
self-control, 10, 22–3, 38–40, 42, 58,
　65, 113, 126, 185, 192
　and *akousmata*, 69
　Alexander the Great and, 83–4
　in ancient Rome, 131, 134, 136, 139
　and the *Bacchae*, 48–50
　Plato and, 71–4, 77–80, 178
　St Paul and, 177–8
　and Stoicism, 92–4, 101
Seneca, 144–5, 150
Seth, 124
Shakespeare, William, 1, 13, 94, 173,
　194
Shamhat, 121–2
Shenoute of Atripe, 188
Simbari people, 5
Skiron, 11
skyphos (drinking cup), 16–17
slaves, 8–9, 12, 18, 21, 36, 47,
　52–4, 68, 74–5, 85, 106, 111,
　221n, 225–6n
　in ancient Rome, 137–8, 143–5, 152
　in the Bible, 163
　eunuchs, 172
　Plato sold into slavery, 66–7, 78
　Spartacus revolt, 158
　transatlantic slave trade, 115,
　206n, 223n
Smith, John, 199
Smith, Morton, 173–4

Socrates, 40, 45, 64–6, 71–6, 91, 94–5, 141
Sodom, 116–18, 173, 188
sodomy, 109, 118, 191–4, 196, 221n, 234n
Solon, 19–21, 57, 171
Song of Songs, 119
Sophocles, ix–x, 15, 98
Souk Ahras, 185
sparagmos, 183
Spartacus, 158
Spartan Lawcode, 23
Spartans, 21–3, 25, 29, 78, 134
  Peloponnesian War, 37, 47–8, 64
  weddings, 17
Sporus, 148
stathmós (farmstead), 13
Stoicism, 92–4, 96, 101, 123, 125, 127, 139, 153–5, 185
  St Paul and, 175, 177
Strato's Tower, 160
stuprum, 140
Suetonius, 147–51, 196
suicide, 65, 109
Sumerians, 103–5, 109, 111, 121–2
swastikas, 17
Symeon the New Theologian, 188

Taormina, 3
Tarquin the Proud, King, 131
Tarsus, 175
Taureas wrestling school, 71–2, 214n
Thagaste, 185
Thales, 67
Thatcher, Margaret, 38, 201
Theagenes the tyrant, 10
Thebes, 18, 48, 59, 69
Theocritus, 99–100
Theodorus of Cyrene, 95
Theodorus of Tarentum, 84
Theodosios, Emperor, 187
Theognis of Megara, 1, 11–15, 23, 219n
Theopompus, 47, 51–2, 59, 61, 126
Theramenes, 48
Theseus, 92
Thespis, 18, 32

Theudas, 168
Thomas the Disciple, 188
Thucydides, 29, 209n, 210n
Tiberius, Emperor, 129, 146–8, 161
Tiberius Gracchus, 132–4
Timarchus, 57, 73, 137, 212n
Titus, Emperor, 154
tolerance, spectrum of, 8–9
trans people, x–xi, 41, 114, 202, 232n
Turing, Alan, 200
Turner, Reggie, 3

Ubertini, Lorenzo di Francesco, 192
Uruk, 121–2
US Supreme Court, 109

vagina, 142
van Baden, Gilles, 195
van Wijck, Adrianus, 195
Villa of the Papyri, 97
Villiers, George, 194
Virgil, 139–42, 162, 174, 185
Virgin Mary, 158–9
Visigoths, 187
von Gloeden, Wilhelm, 3, 6
Vose, Roger, 183, 197–8

Warren Cup, 145–6
wet nurses, 179
White Monastery, 188
Whitman, Walt, 198
Wilde, Oscar, 1–3, 6, 118–19, 199, 201
Wilhelm II, Kaiser, 3
Wils, Josua, 195
Wilsma, Zacharias, 195
Woman's Own magazine, 201

Xanthippe, 65
Xenophanes, 68
Xenophon, 16–17, 21–2, 31, 65, 71, 76–9, 83, 89, 91, 181, 208n
Xerxes, 27

Zedekiah, king of Judah, 106
Zeno, 90–4
ziggurats, 103–4

Note on the Author

Dr Harry Tanner, PhD earned his PhD in Ancient Greek at the National University of Ireland, Galway. As a teenager, he was an evangelical Christian and came to believe homosexuality was a sin. After a period as an atheist, he is open once again to spirituality and religion, and lives a fulfilled gay life in London where he writes and teaches ancient languages and history. *The Queer Thing About Sin* is his first book.

Note on the Type

The text of this book is set in Joanna, a transitional serif typeface designed by Eric Gill (1882–1940) in the period 1930–31, and named for one of his daughters. The typeface was originally designed for proprietary use by Gill's printing shop, Hague & Gill. The type was first produced in a small quantity by the Caslon Foundry for hand composition. It was eventually licensed for public release by the Monotype foundry in 1937.